ABILITY PROFILING
AND SCHOOL FAILURE
ONE CHILD'S STRUGGLE
TO BE SEEN AS COMPETENT

Chpt 1 - Sociocultural Theory

Chpt 2 - Grandparent-Teacher Conference

Chpt 3 - Sitting Ned, Scott & Jay
together

Chpt 4 - The Cartesian Diver System
Jay's success vs. Laura's
reflection

p.49 20% of time goes to Jay

Bring in Niles's
Diver !!!→ Chpt 5 - Class-wide discussion of
the Diver System
Laura "positions" Jay outside
the circle of discourse →

Chpt 5 continued

→ Is Collins' explanation on the bottom of
p. 62 correct? Alternative explanations?

Chpt 6 - Laura + Jay one-on-one

→ Laura "Scaffolds" Jay's learning one-on-one
for an extended period of time

Chpt 7 - GroupWork -
→ Shut up / I'dd'ja
→ Jay sent out of class

p. 82 → "At this point, I make the
decision to get involved in this
research..."

Crosses Line

p. 84 → Laura's perception vs. Kathleen's Perception

_____

Chpt 8 → Faith Clewinson - Jay's Previous Teacher
"And he was disruptive"
→ Debrief w/ classmates
"About half the time, I had no idea
what you were talking about"
→ Collins - No Longer Researcher
"perhaps I could influence it ..."
p. 97 Bordieu - Social Capital

Chpt 9 - p. 107 Vygotsky "Zone of Proximal Development"

Chpt 10 - p. 119 Bakhtin "Social Language & Speech Genres"

p. 119 "Informed by [my brilliance], I viewed

ABILITY PROFILING
AND SCHOOL FAILURE
ONE CHILD'S STRUGGLE
TO BE SEEN AS COMPETENT

copying and mimicry as potential scaffolds for Jay."

by
Kathleen M. Collins
University of San Diego

Chpt 12 - p. 140 "Reductionist Dev'l Model"

Chpt 13 pp. 156-157 Dewey & Vygotsky

LAWRENCE ERLBAUM ASSOCIATES, PUBLISHERS
2003   Mahwah, New Jersey   London

Poems appearing on pages 149, 150, and 151 are from *The Collected Poems of Langston Hughes* by Langston Hughes. Copyright 1994 by the Estate of Langston Hughes. Used by permission of Alfred A. Knopf, a division of Random House.

Lawrence Erlbaum Associates, Inc., Publishers
10 Industrial Avenue
Mahwah, NJ 07430

Cover design by Kathryn Houghtaling Lacey

Library of Congress Cataloging-in-Publication Data

Collins, Kathleen M.
   Ability profiling and school failure : one child's struggle to be seen as competent / Kathleen M. Collins.
       p. cm.
   Includes bibliographical references and index.
ISBN 0-8058-4155-5 (cloth : alk. paper)
ISBN 0-8058-4156-3 (pbk. : alk. paper)
1. Ability grouping in education—United States—Case studies. 2. Discrimination in education—United States—Case studies.   I. Title.

LB3061 .C615 2003
371.2'54—dc21   2002040849
                                                        CIP

Books published by Lawrence Erlbaum Associates are printed on acid-free paper, and their bindings are chosen for strength and durability.

Printed in the United States of America
10   9   8   7   6   5   4   3

For "Jay,"
a boy who loves his family,
poetry,
entomology,
the blues,
football,
dancing,
playing the saxophone,
and going to church,
and who won't let the world forget
that he has something to say.

And for my family,
who taught me to honor
the voices of children.

CONTENTS

Society establishes the means of categorizing persons and the complement of attributes felt to be ordinary and natural for members of each of these categories. Social settings establish the categories of persons likely to be encountered there. The routines of social intercourse in established settings allow us to deal with anticipated others without special attention or thought. When a stranger comes into our presence, then, first appearances are likely to enable us to anticipate his category and attributes, his "social identity" ... While the stranger is present before us, evidence can arise of his possessing an attribute that makes him different from others in the category of persons available for him to be, and of a less desirable kind—in the extreme, a person who is quite thoroughly bad, dangerous, or weak. He is thus reduced in our minds from a whole and usual person to a tainted, discounted one. Such an attribute is a stigma, especially when its discrediting effect is very extensive; sometimes it is also called a failing, a shortcoming, a handicap.

—Erving Goffman
Stigma: Notes on the Management of Spoiled Identity *(1963, pp. 2–3)*

Preface

Jay,[1] 11 years old and about to begin sixth grade, looks down at the photos spread across the Formica table in our booth at McDonald's. "That picture right there," he grins and points to a photo of himself holding his insect collection up for the camera, "That was a Kodak moment. Me and my bugs!"

I examine the photo he's pointed out. It's a great picture—Jay's smile bursts forth from it and communicates the unequivocal joy of the moment, and his squared shoulders and the way he leans his face in toward his insect collection hint at his pride in his success as an entomologist. Considering this as I study the picture, I ask him, "Did our entomology work, the insect collecting and working with Harry this summer, make you feel any different as a learner?"

Jay's already-large brown eyes widen as he looks up from the photo and directly into my face. He looks shocked by my question. "I was always a good learner," he says emphatically. "Don't *you* think so?"

Yes, after working with Jay for 18 months in various teaching and learning contexts, I do think so. I have seen him compose long blues poems quickly and without apparent effort and heard him sing them out loud—and in tune—while dancing and letting the music's energy move his body. I've read his carefully written work—poems, letters, a research report, and entomology notes—in field notebooks, on computer screens, in a journal, and on looseleaf paper. Together we have read and discussed science books, biographies, novels, insect guides, poems, and newspaper articles. I've been stunned and sometimes envious at this articulate 11-year-old's ease and con-

---

[1]"Jay" originally selected the pseudonym "The Amazing Dr. Jay." When I explained the rhetorical awkwardness created by inserting this title within the text of this research, he agreed to be called simply "Jay," as long as I agreed to insert this footnote.

fidence when talking with others, both adults and children, in schools, his church, at museums, in restaurants ranging from McDonald's to establishments of fine dining, and at a major research university. Jay is a child who listens to what others say and really attempts to reach intersubjectivity in conversation. He is able to appropriate and adapt various oral and written social languages at will. Yes, I think he is "a good learner."

However, Jay's school records do not paint a similar portrait of his abilities. Instead, Jay's institutional biography (McDermott, 1993) for second grade through fifth grade chronicles a history of near-failing grades and interactional difficulties. Through labels ranging from "crack baby" to "emotionally impaired" to "learning disabled," Jay's teachers have consistently located the responsibility for his low academic achievement within Jay. He is, the institutional biography asserts, deficient. Jay's second-grade teacher wrote on his report card, "Jay must have his materials/books to work. He must also control his mouth." In third grade, at a different school, his teacher asserted, "Jay did not do his work and his grade reflects it." In fourth grade, Jay's classroom teacher created computer-generated bar graphs indicating Jay's failing grades in every academic subject. Yet, that same year, Jay took a state-mandated achievement test and his reading score was rated "moderate" as compared with those of other fourth graders in the state. Jay's reading score was further described, revealing that on the narrative text section of the test Jay answered 85% of the questions correctly (17 of 20), whereas on the informational text section of the test he answered only 20% of the questions correctly (4 of 20).

For educators, parents, and scholars concerned with social justice and educational equity, these different portraits of Jay raise questions that we must not ignore. What constitutes ability and disability? What factors contribute to a child's appearance as either a good learner or as learning disabled? Under what contextual circumstances does a difference become a disability? How do sociocultural factors such as ethnicity, gender, class, and language influence the identification of ability and disability? These questions seem even more pressing when we consider that students of color, particularly those who are, like Jay, Black[2] and male, are overrepresented in special education programs (Artiles, 1998; Artiles & Trent, 1994; Harry & Anderson, 1994, 1999) and are the recipients of a disproportionate number of corporal punishments and suspensions from school (Harry & Anderson, 1999).

---

[2]Jay's family describes themselves most often with the identifier *Black* and, occasionally, *colored*. In deference to their preference, I use the term Black in this research.

Research Questions

In this book, the result of 18 months of research and 700 hours of data collection, I address these questions through a narrative case study of the ways in which Jay was interpreted to be either learning disabled, emotionally impaired, or a good learner in the various teaching and learning contexts of his life. Guided by sociocultural and social constructivist perspectives on learning, this book is a powerful challenge to deficit notions that locate ability and disability within individuals. Jay's story makes visible the ways in which ability and disability are constructed interactively and discursively within specific activity contexts.

In doing so, Jay's story illuminates the differential responses of various participants within and across the various learning contexts to his positive learning performances and demonstrates the subsequent effects of these differential responses on the success of Jay's attempt to rewrite his narrative of disability. For example, despite invitations to consider evidence of several of his positive performances in and out of school, Laura still responded to Jay as though he were less than capable. This process of responding to a student as though he is disabled, (i.e., reading all of his actions and interactions through the lens of deficiency), is what I term *ability profiling.* Jay's story makes clear the ways in which ability profiling contributes to the construction of disability and school failure, and the intimate relationship between such profiling and sociocultural factors such as students' perceived ethnicity, class, family structure, gender, and socioeconomic status. Jay's story thus acts as a counter-narrative to hegemonic discourses that situate students of color, as well as those from low-income and poor families, as "less than"—less capable, less intelligent, less talented—their White middle-class and upper-class peers.

THE AMAZING DR. JAY AND ME: HOW THE ADVENTURE BEGAN

My interest in understanding the relationship between contextual factors and identities of academic success has roots in my experiences teaching high school students who were labeled "at risk" and placed in my lower track, inclusion-oriented language arts classes. My students, primarily students of color from low-income families, taught me, their White middle-class teacher, valuable lessons about the situated nature of ability and disability and about the ways in which class, race, gender, and languages intersect with power and privilege to shape opportunities in and out of school. Through their competence and resilience, they taught me to question my place within an educational system that had rewarded me with high grades, scholarships, and opportunities to pursue advanced degrees, but positioned them as at-risk, low achieving, emotionally disturbed, learning disabled, and, in some cases, simply dangerous.

I returned to graduate school to pursue deeper understanding of social contexts and literacy education, and my interests drew me to the Guided Inquiry research team. Here, along with lead investigators Annemarie Palincsar and Shirley Magnusson, I explored the constraints and affordances of a particular orientation to teaching science, Guided Inquiry supporting Multiple Literacies (GIsML), for students with special needs (Palincsar, Collins, Marano, & Magnusson, 1998, 2000; Palincsar, Magnusson, Collins, & Cutter, 2001; Palincsar, Magnusson, Collins, Marano, & Hapgood, 1999).[3] In the fall of 1997 our task was to develop case studies of the participation of students identified as having a learning disability in a program of study designed and implemented from a GIsML perspective. As the school year began, I was poised to pursue this line of inquiry in the classroom of fifth-grade teacher Laura Bozek.[4]

Prior to conducting research in her classroom, I had known Laura for a year in the context of her participation in our GIsML research. Laura was one of 18 teacher members of a professional development effort focused on improving elementary science instruction, the Guided Inquiry Community of Teacher Practice.[5] During the year prior to my entry into her classroom, Laura had often reflected passionately and articulately about her teaching and her students during GIsML meetings, and she had garnered the respect

---

[3]The GIsML orientation to teaching science was developed to support the engagement of individuals in sustained inquiry about the physical world, and to provide opportunities for social interaction in ways that mirrored the knowledge-building practices of the scientific community. The goal of this instruction was to provide "a context in which learners can practice the language and tools of scientific problem solving in socially situated activity" (Magnusson & Palincsar, 1995, p. 43). The Guided Inquiry orientation had four phases: engage, investigate, constructing/revising explanations, and reporting. These phases were visited recursively as the students created and deepened their understanding of phenomena. The multiple literacies aspect of the GIsML orientation was intended to signal its potential to support diverse modes of expression. For example, within just one cycle of a guided inquiry investigation, students may have employed graphic documentation, informal writing in lab notebooks, formal writing of presentation materials, reading of second-hand investigation materials, individual and small-group oral presentation, and whole-group discussions. For studies exploring the enactment of GIsML in classrooms, see K. M. Collins (1998); Collins, Palincsar, and Magnusson (1998); K. M. Collins, MacLean, Palincsar, and Magnusson (2000); Palincsar, Collins, Marano, and Magnusson (2000); Palincsar, Magnusson, Collins, and Cutter (2001).

[4]With the exception of the GIsML researchers, all names of people and places are pseudonyms.

[5]The teacher members of the community taught kindergarten through fifth grade in schools located in different districts within the same Midwestern county. Over a period of 3 years, they came together, along with the university-based members, bimonthly to develop the GIsML orientation to teaching. The development of the Guided Inquiry Community of Practice is discussed in more detail elsewhere (see Brown, Palincsar, & Magnusson, 1999; Marano, Palincsar, & Magnusson, 2000; Palincsar, Magnusson, Marano, Ford, & Brown, 1998).

But was this research? She's already drawn her conclusions!!

of the other teachers in our community. Although we had yet to work closely together, I was excited about the opportunity to conduct research in Laura's classroom.

I met Jay in August 1997 when he began fifth grade in Laura's classroom. Like me, Jay was new to Axleton Middle School. Only a few weeks into the school year, Laura expressed frustration with Jay's manner of classroom participation, which she perceived as disruptive and indicative of a learning disability. For this reason, she recommended that Jay, along with five other students she also identified as learning disabled, become the focus for our GIsML research in her classroom that fall.

As the research unfolded, I was increasingly puzzled by Laura's assessment of Jay as learning disabled and disruptive. In my observations, it appeared that, rather than being disruptive, Jay's participation provided opportunities in support of his classmates' construction of understanding of the nature of floating and sinking. I was particularly struck by the collaborative nature of Jay's participation as he worked to make his thinking available for his peers. Jay reminded me of so many of my high school students whose gifts were not recognized in school, and I could not bear to stand by and simply record events as an identity of disability was assigned to him. Although I knew the choice to do so could jeopardize my research in the eyes of those who see inquiry and advocacy as separate enterprises, I made the decision to get directly involved in the classroom research site, and, later, to create and study alternative teaching and learning sites, contexts in which Jay was seen as "at promise" rather than "at risk."

I hoped that these data would become the basis for a collaborative inquiry with Laura that would involve our joint reflection on her teaching and, most particularly, collaborative analysis of her interactions with Jay. Reflecting with me on Jay's participation would, I hoped, motivate Laura to consider the ways in which different instructional and interactional factors shaped her interpretation of Jay's ability. I thought that this research project could interrupt the institutional biography of Jay as a child with a problem. At the very least, I was sure that Laura would see him differently.

However, my efforts to interrupt Laura's narrative of Jay as learning disabled or emotionally impaired were unsuccessful. It became clear that her assessment of Jay was unlikely to permanently change based only on my work with him relative to GIsML instruction. Rather, it seemed to fluctuate and change in response to the contexts in which they both participated. In an effort to further understand this, I continued to videotape, one day a week, Jay's participation in other school-based instructional contexts after Laura's guided inquiry investigation concluded. For the rest of the school year, January through June, I was present and videotaped the activity in Laura's classroom at least one full day each week (usually Wednesday). During this time I observed an increasing push toward homogenization in Laura's instructional practices, which resulted in the increased exclusion of those students she perceived as different from the classroom learning community. As a result, I continued to try to engage Laura in discussion and collaborative inquiry regarding Jay and the other students who were becoming increasingly marginalized, but these efforts were unsuccessful.

During the same time frame, I continued to meet with Jay once a week after school. We began our work together by working on a research report that he was assigned by Laura. At this time, I loaned Jay a pocket tape recorder as part of a writing strategy. After that, we moved on to composing blues poetry and songs, which were particular interests of his. During this time, Jay brought me a tape that he had recorded at home. His spontaneous observations of insects, recorded on the tape, launched our entomology inquiry, which we continued over the summer and the following fall. As my relationship with Jay deepened, I learned about his personal and family histories, and I had the opportunity to conduct informal interviews with his aunt and uncle, his cousin, his great-grandmother, and his grandmother. I was also invited to attend his church and observe his interactions in that context.

Thus, what began as a classroom-based case study of the constraints and affordances of guided inquiry science became a multisited ethnographic portrait of the ways in which contextual features, including participants' ways of interacting with one another, shaped Jay's opportunities to be seen as competent or as disabled. For example, in the context of Jay's church, achievement and ability were represented by lively participation in numerous forms of oral and physical interactions that were active and dialogic, and reflected joint, cooperative activity. In contrast, in the context of Laura's typical classroom instruction, achievement and ability were reflected through triadic discourse patterns (Mehan, 1979) and very little physical movement. The tools and activities, such as individually completed worksheets and silent reading, in Laura's classroom reflected an individualistic definition of achievement that contrasted with the jointly accomplished practices of Jay's church.

ORGANIZATION OF THIS VOLUME

In this book I present my work with Jay in the form of a narrative case study (Sacks, 1970, 1995). Narrative analysis provides a means to analyze the cultural, social, and contextual features of shared activity while attempting to include the voices and insights of all participants. The use of narrative also allows me to make visible my position as "vulnerable observer" (Behar, 1996), and not one who was silent, passive, or whose more active role is hidden behind a curtain of academic prose (see the Appendix for a detailed discussion of my methods of data collection and analysis).

In chapter 1, I introduce and discuss the implications of sociocultural theory for my work. Sociocultural theory asserts that social and individual cognitive processes are mutually constitutive, interdependent, and mediated by mediation of semiotic and technical tools (Palincsar, 1998; Vygotsky, 1978, 1981a, 1981b, 1987; Wertsch, 1991, 1998). An important implication of this dialectical relationship is that identities of competence or of disability are not static properties of individuals. Rather, they are constructed in the relation between individuals and in opportunities and tools provided by activity settings in which they engage (Wertsch, 1998).

Chapter 2, "The Boy Who Had Something to Say," is drawn from an audiotape of a conference between Jay's grandparents and his sixth-grade teachers that took place on October 13, 1998. Chapter 2 depicts the central themes present in the rest of the narrative. The imbalance of power present in the interactions between Jay's home and school lives, the ways in which this imbalance influences the construction of Jay as "disabled" in school learning contexts, and the role of academic and cultural literacies in shaping contextually situated identities are demonstrated in this chapter. The reader is thus poised to inquire into the social, cultural, and institutional factors that led to these tensions, and their effect on Jay's life and educational opportunities.

Each subsequent chapter, 3 through 16, consists partially of narrative text through which I depict my unfolding relationship with Jay in the various teaching and learning contexts of his life. In addition, within each chapter I also include discussions of relevant theoretical and research literature. These discussions serve as interpretive lenses to assist the reader in viewing and making sense of Jay's story in the larger context of educational research. Through the use of narrative and academic discourses, I aim to engage readers in informed inquiry about Jay and the teaching and learning contexts of his life.

In chapter 17, "Ability Profiling and School Failure: Learning From Jay's Story," I provide a theoretical overview and analysis of the project as a whole. This chapter also includes a discussion of the implications of Jay's story for understanding the situated and coconstructed nature of ability and disability through an examination of Jay's role and positioning within each teaching and learning context. Further, in this chapter I also discuss the lessons this work provides for teacher practice and for teacher education programs.

Finally, the book concludes with an Appendix in which I discuss the methodological choices I made in data collection, analysis, and presentation. This includes discussions of the strengths and limitations of narrative analysis, as well as reflections on the implications of my representational choices.

ACKNOWLEDGMENTS

The completion of this book was supported by a host of scholars and friends who gave freely of their time and insights. Any remaining errors are, of course, my own. I wish to acknowledge the contributions of the following people.

First, my heartfelt gratitude goes to Jay and his family. I was profoundly moved by Jay's resilience, persistence, and confidence in the face of an educational system that constructs him as less able than his peers. I am convinced that the deep and supportive love of his family is what makes this possible, and am indebted to them for their collaboration with me and for their support of this work.

It is an act of no small courage to allow one's teaching practice to be videotaped, analyzed, and made public as part of a research project, and I wish to thank Laura for allowing me to conduct this research in her classroom.

Harry, the university-based entomologist who volunteered his time and insect-collecting equipment to work with Jay and me, the citizens of Axleton who participated in the various interviews I conducted, and the members of Jay's church who welcomed me into their midst each deserve a special word of gratitude as well. I could not have completed this work without the contributions of these participants, and I am very grateful for their assistance and support.

During the course of this inquiry, I had the great gift of working with a team of talented and supportive scholars who guided my efforts. Annemarie Palincsar, my advisor, mentor, and role model, was and remains a constant source of personal and professional inspiration. Jean McPhail's artistic sensibilities gave me the courage to venture away from traditional forms of academic writing, and her research regarding interest-based apprenticeships influenced the multisited ethnographic design of my work with Jay. Additionally, Deborah Keller-Cohen, Elizabeth Moje, Lesley Rex, and Sharon Stephens were generous with their time and their intellectual insights, and their feedback on numerous earlier drafts was invaluable in shaping the final version of this volume.

My colleagues and students at the University of San Diego contributed to my thinking about this work in a variety of ways. I am especially grateful for encouragement and support provided by Paula Cordeiro, Ana Estrada, Steve Gelb, and Cheryl Getz. Additionally, conversations with Laura Apol, Patricia Edwards, Susan Florio-Ruane, and Victoria Purcell-Gates during a visit to Michigan State University were helpful in honing my thinking about issues of inquiry, advocacy, and subjectivity.

I wish also to thank Carol Sue Englert and Alfredo Artiles, along with several anonymous reviewers, for their carefully written reviews of an earlier draft of this volume. Encouragement from Carol Sue and Alfredo helped me to go forward, and their feedback improved the scholarly depth of this work. Naomi Silverman, my editor at Lawrence Erlbaum Associates, helped me stay focused and apply these reviews to my manuscript in ways that have improved its readability.

I am also grateful for the love and care of my dear friends and fellow scholars Elizabeth Dutro, Susanna Hapgood, Nancy Marano, Fé MacLean, and Jennifer Sinor. In addition to the gift of her friendship, Elizabeth was always ready with just the right article, book, or word of encouragement at the moment when it was most needed. An elementary teacher researcher, Fé provided valuable insights into the classroom data as well as personal encouragement. Additionally, I am indebted to Luci Kovacevic, Pete Lopez, Georgia Sparkman, and Lisa Woods for providing support and friendship.

Like Jay, I am blessed with a family that has supported my endeavors with unflagging love and confidence in my capabilities. My mother, Roma Collins, an elementary school special educator, provided both personal understanding and professional insight. My father, James Collins, a professor of literacy, helped me develop my own approach to scholarship and gave me my start as an educational researcher. Jamie Collins, my brother, provided emotional sustenance and motivation via weekly phone calls and his expressed faith in the value of this work. My sister-in-law, Jennifer Patton Collins, was a source of encouragement, kindness, and shared laughter.

The research reported in this book was supported in part by a grant from the U.S. Department of Education (H023V70008) to the REACH project

(Research Institute to Accelerate Content Learning through High Support for Students with Disabilities in Grades 4–8). My writing was further facilitated by a Warriner Scholarship awarded by the School of Education at the University of Michigan (1998), a Rackham Graduate School Dissertation Fellowship awarded by the University of Michigan (1999), and two Faculty Research Grants awarded by the University of San Diego (2000–2002).

1

Introduction: A Sociocultural Perspective on [Dis]ability

It is well documented that children of color are overrepresented in special education programs (Artiles, 1998; Artiles & Trent, 1994; Harry & Anderson, 1994, 1999), and underrepresented in gifted education programs (Ford, 1998). For example, in 1991, Black children comprised 16% of the overall school population and 35% of the special education population in the United States (Harry & Anderson, 1994). Black boys, like Jay, are especially overrepresented in special education programs and are the recipients of a disproportionately high number of disciplinary procedures, such as corporal punishments and suspensions (Harry & Anderson, 1999). Other educational sorting practices, such as ability grouping and tracking, have resulted in similar forms of school segregation and unequal educational opportunities for students of color (Green, 1999; Oakes, 1985, 1995; Oakes, Wells, Jones, & Datnow, 1997). Further, in an analysis of the variables examined in educational research on overrepresentation, MacMillan and Reschly (1998) concluded that ethnicity serves as a "proxy" for socioeconomic status, and they called for increased attention to the role of social class in special education referral.

Despite this knowledge, there is a dearth of special education research that attempts to examine the ways in which the identification of disability is influenced by sociocultural and contextual factors such as students' perceived race, class, gender, language use, and the mediational features of activity contexts (Artiles, Aguirre-Munoz, & Abedi, 1998, Artiles & Trent, 1994; Artiles, Trent, & Kuan, 1997; Guitierrez & Stone, 1997;

Pugach, 2001). The result of such inattention to sociocultural factors in shaping identification practices is that an inherently social process, the display and recognition of successful participation in classroom learning, has been largely portrayed as an objective means of identifying "deficits" within individual learners.

It is therefore imperative that we begin to identify and understand the influence of sociocultural factors on the identification of children as gifted, average, or learning disabled. Until we do so, we will continue to fail to interrupt the processes that result in the overrepresentation of students of color and those from low-income and poor households in special education programs (Artiles & Trent, 1994; Pugach, 2001; Pugach & Seidl, 1996, 1998; Sleeter, 1986). Let us begin by considering the lenses through which scholars and educators have viewed the causes of low school achievement.

THREE LENSES ON SCHOOL
SUCCESS AND FAILURE

Scholars of teaching and learning have presented differing views regarding what contributes to school success and school failure. One common model has become known as a *deficit or medical model* approach to understanding low achievement. This model emerged from special education's roots in the medical field and the diagnoses of brain injury (Trent, Artiles, & Englert, 1998; Poplin, 1988b). Poplin (1988b) identified deficit approaches (including four models of disability: medical, psychological process, behavioral, and cognitive/learning strategy) as part of a reductionist paradigm, which isolated aspects of teaching and learning from their situated occurrence in social interactions. Reductionism, particularly as manifested by deficit, medical, and mechanistic metaphors for learning, assumed human learning could be broken into component psychological processes and observable behaviors, and that these processes and behaviors could be isolated and treated (Gavelek & Palincsar, 1988; Poplin, 1988b). This assumption led to the most severe limitation of the reductionist paradigm; that is, its failure to consider the contextual and social aspects of human learning as a complex process.

A second perspective on understanding low school achievement is known as the *communication process* or *cultural difference* approach. Scholars explicitly concerned with the educational underachievement of minority children and those from low-income families employed this lens to conduct extensive research into the dynamics of discursive interactions of classrooms (see reviews in Cazden, 1986; Hicks, 1995). Such studies demonstrated that low achievement in school was often linked to culturally based communicative differences (Erickson, 1996; Heath, 1983; Michaels & Collins, 1984; Philips, 1972; see also discussions in Cazden, 1988, and Hicks, 1995), and that when instructional discourse was made more culturally congruent, achievement improved (Au, 1979, 1980; Au & Jordan, 1981; see also discussions in Erickson, 1987, and Gee, 1996).

A third lens, one that broadens deficit and communication process perspectives on understanding the dynamics of low school achievement, is provided by social constructivist and sociocultural theories. Social constructivist theory challenges the assumption of the deficit approach that locates ability, or disability, solely within an individual student or group of students (Vygotsky, 1978, 1987). Further, a sociocultural perspective challenges the communication process approach to move beyond a focus on spoken interactions to consider how these interactions both reflect and are shaped by larger cultural practices, sociopolitical interests, and social positioning.

Social constructivist and sociocultural theories ask us to consider how we define ability and competence in our classroom and our research, and how our own teaching, assessment, and interactional practices might shape the interpretations we reach about a student's learning, about their competence and incompetence. Rather than looking for a deficit or impairment within learners, a sociocultural perspective suggests examining the intersection of environment and individual to understand how they mutually construct each other. Ability and disability are thus not constant or perceived as solely located within individuals. Rather, they are constructed in the relation between individuals and the opportunities provided by the activity setting in which they are engaged. School success and school failure are therefore viewed as cocreated in situated activity.[1]

SOCIOCULTURAL THEORY

Jay articulated one of the central tenets of a sociocultural theoretical framework when I asked him to describe his own learning process:

> When somebody else say something, I just like take what they're saying and […] remember what I, what I had learned from the year, and combine that. And when I think about it real hard it just comes out. It's like a burst, a burst of fire. (Jay, interview, January 9, 1998)

---

[1]The shift to perspectives on ability and disability informed by social constructivist theories is interwoven with the emergence of new definitions of literacy that challenge and extend static, elite, and functional definitions of literacy (Gee, 1991; see discussions in Au, 1998; Keller-Cohen, 1994; Sleeter, 1986; Trent et al., 1998; see also Anderson, Holland, & Palincsar, 1997, on science literacy).

Jay's reflection captures the notion that social and individual cognitive processes are mutually constitutive and interdependent. The interdependent nature of individual and social development was posited in the work of Soviet psychologist Vygotsky, whose scholarship provided the foundation for many of the constructs of social constructivist and sociocultural theory. Vygotsky (1978, 1981a, 1981b, 1987) described learning as a process of change, a complex dialectic between an individual and his or her social and cultural contexts in which they mutually construct and transform each other.

Wertsch (1991) proposed consideration of three themes in Vygotsky's work that each explicate different aspects of the mutually constitutive relationship between individuals and their social and cultural contexts (see also discussion in Palincsar, 1998). These themes include: (a) individual development stems from social resources; (b) semiotic tools, both physical and conceptual, shape and define (mediate) action; and (c) human development is best understood through genetic analysis. Although foregrounding each theme separately is somewhat artificial because of their interdependent nature, it is also a useful analytic approach because it allows me to illuminate some of the complexities and implications of sociocultural theory. Therefore, in the rest of this section I discuss each of these themes and the ways in which they informed my research with Jay.[2]

Individual Development Stems From Social Resources

The assertion that individual development stems from social resources is a key tenet of Vygotsky's work. In Vygotsky's model, individuals take up the conceptual and physical tools and signs (the social resources) that are available to them within their cultural contexts. In the process of taking up and employing these tools, an individual transforms both his or her own understanding and the shared understandings of the community. The process of employing a cultural tool thus changes or transforms the forms of thought possible at the institutional, social and cultural, and individual planes of development. Vygotsky described this process as the general genetic (developmental or historical) law of cultural development:

---

[2]In the section that follows, my discussion of sociocultural theory is grounded in and illustrated through my research with Jay. Readers interested in additional empirical studies in education conducted from a sociocultural perspective would be well-served by beginning with recent volumes edited by Hicks (1996), *Discourse, Learning and Schooling;* Forman, Minick, and Stone (1993), *Contexts for Learning;* and Moll (1990), *Vygotsky and Education: Instructional Implications and Applications of Sociohistorical Psychology.* Each of these volumes begins with an introductory essay that further explicates sociocultural theory.

We could formulate the general genetic law of cultural development as follows: Any function in the child's cultural development appears twice, or on two planes. First it appears on the social [intermental] plane, and then on the psychological [intramental] plane. First it appears between people as an interpsychological category, and then within the child as an intrapsychological category. This is equally true with regard to voluntary attention, logical memory, the formation of concepts, and the development of volition. We may consider this position as a law in the full sense of the word, but it goes without saying that internalization transforms the process itself and changes its structures and functions. Social relations or relations among people genetically underlie all higher functions and their relationships. (Vygotsky, 1981a, p. 163)

Thus a sociocultural perspective posits that cognition is mediated by the social interactions that occur within the cultural context of development. Even when an individual is engaged in activity that appears to be solely intramental, such as thinking or writing alone, he or she is engaged in a social process because his or her action is mediated by interactions and tools first experienced intermentally. Vygotsky's concept of mind thus extends "beyond the skin" (Wertsch, 1991, p. 14) to include the ways in which thought and action are mediated by tools, signs, and other agents (see also Wertsch, 1998, on socially shared cognition).

One implication of this concept of mind for classroom research is that measures of individual conceptual change are insufficient for reflecting the process of dialectical transformation and development posited by sociocultural theory. The mediational means and habits of mind of the learning community, the opportunities they afford, the constraints they impose, and the transformations that they undergo must all be considered. For example, from a sociocultural perspective, it is not enough to examine only Jay's pre- and posttest scores on the conceptual assessment of floating and sinking, or even to examine his scores in relation to those of the rest of his class. To more fully appreciate these measures of Jay's understanding of density, one must examine the sociohistorical aspects of their construction. Among these aspects are the contextual elements that supported Jay's construction and expression of understanding, such as his participation in the instructional conversations during public sharing time, the responses of his classmates and his teacher to his participation, and the physical and conceptual tools that mediated these interactions.

Vygotsky's description of the dialectical relationship between individuals and their social and cultural contexts is often described as *internalization*, with an emphasis on "the internal reconstruction of an external operation"

(Vygotsky, 1978, p. 56). However, Vygotsky also emphasized the ways in which internalization involves the both taking up of a tool or participation in an activity, and *transformation*. In Vygotsky's view, the very process of participating in social and cultural activity transforms an agent intramentally, and the participation of that agent in the community then transforms the tools and constructs available for appropriation. Depicting Vygotsky's thinking about internalization as involving only the taking up of mediational means misses the dynamic nature of the relation Vygotsky described, and contributes to claims that sociocultural theory is concerned primarily with transmission or transference (cf. Cobb, 1994). As John-Steiner and Mahn (1996) noted, this portrayal of sociocultural theory overlooks the notion of learning as *mutual transformation* that characterizes Vygotsky's work.

Wertsch (1998) explicated the concept of internalization further, claiming that the use of the term perpetuates the very mind–body, individual–society dualism that Vygotsky, through the development of sociocultural theory, sought to overcome. To avoid this dualism, Wertsch introduced alternative terminology to describe the dialectical relationship between individuals and their social and cultural contexts. He identified two different forms of internalization, internalization as mastery and internalization as appropriation.

Wertsch's (1998) consideration of internalization as mastery emphasizes knowing how to use a cultural tool. In this case, the operation involving the tool might never move inside as implied by the term internalization, but rather remains visible. Wertsch discussed examples that include the use of physical tools, such as pole vaulting; conceptual tools, such as mathematical operations; and relationships with other agents, as in studies of socially shared cognition.

In my work with Jay, several striking examples of internalization as mastery took place in the context of our entomology inquiry. For example, knowing how to engage in the various field-based practices of entomology, from preparing a "kill jar," catching insects and transferring them to jar, removing them, mounting them, and recording our field notes, was critical to our inquiry, and although we both mastered this range of practices, they never moved inside in the sense that they were always performed externally, with physical tools. Further, there were many instances of distributed cognition in this context as we were joined first by Jay's cousin and then by a university entomologist, who each brought their own understandings and skills to the inquiry and took up different roles. At one point in our field collection, for example, Jay assigned his cousin the task of recording our entries in our field guide because he thought she could write better (more neatly) than he could. In this context, knowing how to complete different tasks, individually and collectively, demonstrated internalization as mastery of insect collecting.

Wertsch (1998) drew on the work of Soviet scholar Bakhtin to explore the notion of internalization as appropriation. Like Vygotsky, Bakhtin emphasized the dialectical nature of communication and cognition, although Bakhtin focused more exclusively on language. Bakhtin's concept of dialogicality posits that a speaker appropriates his or her words from interactions with others, and that the process of appropriation involves one of transformation:

> Language, for the individual consciousness, lies on the borderline between oneself and another. The word in language is half someone else's. It becomes "one's own" only when the speaker populates it with his own intention, his own accent, when he appropriates the word, adapting it to his own semantic and expressive intention. Prior to this moment of appropriation, the word does not exist in a neutral and impersonal language (it is not, after all, out of a dictionary that a speaker gets his words!) but rather it exists in other people's mouths, in other people's contexts, serving other people's intentions: it is from there that one must take the word, and make it one's own. And not all words for just anyone submit equally easily to this appropriation, to this seizure and transformation into private property: many words stubbornly resist, others remain alien, sound foreign in the mouth of the one who appropriated them and who now speaks them; they cannot be assimilated into his context and fall out of it; it is as if they out themselves in quotation marks against the will of the speaker. Language is not a neutral medium that passes freely and easily into the private property of the speaker's intentions; it is populated—overpopulated—with the intentions of others. Expropriating it, forcing it to submit to one's own intentions and accents, is a difficult and complicated process. (Bakhtin, 1981, pp. 293–294)

Following Bakhtin, Wertsch (1998) argued that internalization as appropriation involves resistance, "a 'friction' between mediational means and unique use in mediated action" (p. 54). As discussed more fully in the next section, this friction is not unrelated to the argument of discourse theorists that forms of discourse are intimately linked to issues of identity (see also Bakhtin, 1981, on ventriloquation).

Some of the most interesting examples of internalization as appropriation in my work with Jay began in the context of our writing together and carried over into other activities. For example, when Jay and I composed blues poetry together, we began by adhering strictly to the rhythm and rhyme of 12-bar blues music (see Greenfield, 1988, and Hughes, 1994, for descriptions of this form). Jay's enthusiastic response to this format was immediate, and physical as well as verbal: He began dancing and composing his poetry simultaneously. He quickly adapted the 12-bar blues format for his own meaning-making purposes and composed several song-poems orally. Several months after our first collaborative efforts, unprompted by me, Jay taught his cousin, Tasheka, how to compose 12-bar blues song-poems. The recording of their interaction in this activity (I was not present) offers an illustration of internalization as appropriation in the sense posited by Wertsch (1998). In their discourse together, it is possible to discern Jay's appropriation and transformations of the 12-bar blues format. This interaction is depicted and discussed more fully later in this volume, but here a brief excerpt of the transcript illustrates my point:

Jay: Hello, Kathy. This is Jay and
Tasheka: Tasheka.
Jay: Welcome to our basement, where we're ready to go. And a 1, 2, 3, and action! What we're going to be talking about today, we're going to talk about how to make up a blues song. You know what I'm sayin' Tasheka?
Tasheka: Hmm-mmm.
Jay: When we are making this song, you're not s'posed to, well, you can play around but sometimes you have to be serious. You know? Make a line, you know, and make it sad. ((singing)) ding-ding-ding-ding
Tasheka: Sad?
Jay: Yeah. The blues are usually sad. You didn't know that? Did you?
Tasheka: Not really.
Jay: Like, ((singing))
           I been in my bed
           sick I count the days
           and in a little while
           I think I gonna be dead.
           Cause I got the blues
           The blue-wooo-wooos
           I think I got the blues.
Tasheka: I think it's s'posed to rhyme.
Jay: Nu-huh. It's not. I just made it up.

Jay's instructions to Tasheka about the activity of composing a blues song, "You can play around but sometimes you have to be serious," illustrated his understanding and transformation of an activity he initially engaged in with me. He then adopted the role (and discourse) of teacher and tried to give directions to Tasheka: "Make a line, you know, and make it sad." His role as teacher also included modeling of the composing process. In addition, it was possible to identify his appropriation of what might be termed "movie director talk" as he encouraged Tasheka to participate in the performative aspects of the activity, "And a 1, 2, 3, and action!" In the interactions that followed, Tasheka made her own transformations to the 12-bar blues format as she appropriated it for her own use.

Semiotic Tools Shape and Define Action

The dialogue between Jay and Tasheka discussed in the previous section also signals the importance of a second theme in Vygotsky's work, his discussion of mediated action and tool use. In work related to this theme, Vygotsky asserted that individual and social development are inextricably bound through semiotic tools. Thus, in the preceding example, the rhythm and rhyme of blues music, the 12-bar blues composition pattern, and the tape recorder constitute different tools that mediate Jay and Tasheka's action and interaction. Vygotsky (1981a) posited that forms of mediation such as these are both products of their sociocultural context, and serve to facilitate, shape, and define the activity contexts in which they are applied. Certainly that is the case in the preceding example: Jay and Tasheka defined their activity together in relation to the tools they employed ("we're going to talk about how to make up a blues song") and the tools then shaped their activity.

Although much of his work centers on explicating development of speech as a semiotic tool, Vygotsky (1981b) viewed "various systems for counting; mnemonic techniques; algebraic symbol systems; works of art; writing; schemes; diagrams; maps and mechanical drawings; all sorts of conventional signs; and so on" (p. 137) as forms of semiotic mediation. Further, Vygotsky (1978) explored the representational uses of drawing and gesture by young children. As we have seen with Jay and Tasheka, additional forms of semiotic mediation could include technological tools such as computers, calculators, and tape recorders, and artistic forms of expression such as dance and drama (Palincsar, 1998; Wells, 1999). The critical feature shared by these diverse forms of mediation is that they fundamentally shape the activity in which they are applied. Vygotsky asserted that mediational means do not simply facilitate action that would have other-wise occurred in a more cumbersome fashion; rather mediational means create possibilities for action that would not have existed otherwise:

> By being included in the process of behavior, the psychological tool alters the entire flow and structure of mental functions. It does this by determining the structure of a new instrumental act just as a technical tool alters the pro-cess of a natural adaptation by determining the flow of labor operations. (Vygotsky, 1981b, p. 137)

Each of the activity settings and contexts portrayed through Jay's story presented its own array of semiotic tools and mediational means. Within the Guided Inquiry Supporting Multiple Literacies (GIsML) inquiry of floating and sinking, the semiotic tools included graphic illustrations of the materials of the inquiry, such as a Cartesian Diver System, as well as textual and spoken forms of language, such as the specialized forms of discourse employed dur-ing public sharing. Mediational means within the entomology inquiry in-cluded the physical tools of the lab, such as the microscope, as well as the different forms and genres of written documentation recorded in both the field and the lab. Music was an important semiotic tool in Jay's church activ-ity, and in this setting music and words were accompanied by expression through dance and movement. In each activity setting, the mediational tools available for appropriation shaped Jay's participation by enabling and con-straining certain forms of action and ways of constructing meaning. Further, across the settings a kind of macrocontext was formed by my engagement with Jay in a biographical research project. Engagement in this project pro-vided tools, such as notebooks, tape recorders, microphones, and video cam-eras, across contexts that might not have otherwise been available and that created different opportunities (and constraints) for Jay's participation.

Emphasizing the role of mediational means (semiotic tools) in enabling or constraining action and thought (mental action) means that the unit of analy-sis for a study informed by sociocultural theory is the agent acting with the mediational tool (Palincsar, Collins, et al., 1998; Palincsar et al., 2000; Wertsch, 1998; Wertsch, Tulviste, & Hagstrom, 1993). Jay's participation in church, for example, could not be considered without attention to the ways in which the semiotic tools of this activity setting—music, call-and-response speech patterns, movement, and dance—shaped his participation. Wertsch (1998) referred to this as an "irreducible tension" between agents and mediational means and asserted that "the essence of examining agent and cultural tools in mediated action is to examine them as they interact" (p. 25).

Assessments of ability and achievement are therefore always situated within specific activity settings and are reflective of an agent's "skill in functioning with a particular cultural tool" (Wertsch, 1998, p. 45).

This was an important assertion for my research with Jay. Why did Laura assess his abilities differently in different instructional contexts? An analysis informed by sociocultural theory would suggest that at least part of the answer to this question must lie in an examination of the mediational means and practices offered within each activity setting. From this perspective, we must ask this: Within each activity, what physical and conceptual tools were available for appropriation, and how did Jay act and interact with them? What were the conventional practices for the use of various mediational means within each setting? What abilities (and disabilities) were made visible by Jay's use of these tools and participation in these practices? These questions informed my choices in creating the plot for the narrative analysis of my work with Jay (a process described more fully in the Appendix).

Within each activity context, it was evident that different tools did indeed facilitate Jay's demonstration of different actions, abilities, and disabilities. For example, the physical tool of an Australian ("upside down") Cartesian Diver System (CDS), along with spoken interactions with his teacher, Laura, mediated Jay's articulation of understanding in the following excerpt. This excerpt was taken from the fourth day of the class's inquiry about floating and sinking. Laura had just helped Jay by holding the CDS while he wrapped a rubber band around the top. Jay then tested the operation of his system, and noticed that the water was entering the small test tube, the diver. Laura then used the CDS and her questions to mediate Jay's understanding of the system:

Laura:	So where's the water coming from and why's it going in?
Jay:	The water's coming from the test tube.
Laura:	OK.
Jay:	And how is it comin' in?
Laura:	Yup. [Why is it going in?]
Jay:	[I don't know how it's] going in.
Laura:	What's different between now and now? ((Laura presses and releases on the top of the CDS, making the diver float and sink)) Now and now? Now, what have I done?
Jay:	You have pushed it, and then probably pressure pushed it up, [and pushed it in there.]
Laura:	[OK, so when I pushed it,] you're calling that pressure?

Jay: Yeah.
Laura: So where's that pressure go?
Jay: It goes into the water, in there, and it, um the water makes it,
           I mean the pressure makes the water go up.
Laura: And then because the water is going up
Jay: It gets heavier and it goes down.

In this example, the CDS as a physical tool worked with specific forms of discourse, expressed through Laura's questions, to facilitate and mediate Jay's understanding. This kind of interaction, in which aspects of an activity out of a learner's range are controlled by a more knowledgeable other, is often referred to as *scaffolding* (Wood, Bruner, & Ross, 1976). One of the features of scaffolding is that a learner's attention is focused on specific aspects of the activity or problem. In this case, Laura used both the CDS and her language to focus Jay's attention on the changes within the system.

As Stone (1993) argued, "a persisting limitation of the metaphor of scaffolding relates to the specification of the communicative mechanisms involved in the adult–child interaction" (p. 170). Drawing on the work of Rommetveit (1974, 1979), Stone proposed the process of prolepsis as one such mechanism. Prolepsis occurs when the speaker "presupposes some as yet unprovided information," which creates "a challenge which forces the listener to create a set of assumptions in order to make sense of the utterance" (Stone, 1993, p.171). In her interaction with Jay, Laura's questions were proleptic in that they required Jay to make assumptions about the movement of the water within the CDS.

In addition to prolepsis, the interaction depicted here illustrates another communicative mechanism of scaffolding interactions, the mutual appropriation of semiotic tools. Laura drew on Jay's own use of language to mediate his understanding to encourage him to express further understanding of the CDS:

Laura: OK, so when I pushed it, you're calling that pressure?
Jay: Yeah.
Laura: So where's that pressure go?
Jay: It goes into the water, in there, and it, um the water makes it,
           I mean the pressure makes the water go up.
Laura: And then because the water is going up
Jay: It gets heavier and it goes down.

Laura's use of Jay's own language allowed Jay to build on his present observation to express new understanding. Jay was the first child in Laura's class to build a working CDS and had articulated similar ideas about the water "going in" the diver 2 days earlier. However, it was not until this interaction, when his observations were mediated by Laura's questions using his own semiotic tool, that Jay extended the concept of water going in or going up to make the claim "It gets heavier and it goes down." In this example, it was not just the learner who appropriated the teacher's discourse.[3]

Narrative analysis of Jay's interactions across contexts also illustrated that what appeared to be the same semiotic tool was defined, used, and thus shaped participation differently in different activity contexts. For example, when Laura identified Jay as possibly learning disabled, she emphasized his perceived inability to communicate in writing and his preference for oral expression. Laura's assessment of Jay's writing was based on the forms that writing took in class. However, in two contexts outside the classroom, Jay demonstrated willingness and capability as a writer. With the computer as a mediational tool, Jay composed, revised, and edited a research report on eagles. In the university entomology lab, Jay learned the importance of documenting research notes soon after a specimen was collected. He then sat for an hour documenting his observations, writing by hand in his lab notebook and using the microscope to aid his observations. The different forms of writing employed in each context, as well as the different social and cultural meanings assigned to writing, shaped Jay's demonstration of ability (and disability) as a writer.

As the examples I've shared thus far make clear, oral discourse was an important mediational means in the teaching and learning contexts of Jay's life. In addition, within each context, there were differences in the conventional uses and purposes of discourse. Discourse, then, was a socioculturally situated, semiotic resource in each of the contexts I studied. This observation is consistent with those of other scholars of sociocultural theory and discourse analysis (cf. Gee & Green, 1998).

---

[3]In another study (K. M. Collins, 1997) I explored a similar case in which successful scaffolding interactions (those leading to apparent intersubjectivity) involved this type of mutual appropriation, and unsuccessful interactions were characterized by the lack of agreement on the use and meaning of a particular semiotic tool. That is, in interactions that led to apparent misunderstanding, even when the tool itself was the same, participants were using it as part of different semiotic systems.

Human Development Is Best Understood
Through Genetic Analysis

The third theme Wertsch identified in Vygotsky's work concern developmental or *genetic analysis*. Genetic analysis brings together the other themes of Vygotsky's work through proposing a historical examination of change over time. As Palincsar (1998) summarized, "It is with the use of genetic analysis that the complex interplay of mediational tools, the individual, and social world is explored to understand learning and development and the transformation of tools, practices, and institutions" (p. 354).

Palincsar (1998) identified four levels of developmental analysis in Vygotsky's work and emphasized their interrelated nature. The broadest is *phylogenetic,* which is concerned with the human use of tools, especially psychological tools such as language (Palincsar, 1998; Vygotsky & Luria, 1930/1993; Wertsch, 1998). The next level of analysis explores influences at the level of particular cultures and communities people belong to, and is referred to as *cultural/historical* (Palincsar, 1998). Individual characteristics, such as interests, learning styles, and personal life histories, are explored at the level of *ontogenetic* analysis (Palincsar, 1998). Finally, *microgenetic* analysis explicates interactions between individuals and their activity settings and therefore considers the interplay of influences at each of the other levels (Palincsar, 1998; Wertsch, 1998).[4] These levels of analysis are woven throughout this narrative in a manner that shows their interrelated nature.

POSITIONING AND SOCIAL IDENTITIES

Sociocultural theory thus offers a different way of seeing the problem of low achievement in school. Rather than focusing on locating a deficit within Jay, or on identifying the cultural differences present among Jay, his classmates, and Laura, sociocultural theory illuminates the mutually constitutive and interdependent nature of social and individual cognitive processes (Cole, 1996; Vygotsky, 1978, 1981a, 1981b, 1987). The challenge in this work was to identify and make visible the interactions, discourses, practices, and tools that influenced the coconstruction of identity, achievement, and ability.

---

[4]Rogoff (1990, 1994) developed the application of these levels of analysis in a slightly different way, arguing for the characterization of development as participation in the activity of a community. Participation in the activity leads, in Rogoff's view, to transformations at each of three levels or planes. Changes an individual's participation are considered at the *personal plane,* changes in the relationships among individuals are considered at the *interpersonal plane,* and historical changes in the availability of tools and practices are considered at the *community* or *institutional plane* (Cole, Engestrom, & Vasquez, 1997; Rogoff, 1990, 1994).

One way in which I sought to meet this challenge in my analysis was through my use of the construct positioning. As developed by Davies and Harré (1990), the construct of *positioning* offers a way to describe the process through which people are placed into different identities (roles, categories, storylines) through culturally and historically situated interactions, and the ways in which they respond by taking up that identity or by attempting to *reposition* themselves.

Davies and Harré (1990) noted that positioning is not always a conscious or intended process:

> Positioning, as we will use it, is the discursive process whereby selves are located in conversations as observable and subjectively coherent participants in jointly produced storylines. There can be interactive positioning in which what one person says positions another. And there can be reflexive positioning in which one positions oneself. However, it would be a mistake to assume that, in either case, positioning is necessarily intentional. (p. 48)

The assertion that positioning may be unintentional is an important one: Because of a speaker's own location in a specific cultural, historical "space," certain discourses and hence forms of positioning are more readily available, and might seem more "natural" than others. A speaker (or producer of any form of text) might be unaware of how those discourses position those who are its subjects.

My analysis of Jay's story suggests many different forms of positioning were present in the interactions among him, his family, and teachers at Axleton Middle School. Most obvious, perhaps, were the physical forms of positioning through which Jay and other students who manifested various forms of difference were literally positioned at the margins of the classroom community, their desks pushed to the fringes of the room. Such physical positionings embodied the somewhat more subtle discursive practices through which participants positioned each other during face-to-face encounters, as well as during reflective or descriptive conversations where the person as subject was not present. An additional dimension of positioning in this work relates to the ways in which I was positioned by Laura, Jay, and Jay's family, and the ways in which these positionings influenced the work I was able to do and the interpretations I reached.

2

The Boy Who Had
Something to Say

October 13, 1998
Gray clouds slide swiftly toward the boys roller-blading on the blacktop bas-
ketball court. Here, the unbroken Midwestern horizon enables you to see the
weather before you feel it, if you know how to look. But the boys are absorbed
in their ongoing game of hockey, and are not interested in the impending
storm. Inside, another sixth-grade boy, their classmate, sits in his class-
room, waiting. He is silent as his teachers gather papers and arrange chairs,
preparing for the upcoming conference. Soon his grandparents will enter the
room, and the discussion will begin.[1]

"You all sit over there. Right there." Metal furniture scrapes across the linoleum floor.

"We called you because we thought it'd be best if we all got together to try
to help Jay have a successful school year. He's starting off sixth grade having
some problems. Self-control. He's quite disruptive. He'll call out, or not raise
his hand. Constantly just talkin' and whatnot, and comments and whatever.
So we're trying to, you know, get some help in curbing that. So we can get
some instruction done in the classroom without any disruptions."

"And it's also happening with, she has him half the day and I have him the
other half, and it's definitely in my classroom also. Jay has a lot of good
ideas. Sometimes, you know, like I said, he likes to share his ideas, and I
don't mind him sharing those with us, but there's an appropriate way to do

---

[1] I reconstructed this opening scene in collaboration with Jay. The dialogue was drawn from my
transcription of the audiotape of the meeting recorded by Jay. Where indicated, segments of the dialogue have been summarized. Otherwise the whole conversation is presented as it appears on the
tape. Please see the Appendix for details regarding my approach to transcription and representation.

that, you know. I'd like to see him raise his hand, just not yell out things. And just, you know, like I said, it's becoming really disruptive in class. I'm sure you folks don't send him to school to do that. He's here to learn and get an education. It's important. And, he just, he wants to argue everything. I'm not sure if you ever see that at home or not but he wants to make an issue out if it and argue about it. Since we're all on the same team, we wanted to get you folks in here and see if we could come up with some solutions so we can avoid that. And so you're aware of the problems that he's having here, and so we can have a good school year." Mrs. Armstrong addresses Jay, "Anything you want to ask, add, or put in there? Do you agree with what Mrs. Simpson and I are saying?"

"I guess."

"Why are you behaving like that?" Mrs. Armstrong continues.

"I mean, I like, I have something to say, and I just say it."

"You just shout it out. Now what would happen if everyone in the classroom just had something to say and they just started shouting out things? Would any work get done here?"

"I don't know. They'd hear each others' ideas."

"But would they be able to hear each other?" asks Mrs. Simpson.

"Do you feel you can control yourself?" Mrs. Armstrong adds, and Mrs. Simpson's question is left unanswered.

"Yeah."

"Well, then, when you do that, you're choosing to act up. So when Mrs. Simpson and I see you doing something you shouldn't do, that's a choice you're making. Is that correct?" Mrs. Armstrong continues without pausing, "That means you need to make good choices instead of poor choices or there'll be certain consequences you really don't like."

"Hm-mm."

"You understand that?"

"Hm-mm."

"And the arguing back and forth when you do something is really not necessary either. You know just as well as I do … "

" … and the comments aren't necessary," adds Mrs. Simpson

"Yeah, the comments aren't necessary. The arguing," Mrs. Armstrong continues. "That's taking more time. You know we don't have, we have kids we have to teach. That's what we're here for. And the disciplining, and the having to put so much energy towards that, is not, is not a good idea. It takes away from all kids. And it's taking away from you too by, you know, misbehaving." After a 2-second pause, Mrs. Armstrong continues, "Anything you don't understand from what we've said?" She pauses for another second, and then asks, "Has he had these problems before or are they new to sixth grade?"

Jay's grandmother speaks softly, "Last year, too."

"Well, hopefully later on, maybe we can get back together again or um, something like that, touch base." Mrs. Armstrong is speaking swiftly now, "Hopefully we can say, next time we talk to you, maybe in a couple of weeks, or whatever, that Jay has made excellent progress. He's fine. He can control himself."

Jay speaks, "I try to keep myself under control."

"Sometimes," Mrs. Armstrong acknowledges. "What happens in the afternoon when you come see me? Do you waste all your energy trying in the morning and you can't control yourself anymore?"

Jay's grandfather asks, "Is it a all-day process or, you know?"

"Well, she sees him first thing in the morning," explains Mrs. Armstrong. "And I have him in the afternoon."

Mrs. Simpson speaks, "But it's all day long that we're, you know, getting the disruption. Because we talked to Jay before. It's like he wants to be the center of attention … "

" … And, uh, you know I don't understand that," Mrs. Armstrong begins. "You can be a positive leader with our group. But right now, you know, you're not really being a good leader for people to follow you. Is there some reason that you want everybody's attention?"

"I don't want their attention."

"You want to be the class clown, is that what you're trying to do here?" Mrs. Armstrong continues.

"I'm not the class clown."

Jay's grandfather speaks quietly, "That's what it comes out to bein' when you do that though. Everybody, you know, be wonderin' what's goin' on."

Mrs. Simpson begins, "And we have another problem. He's up out of his seat all the time, or over at somebody else's desk. He really does not, or doesn't seem to be able to be quiet … "

" … We'll be workin' and I'll look over at him and he's kinda hangin' out by his chair, kinda movin' around. Just by his desk even. He doesn't sit still very good," Mrs. Armstrong agrees.

"Yeah. We been tryin' to address that issue for a while now. Last year. A little bit the year before. You know," his grandfather responds. "We been seein' it escalate. So far we just haven't been able to, uh, to do anything, you know. We try at home, you know, to give him punishments. Set in his room and read or whatever. Try to get him to be still for a while. But, you know, he do all right for a minute and then he's off and running. I think it's, I think it's like you said, that he like to be around children and get all the attention."

"Hm-mm," Mrs. Armstrong murmurs.

Jay's grandfather continues, "Because he does that with his nieces and stuff. You know, uh, his cousins and whatnot. When they come over he get, you know, he get more excited. When he think he can get some attention, you know. So I think that's the problem with him."

"It might help you, you know the homework assignments we give him during the week? Does he show you those during the week at all? 'Cause we might wanna jot, start jotting in, you know, when we have a problem we'll call you up or something. Maybe jot it down." Mrs. Armstrong addresses Jay again, "Or if you're having a good day, maybe working really well, you know you can bring your planner up and say 'Mrs. Simpson or Mrs. Armstrong, would you sign it.' You know, we're happy to put positive comments in there too. Or the same thing, if you're having an off day, we have to put those in there too."

"And if you're having an off day and we put something down about that, what are you not going to do?" asks Mrs. Simpson.

"White it out," Jay whispers.

"Can't hear you," his grandfather speaks. "Speak up. Speak loud. This is your opportunity."

"I won't white it out like I did last time."

"You whited it out?" Mrs. Armstrong asks. "I didn't hear this part."

Jay's voice is louder now, "I, um, whited it out because I wanted to go to my dad's house."

"Did you make it over to your dad's house?" his grandfather asks.

"Yeah."

"Yeah." Jay's grandfather speaks softly, "That was the weekend."

"She called that Monday," his grandmother explains. "And I asked him. I said, 'Why is this whited out?' 'Oh, that's just something I was doin.' Uh-huh."

His grandfather's voice is louder now, "Because I think the week before that he had got in trouble on the bus. And, uh, uh, I told him he couldn't go over to his father's because he needed to be on punishment and learn some discipline. And, uh, so that following week, I guess that he thought that he wanted to go to his father's so he whited it out."

"Whited it out," his grandmother repeats.

Mrs. Armstrong addresses Jay, "You shouldn't ever ruin their trust in you. So you would think, that. You want somebody to believe you're telling the truth so they can trust you. Is that right?"

"Uh-huh."

"So again, thinking back before you do some of these things. Because you're smart. So what do you think of this, Jay, do you think you're making the right decision?"

His grandmother responds before he does, "Or do you just think you got too much energy you just hafta bust out everywhere? Energy just hafta bust out. You hafta learn how to maintain that energy."

"He hafta learn some discipline and respect. I know that's another issue. I get feedback. He tries to disrespect us sometimes," his grandfather adds.

"Do you try taking, like, no TV for the day or give him extra chores?" Mrs. Armstrong suggests.

"Yeah, we did that," his grandmother answers.

"Some parents try that," Mrs. Armstrong continues. "You know, if he has one of his off days, or does something, you can give him extra chores or extra little jobs around the house."

"We been talkin' about that too," his grandfather explains. "In fact he had some extra chores the other week, when he got in trouble on the bus. I had him doin' extra … "

" … Me too. I did too. That week," his grandmother adds.

"Does he talk on the phone very much, or at all?" asks Mrs. Armstrong. She pauses for 1 second then asks, "What would really bother you if they took it away from you, Jay?"

"Probably the TV. I don't know."

"The TV." Mrs. Armstrong repeats, "Maybe, have you tried some positive rewards too, where if he's having things go his way he can have friend over, or go over somebody's house?"

Jay answers quickly, "No."

"Well, maybe you can talk to them and see if you can work something out. There's all kind of different things," Mrs. Armstrong suggests.

Jay's grandfather speaks, "Well, you know, like, like even his cousins live down the street. And, uh, when it was a little warmer he'd ride his bike. His next-door neighbor is his cousin, and uh, Tasheka, so, uh, sometimes she comes over at night or we let him go over during the day. He has a discipline problem, so."

"Hm-mm." Mrs. Armstrong addresses Jay, "So it sounds like it's basically what you have to earn. You have to earn that people can trust you, that you're not gonna have some problems. That's what I'm understanding here, right?"

His grandfather continues, "Even with his cousins, he'll get in little, he wanna be the center if it's just one person."

"The leader. You know ... " his grandmother begins.

" ... He wanna, he wanna, he wanna control the situation," Jay's grandfather adds.

"I know one thing," Jay's grandmother continues. "The lady that was working with you from the U of M? I guess if you can't control yourself, you like bein' with her. I might have to tell her, she can't work with you no more."

"Was this last year?" Mrs. Armstrong asks.

"This summer ... " his grandfather begins.

"This summer and last year ... " his grandmother adds.

" ... it was like an activity," Jay's grandfather continues. "You go out and, and catch butterflies and pin 'em down, and name 'em. And do recording, recording messages about the, um, the subjects that they, you know the insects and different things. It was a lot of field work ... "

" ... Hm-mm," his grandmother adds, "And she took him to the University. She would take him to the places ... "

" ... and she would buy him, and treat him," her husband goes on, "and you know, kind of spoiled him a little bit. So, I mean, you know, it was interesting. It was educational."

"Did you enjoy that?" Mrs. Simpson asks.

"Yeah."

"He, seemed like he was real interested in it," Jay's grandfather continues. "In fact, he got his cousin involved. And they both participated in it back in the summer. In fact, she gave quite a few positive reports of him."

"Well, good," Mrs. Simpson says.

"She enjoyed it," Jay's grandfather continues, "She seemed to have enjoyed it, when she came and got him. They seemed to get along real good."

His grandmother addresses him, "She want to work with you again, but you got to improve your, uh, attitude."

Mrs. Armstrong speaks quickly, before Jay responds to his grandmother, "Is he gonna ride the bus home or is he coming home with you? They're gonna get out in a few minutes."

Jay's grandfather answers, "He'll come with us."

Mrs. Armstrong continues, "Any suggestions for making his papers legible? His handwriting is, I cannot read it. And sometimes I think I mark things wrong because I can't understand … "

"He knows," his grandfather speaks more loudly.

" … what he's saying" Mrs. Armstrong continues.

"He knows," Jay's grandfather repeats. "I spoke to him on a number of occasions about that."

"Do you have those, uh, like an alphabet thing for children who have problems writing? You know how they have the writing where you connect the dots together to improve your writing? Do they have that?" his grandmother asks.

Mrs. Simpson speaks, "To improve your handwriting?"

"They might. Just some—" Mrs. Armstrong begins.

"Yes. For handwriting," Jay's grandmother answers Mrs. Simpson.

"Just some," Mrs. Armstrong repeats, her voice growing louder, "basic things that I'd like to see him do is when he does an 'A' he doesn't close his 'As.' Closing those letters, you know, 'A'—"

"He has more problems than that." Jay's grandmother raises her voice, too. "'Cause he be writing too close."

"Yeah," his grandfather agrees.

"You can't even see what it is," his grandmother continues.

"Yeah, that's true," his grandfather agrees again.

"Well, first let's try to figure out what some of it is—" Mrs. Armstrong begins.

"It, it connects. He don't break it. He don't form … " Jay's grandfather explains.

"Connects," echoes his grandmother.

" … He don't, he don't take his time," Jay's grandfather goes on.

"He wastes a lot of space," his grandmother adds.

"He write too small, he don't press hard enough, like. Like, I, I have good penmanship, you know. And I try to explain to him, you know, like, how to um, keep 'em separated," his grandfather's voice is rising.

"Space his words out," Mrs. Simpson breaks in.

"Space," his grandfather repeats. "You know, even if you think of spacin' it. You know, one letter at a time. And what Jay do," he pauses briefly, then continues quickly, "Write, write, write a sentence. 'My name is Jay.' Normal."

There is a 5-second pause, and then Jay's grandfather says, "Now that 'n' look kinda funny."

"Well, that's better than it usually is," his grandmother observes. The adults laugh together. Jay is silent.

"Yeah, he's spacin' now," his grandfather chuckles.

"He's takin' his time," his grandmother agrees. "I think that's the problem, too."

"So, I guess what we could do is," Mrs. Armstrong begins, "he could start recopying papers if we can't read 'em. That's a good choice. Also, at home, for some extra activities, maybe you know, if he's having some problems, he could practice his penmanship. In the back of his language arts book there's an alphabet there that shows you how to make the letters and that. So he can look right back there."

"In the back?" his grandmother asks, no trace of laughter remaining in her voice.

"In his English book," Mrs. Armstrong explains.

"Well, you bring your English book home," his grandmother's voice is quieter now.

"And you wanna help kinda him budget his time so he doesn't wait 'til the last minute to do everything," Mrs. Armstrong continues.

"He have a *hour* every day that he have study time whether he have homework or not," his grandmother explains firmly.

"We give him a *hour*," his grandfather repeats.

"So you could slow down here in class, and you know, not, make it so we can read it." Mrs. Armstrong continues, "Another suggestion, maybe once a week or something, when you check his planner if you could help him clean his Trapper Keeper out. 'Cause I know when he comes in, papers are everywhere. And, he's even taken over my couch. And, 'Jay, you can't be all over that couch. That's for people to sit on!' And he's got papers all over the place."

"We just cleaned that out last week," his grandmother explains. "Is it messed up again?"

"He was working on it a minute ago. Let's see what looks like, just out of curiosity," Mrs. Armstrong suggests.

"That's important, to keep organized," Jay's grandfather agrees.

"Well, it looks better than it did last week when I looked at it," his grandmother observes.

"Pretty much, at least reasonable. It looks pretty decent," Mrs. Armstrong acknowledges and then goes on, "but you can still check on it because I know he, lots of times he puts papers all over the place. And I think he has, you know, trouble finding sometimes, just to turn in an assignment, when he can't find it he's doing a paper shuffle."

Mrs. Simpson explains, "If they don't get four stickers in their planner by Friday that means that something is missing. Then they have an assignment to do, basically a reflection statement, they think about what 'I didn't get done this week and how can I improve.'"

"So he's supposed to do that on his own?" Jay's grandfather asks.

"No, they work on it during penalty time, " Mrs. Simpson explains. "But they still have to take it home to get it signed."

"If a kid gets four stickers, and our initials, then he gets to go outside on a Friday for some, um, recess. In sixth grade they don't have recess anymore. And we know kids still like to get out and play and run, so if he gets all his work done, then he gets to go outside. But if he doesn't, then what happens?" Mrs. Armstrong asks Jay.

"I have to go into the penalty room."

"OK," Mrs. Armstrong continues. "So then he goes into the penalty room and he has some kind of reflection to do about changin', changin' his ways and getting organized."

Mrs. Simpson addresses Jay, "Is your language arts done?"

"No, well, I don't know."

"Do you have the dictionary cards done? Do you have a dictionary?" Mrs. Simpson continues.

Jay's grandmother answers, "That's what he was working on Friday."

"Does he use his hour time doing things?" Mrs. Armstrong asks.

"Yeah." His grandmother explains. "I have him sittin' at the table, where I can see him."

"You might wanna check back on him sometimes because he likes to waste time, too, I noticed. Just, say, 'OK, go ahead and work on that a while and I'll check back on ya in a little bit' or whatever."

"That's why I have him sittin' at the table instead of in his room. He wanted to sit in his room. I said, 'Naw, you sit at the table.' 'Cause he be in his room, he could be in there sleepin'."

The adults discuss a free after-school tutoring program that would involve Jay being bussed to another school in the afternoons. Jay is silent during this discussion. Then Mrs. Armstrong reminds Jay that his grandparents will be looking at his planner, stating, "I'm afraid you'll have to write in your planner so they can read it at home." The adults laugh, but Jay does not. Mrs. Armstrong continues, "So, again, slow down. Slow down on you, your writing. Space your words out. Do some practice during that hour time at home.

Clean up your Trapper at least once a week. And, what are we doing about the big problem, the big behavior problem? What's happening with that?"

"I'll come up and have you write in my planner how I did," Jay speaks softly.

"OK. So we want you to bring your planner up at the end of the day. It's your job to bring it up and say, 'Mrs. Armstrong, can you write down what I did today.' And if we don't write anything, then your mom or somebody is gonna think that there must have been a problem today because Jay never got a signature from anybody."

"That's right, " his grandmother agrees.

"Can you remember to do that?" Mrs. Armstrong asks.

"Yeah."

"And let's see if we can get some good comments in there too. OK?" Mrs. Armstrong continues. She lists the homework assignments for that day that should be written in his planner, then continues, "Let's us keep in touch. Maybe in another two or three weeks, we can get back together. If it's convenient for you, come on back in. We'll review how things are going. Hopefully, you'll hear some major improvements. OK?" She addresses Jay, "Any questions you have? Anything you don't understand?"

"Are we asking of you anything that's unreasonable?" Mrs. Simpson asks.

"No-oh," he draws the word out slowly.

"No." Mrs. Simpson repeats, "OK."

Mrs. Armstrong reviews Jay's current grades, and then explains her grading policy. "So like if he gets a worksheet back from me, if he doesn't like it he has one day to redo it and bring it back the next day. But I don't come after him and say, I don't come after him and say, 'Are you gonna redo that?' or 'Where's it at?' You know, it's gotta be his responsibility because it's kinda like an extra plus we're giving him. So he can redo it."

"Hm-mm. Another chance." His grandmother continues, "Another thing too. A punishment, if you don't do good, you won't be goin' on trips, when they have trips."

Mrs. Armstrong agrees. "One of our big trips that we have this year is sixth grade camp. So that's for like a week. Um, so again, hopefully he can join us all, you know, join us for all the trips. But that's up to how he behaves."

"Right," his grandmother agrees.

Mrs. Armstrong addresses Jay, "So that comes down to you. OK?"

"OK."

Mrs. Armstrong continues, "Well, thank you both for coming in and for takin' the time here to help us get him on the right track. Hopefully, like I said, if we meet again in another two-three weeks, hopefully we'll be sayin' all kinds of wonderful things about he listened and is following through with everything he promised he was going to do."

"We hope so," his grandmother speaks softly.

They are in the car, and no one speaks for several minutes. His grandfather breaks the silence, "It look like it gonna rain out here."

"It sure do," his grandmother agrees. "All this wind."

His grandfather begins, "You gotta clean up at school. Them people, they be lookin' at stuff like that. They think our home probably tore up."

Jay begins, "I didn't—"

"Don't say anything," his grandmother tells him.

His grandfather continues, "His problem is he always gotta … "

" … try to justify."

"Yeah. That's what she said. You argue with 'em and stuff in the classroom … "

" … gotta learn how to close your mouth."

"You wanna, you try to be right all the time. Organization. When you get into junior high and high school, they want him to be able to be organized with his notes, to be able to read what he write, and all that kind of stuff. They expect more out you when you get older. I can see at five years old, you know, finger paintin' and stuff—" A loud clap of thunder interrupts Jay's grandfather, and heavy drops of rain begin to bang against the roof and hood of the car.

Jay handed me the tape of this interaction as he slid out of my car one evening after we had spent the afternoon working together on our ongoing research project. When I pushed the cassette into my car's tape deck on the drive home, I expected to hear Jay's voice describing the insects he'd collected most recently. Instead, a woman's voice filled my car.

"You all sit over there. Right there … "

When a second woman began speaking, I realized I was listening to a tape of a conference with Jay's sixth-grade teachers. Listening to the tape left me stunned by the ways in which Jay and his grandparents were positioned by his teachers, and dismayed over the portrait of Jay that was constructed in the meeting. During this meeting, through both the content and discursive style of their talk, the teachers jointly constructed a narrative that depicted Jay as a child who either chooses to be disruptive or who cannot control himself. In this narrative, Jay's grandparents were positioned as either well-meaning but ineffective, or as neglectful of their grandson's education.

After more than a year of working with Jay, this tape made it clear that I had not been able to interrupt the institutional biography constructed about him. Tears—of anger, of frustration, of despair—ran down my face as I ejected the tape and entered my apartment. I felt physically sick. There seemed to be no place in school for the child I knew. The boy who loved to write and perform blues poetry. Who composed and enacted complicated dramas with his cousin after school. Who would spend an entire day catching insects, documenting his finds in his field journal, and then sharing his data with a university-based entomologist. Who loved to dance, sing, and worship in church, and would lead his younger cousins through a service. Who, before a visit to my university office, would change into his best clothes—a long-sleeved, black-and-white flannel dress shirt and black corduroys—even in the heat and humidity of midsummer. Who thought he had something to say, if only anyone would listen.

This is our story, the story of the Jay not reflected in his school records or described by his teachers, and of how I came to know him. It is a story that challenges prevailing notions of ability as a quantifiable characteristic people either have or don't have, a story that requires us to consider how and why communities work to exclude some members and thus position them as disabled or different. It is a story that asks us to examine our own assumptions when we exclude or silence a child "for his own good" or "so he'll learn to behave," or when we decide that a child must be impaired or disabled because he is not learning the way that we teach. It is a story that asks us to reconsider where we place responsibility for failure and for success.

3

"He's What I Would Call 'Out There.'"

August 28, 1997
Thirteen-and-a-half months earlier

It is a bright morning at the end of August, hot enough to remind me that it is still summer vacation in some school districts, when I set out to begin my observations in the classroom of fifth-grade teacher Laura Bozek at Axleton Middle School. Laura and I are both members of a professional development effort, the GIsML Community of Practice. I am working as a research assistant in her classroom, and my role at the beginning of the new school year is to observe and document the routines and practices of Laura's classroom community.

My task this morning is particularly important because of the theoretical perspective that guides our ongoing research effort. GIsML is an orientation to teaching science that is informed by social constructivist perspectives on learning and cognition, which assert that social and individual cognitive processes are mutually constitutive and interdependent (Magnusson & Palincsar, 1995; Vygotsky, 1978, 1981a, 1981b, 1987). In this view, the dialectical relationship between individuals and their social contexts is seen as mediated by physical and conceptual tools through participation in situated activity. The classroom is thus viewed as a learning community with routines and practices for tool use that shape the opportunities and constraints for participation, and thus for learning (Rogoff, 1994).

It is this theoretical orientation and attention to the larger context of the inquiry, the classroom learning community, that distinguish the GIsML orientation from other discussions of inquiry-based science and that call for my presence in Laura's classroom at the beginning of the school year. My observations in Laura's classroom as she begins the new school year are intended to help us understand how Laura establishes the routines and practices of her classroom community, and to what extent these practices may enable or constrain the development of a classroom learning community.

Even with a head full of thoughts about how I will watch for and document classroom practices and forms of student participation, it is impossible not to take note of the changing landscape outside my car. As I approach Axleton, apartments, shopping malls, restaurants, and generic urban sprawl yield to houses whose yards grow larger and larger. Finally the yards merge with fields of soybeans and corn that ring the town on all sides, as though Axleton was a giant bull's eye on a dartboard.

Axleton was constructed in 1831 at the intersection of two Native American trails that were first widened by the passage of wagons and horses then, their utility clear as Axleton's population grew, made "permanent" by lining their muddy bottoms with wooden planks or "timber." During the hardest part of the cold Midwestern winters, the first White European settlers of Axleton tore up the planks and burned them for fuel, so that they had to be replaced each spring (which all but destroyed the area's native population of oak trees). The highway I travel on deposits me onto what is still one of two main roads into town, paved now for many years but still called Timberland Road.

I drive past the McDonald's, Arby's, Big Boy, gas stations, and strip malls that cluster near the highway exit and announce their presence in plastic, primary colors, and approach Main Street. Houses begin to line Timberland Road just past the entrance where, having been refueled and fed, a traveler can get back on the freeway. These houses have wide front porches and American flags blowing in the breeze, and many were constructed on the foundations of the earliest buildings erected in Axleton. One rests on the foundation of Axleton's first school. Within a mile of the highway exit, I am at the intersection of Timberland Road and Main Street, at the entrance of downtown Axleton, the core of the community.

Axleton, population 4,040, straddles two counties, and at the intersection of Timberland and Main I have half my car in each. Coming from my home I approach from the north, so that the back end of my car sits in Jessup County. Seventy-two percent of Axleton's residents live on this side of town, where the average household income is $36,561. The front half of my car rests over the border of Walden County, where 28% of Axleton's residents live and the average household income is $29,934. Part of this discrepancy may be connected with educational differences across the two counties: In Jessup County, 41.9% of the residents have a bachelor's degree or higher, whereas in Walden County the number is far lower, at 10.5%.[1]

Turning right, I enter Main Street and downtown Axleton. This view of Axleton always reminds me of the New England town I was born in, with its brick buildings, pots of geraniums on the sidewalks, and shops lining either side of the street. There is a barber shop with a red-and-white pole out front, a drugstore that sells a little of everything, a coffee shop and a bakery that are both locally owned, and a franchise pizza shop housed within the structure that was once Axleton's first apothecary (herbs and medicinal plants were grown in the small backyard). This street also boasts Axleton's first and only movie theater, which opened in 1939 with a showing of *Snow White* but is now a hardware store; in 1999 if you want to see a movie you need to drive about 30 minutes to the more urban Andover City.

The necessity of driving is one of the limitations of life in Axleton. There is one large grocery store one the edge of town and two quick-stop minimarkets off of Timberland Road. With the exception of a second-hand catch-all shop on Main Street that sometimes has children's clothes, there are no clothing, shoe, housewares, or department stores. No public transportation system exists. Beyond the downtown area, Axleton becomes very rural very quickly, and a working vehicle is necessary for transportation to and from employment, shopping centers, places of worship, medical offices, and any after-school activities children might want to be involved in.

It is a short drive from Main Street to Axleton Middle School, and when I pull into the school parking lot at 7:20 in the morning, buses are still parked out front. Excited children wearing their back-to-school best spill through the school bus doors and onto the sidewalk. They rush about excitedly, greeting old friends and exclaiming over new classes, teachers, and routines. It is August 28, 1997, the third day of school.

Laura is standing outside her room when I get there, greeting children as they enter. Her short, stylishly cut, light brown hair is freshly trimmed for the new school year and she wears pressed slacks and a sweater set that suits her athletic build. I say hello and slip into the classroom, wanting to get settled before the children fill the room. There are three bulletin boards in the classroom, one on either side of the chalkboard in the front and a larger one across part of the back wall, directly behind the couch I am sitting on. One

---

[1]I used 1990 census data, provided to me by the city's development office, for all of the demographic information about Axleton. The Axleton Historical Society provided historical information.

bulletin board in the front is devoted to "Axleton Middle School News." It holds lunch menus, a bell schedule, and a map like the one I have in my hand. The other, titled "Fast Facts," holds a chart with all of the children's names listed vertically. The row next to each name has a space for each of 12 timed math tests that the students will take; as each test is mastered a star will be entered on the chart. The bulletin board in the back of the room holds letters from Laura's previous class, and large blue-construction-paper letters across the top announcing "How to survive fifth grade."

The student desks are pushed together to form six tables of four desks each, and one table with three desks. As the students take their seats I notice that they are sitting in gendered pairs at the tables. There are two exceptions to this pattern: Danny, a child with Down syndrome, sits in the back of the room with a table of three girls, and three boys sit together in the front of the room near the windows. There are 15 boys and 12 girls in the class. Like Laura and myself, most of the students appear to be White and of European descent. Three appear to be Black or of mixed ethnicity (Jay, Cynthia, and Jessica),[2] and one boy (Matthew) is from Korea. Laura's classroom reflects the student population of Axleton fairly accurately: Based on families' self-identification of student ethnicity at enrollment, 91.5% of Axleton's 2,400 students are White, 8.0% are Black, and .5% are Native American or "other."

A sagging couch is pushed against the back wall of the room, next to a small bookshelf and worn armchair. I settle into the couch and begin to take notes in a small yellow notebook, beginning with a sketch of the seating arrangement; shown in Figure 3.1.

On the chalkboard Laura has posted the "morning work"—three sentences with grammatical and syntactic errors that the students are supposed to correct as they write the sentences on lined paper in their morning work folder. As the students work on this, Laura takes attendance and attends to

---

[2]Jessica left Axleton and moved to Andover City in early December. Like Jay, Jessica was a highly active participant in class discussions, especially during guided inquiry. Prior to Jessica's move, Laura suggested we follow her as a case study student as well: "There's one girl in particular, Jessica, who's not one of the case study kids, who would possibly be an interesting one. Um, she has a lot of really good leadership capabilities. I mean, Jessica's just a natural leader, but she's one of these kids that will go either way. She'll either fall in with kids who are either sort of gang oriented, uh, smoke, drink, party, or she could go the other route, you know if she decides that she's gonna, you know, be a good kid. And she's having a, a real problem deciding which way for her. Right now she's, she's, the first probably two months, month and a half of school, she was turning all of her assignments in. This last, I just did progress reports yesterday, and she's turned nothing in. So she's doing kind of a switch around here on me. But she's also very, I mean she will not miss a trick. She's the one who will say, well, um, the, we were talking about criminals or something on some assignment, and I made the comment, 'When you, um, describe what this criminal is doing, you could say, 'He did this' and she said, 'Well, criminals could be women.'"

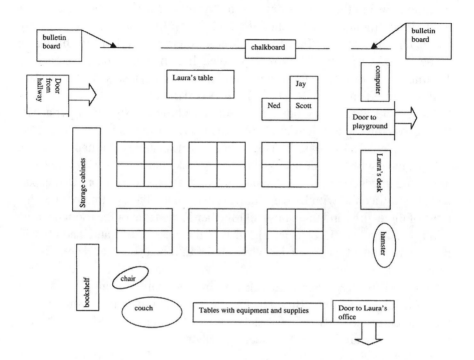

FIG. 3.1.   Seating Chart 1. Jay's fifth-grade classroom, September.

other administrative tasks, sitting at a long table in the front of the room. Also posted on the board is the daily schedule:

>   1st hour—Morning work/posters
>   2nd hour—Math
>   3rd hour—Social Studies
>   4th hour—Exploratories
>   5th hour—Timed test/lunch/story
>   6th hour—Science/recess
>   7th hour—Spelling/journals

Although the students will only leave Laura's room for lunch, recess, and "exploratories" (either art, gym, or music depending on the time of year), Laura adheres to the middle school bell schedule when changing subject to, as she asserts, "prepare the students for sixth grade."

Four students—the table of three boys (Jay, Ned, and Scott) and a girl named Molly—are eating school-supplied breakfasts. Doughnuts—the miniature kind covered in powdered sugar and packaged in cellophane—and chocolate milk are the popular choices. One of the boys, Jay, stands up, slurps the last of his milk noisily, wipes a napkin through the powdered sugar on his desk with a flourish, and marches across the front of the room to the trash can. He stands for one more moment, slurping the very last drop of chocolate milk up through his plastic straw, before he disposes of his breakfast wrappings. Laura watches him do this, as do several of his classmates. He appears totally unaware of their gazes and walks briskly back to his seat, where he opens his notebook and begins the morning work.

Fifteen minutes into the school day Laura stands up and addresses the class, "Good job coming in this morning. It looks like everyone is doing their morning work. Breakfast students, remember your job is to eat *while* you are working." Laura pauses and glances to her left, at Jay, who is looking down at his morning work and seems unaware that this public announcement seems directed toward him. Laura continues, "Now, as we go on in the school year we won't be spending a lot of time on morning work. You should be able to complete it in 10 minutes." She introduces me to the class as "Kathleen, a research assistant from the university," and then tells the students to exchange their morning work papers with a classmate at their table. There is some paper shuffling and discussion as the boys at the table of three exchange papers twice, figuring out an equitable trade with an uneven number of participants.

As the day goes on, Laura consistently emphasizes that, even though this is fifth grade, they are middle school students now, and must be organized and responsible for their own work and their own behavior. She stresses that it is her job to prepare them for the demands of sixth grade. After each subject area lesson, she has the students update, on a calendar, the work they completed in that subject area and any unfinished work or homework to be completed that evening.

Bathroom trips are taken together—the class files out in a line but students return individually—and there are two during the course of the day. After one such break, the children appear to have some difficulty transitioning to social studies, and are instead talking quietly to each other as they straggle into the room. Laura reminds them to look at the board and check the schedule to see what they should be doing. Then she tells them to "Think about moving from one subject to another. What is the proper way to prepare?" Students raise their hands and, when they are called on, make suggestions, which Laura writes on the board:

1. Put away old materials.
2. Get out new materials.
3. Stay in your seat.
4. Do things quietly.
5. Make eye contact with the teacher.
6. Be quick.

The students then practice getting ready for social studies. After the third try, Laura congratulates them for making the transition appropriately. They begin the social studies lesson, each student reading a paragraph of the text out loud to the class. When a student stumbles over a word, Laura supplies the correct pronunciation.

Over the course of the next few weeks I make three additional visits to Axleton Middle School and continue to document the routines and practices of Laura's class. Gradually jobs that she completed on the first day, such as passing out papers, are assigned to student helpers. Also gradually the practice of a biweekly class meeting is introduced and evolves from a brief meeting led by Laura to a longer one where students take turns—the speaker holding a stuffed penguin in her or his lap—complimenting each other. Danny, the boy who has Down syndrome, spends much of his school day out of the classroom with his aide, but consistently receives the most compliments in these meetings.

On my last observation before Laura begins her guided inquiry investigation of sinking and floating, I observe a science lesson that elicits more interactive discussion and enthusiastic student participation than any lesson I have witnessed thus far. In this lesson, Laura is trying to impress on the students the importance of making and recording detailed observations of phenomena. Working with a partner, they have already performed a variety of tests on a white "mystery powder" and on salt, sugar, baking soda, baking powder, and flour, documenting the reaction of each substance to water and to vinegar. Their overall objective is to identify the mystery powder. During this lesson, the students are sitting at their desks with their science notebooks out.

"I looked over your data sheets," Laura is standing in front of the chalkboard, "and some of you are really going to benefit from taking notes when others share today. And when you share, I want you to share what you wrote, not what's in your head. Today, work on fixing up your notes when others share. And think about how to improve your own notes the next time around." Laura explains that they will be allowed to use their notes, "but only your own notes," for an upcoming exam.

The "passer-outers" for the week, Ned and Maria, distribute the data sheets. As Ned takes his seat again, I notice that his data sheet is nearly blank. His short blond hair pokes up in several directions and he kneels on his chair, a bundle of barely contained energy as he leans toward Jay, who is sitting diagonally across from him. "Jay! Jay! Hey, partner!" Ned grins as Jay looks up. Jay grins back quickly, a bright white flash against his ebony skin. Then he turns to face Laura at the front of the room. The seat next to Jay is empty: Scott, who is identified as emotionally disturbed, has forgotten his morning medication, and as a result spends most of the day in the assistant principal's office.

Laura writes "Number 1 with Water" on the chalkboard, and the students begin to share their observations, first raising their hands to be called on. Ned is recognized first, and announces clearly, "It turned mushy."

Danny, prompted in a loud stage whisper by the girl sitting next to him, Molly, offers, "It turned liquid."

"It, like, made the water all cloudy," Catherine, Maria's tablemate, observes.

"The color changed to yellowish-white," Maria adds.

Several more observations are offered, and then Laura reminds the students that they should be very specific in their observations, "I'm going to press you a bit on that." She turns to the list on the board, and then asks Ned, "What did you mean by 'mushy?'"

"When you pressed down on it, it was kind of sticky, like mush," Ned explains.

"Can you say more? Did it bounce, or sink, or spread?"

Ned hesitates, looks at his blank paper, and then at Jay. Without raising his hand, Jay offers, "It was like a sponge is. A wet sponge."

"I like that," Laura nods to Jay. "When you think of something that it's like, everyone knows what you mean."

"Yeah!" Ned agrees enthusiastically. "Like bread!"

Several hands are raised at once now. Laura calls on Matt, who adds, "It was wet but not all the way, like when your clothes are washed but not all the way dry."

The class spends the next 40 minutes enthusiastically generating a long list of analogies for each substance. Although Jay and Ned don't have much written on their papers, I note that they participate extensively and that their analogies are particularly vivid. They also seem to work to clarify and extend each other's contributions, as they did on the first exchange. For example, when Jay notes that when the second substance was mixed with water, it "turned kind of mushy," Ned adds, "like a sponge." Jay clarifies, "No, not like a sponge. Like cereal that got soggy. Corn flakes." Later, when the class is listing their observations for the third substance mixed with water, Ned observes, "It turned doughy like gum. Like chewed, ABC gum."[3] Jay agrees, adding, "Yeah. It got soft and gooey like a marshmallow."

When the students leave for lunch, I meet briefly with Laura and share my observations and notes with her. Laura is surprised when I share my thinking about the nature and extent of Ned and Jay's participation. She comments that she thinks Jay is having difficulty "fitting in" at Axleton Middle School because he moved to this small, rural community, from a larger, more urban school district, Andover City, just before the school year started. She cites his recent confrontation with another student in the cafeteria as evidence, and states that she thinks "he's really EI [emotionally impaired]" but she is frustrated because it is the beginning of November and she has yet to receive his school records. She explains that she recently referred him for psychological assessment to see if he qualifies for special education services, but that his grandmother (his guardian) has not yet given her consent for the assessment to take place.

Two weeks after the mystery powder investigation, Laura and I meet again to discuss her plans for her upcoming guided inquiry investigation of floating and sinking. As part of my work with the GIsML research team, my role in Laura's classroom during her guided inquiry teaching will be documenting the experiences of the students she identified as having special needs. I begin this meeting by asking her to describe what she perceives to be the strengths and weaknesses of each of these students, and she starts with Jay, "He's, well, you know him. He's what I would call 'out there.'" She pauses, chuckling softly, "He's just all over the place. But I, I've suspected all along that he's actually got quite a bit going on in here." She taps her head, and smiles. "But it's just interfered with on so many other levels, emotionally, and socially. And, um, that he doesn't have time to just think about things. And his responses [on the subject matter pretest] were quite interesting to read, and he wrote a lot."

"Oh, I haven't seen those yet," I respond.

"He'll be working with two other kids who are pretty severe. So that group, I have my aide working with that group."

"Right. Danny and Ned."

"I think Jay's probably much more capable than what he's showing on paper. Um, his grandparents are his guardians and they've been coming in every day, every other day actually, to see how he's doing at the end of the

---

[3]Jay told me at a later date that "ABC" is a stand-in for "already been chewed."

day, and get a personal update, the last two weeks, but I think that might be going by the way sidesoon."

"Now he moved here from Maple Cove?" I ask.[4]

"No, Andover City. Yeah, he went to Thomas Jefferson Elementary."

"OK, OK." I am writing quickly in my notebook. Maple Cove is an urban school district bordering the Andover City School District, and both are within an approximately 30- to 45-minute drive of Axleton. The students enrolled in Andover City schools, where Jay moved from, are identified as 49% Black, 47% White, and 4% "other," and Maple Cove's students are 45% Black, 52% White, and 3% "other" (Miller, 1999).

Laura continues, "Yeah, for a while I thought, 'Oh, maybe he was from one of the schools, you know, of our folks.'" Laura laughs and I smile. "Our folks" is a reference to the community of elementary teachers Laura and I both work with. "But," she continues, "it was Andover City, not Maple Cove, so." She pauses, then goes on, "And he actually was retained last year in fourth grade because he missed about 26 or 27 days. But they brought him here and said, 'Nope, he belongs in fifth grade' before we had a chance to get his records or talk to the principal, so we didn't find out he was supposed to have been retained until about three or four weeks ago. And at this point, you know. It's kinda late to send him back down to the elementary school. He'd really go off the wall." Laura chuckles softly and then adds, "But I think he's got something to add, so it'll be interesting to see how much he gets out of this. If his behaviors don't get in the way."

"OK." I nod, still writing. "Did you have a sense of the strengths of, ah, Ned, or any of the others?"

"Um, Ned can be very verbal. Um, but he also has a pretty short fuse in terms of other people. He'll get annoyed and frustrated real quickly with Jay. And, uh, Jay will feed into that."

"Mmm."

"That's why I told my aide, I said, 'I'm just gonna plunk you right here.' The problem is both, neither one of those kids can work with anybody. And nobody, at this point in the year, it's like, 'I'm not gonna work with that child. He'll destroy my project.' They, they've got more of a, um, you know they're less tolerant. So, Jay and Ned chose to work together, but I knew it was going to be difficult, and that's why I had my aide work with them."

"Hm-mm."

---

[4]My concern at that time was documenting what we knew about the identified children. I wish, in hindsight, that I had asked Laura why she thought the visits from Jay's grandparents "might be going by the wayside soon."

"But Ned is very interested in science."

"Good."

"Very interested in science. He just loves doing these kinds of, um, activities, and he will sit and think about it. He has some real trouble with written expression. Um, he's one of the kids I'm having tested, along with Jay."

"Hm-mm."

"For, um, I think Ned has probably got ADHD, because he tends to be, you know, really easily distracted. Up and down, talks a mile a minute, and his writing is one of these." Laura demonstrates a scrawling motion, sweeping her hand quickly across her notebook. "You know, kind of looks like an ADD kid, that they can't slow down enough to get the writing in between the lines, and usually by fifth grade they've accomplished that much."

My observations of Laura's classroom practices as she began the school year suggested that the development of her classroom culture emphasized orderly, structured, routines where each of the students was working on the same activity or assignment, individually, at the same time. This was demonstrated through a range of practices, from going to the bathroom as a group to following along individually in their social studies text. The mystery powder activity stood out because of its emphasis on dialogic, active participation, and it was in this context that Jay and Ned, students Laura identified as "different," seemed to participate most effectively. However, even in this context, there was no attempt to pull together the different observations made by individual students. There was no attempt to encourage students to build off of each other's ideas and construct a group interpretation or explanation of their observations.

This pattern in the types of routines, practices, and activities Laura supported in her classroom suggested a view of learning based on values of individual achievement, and did not reflect the values of a learning community engaged in responding to each other, not just the teacher, and in actively learning from each other. I wondered, then, what the implications of Laura's type of classroom culture would be for her enactment of GIsML, which was designed on the model of a learning community. Would her students be able to respond to each other and build explanations together? Would Laura be able to scaffold the forms of participation necessary for them to do so?

Another issue raised in these early observations was Laura's rapid identification of Jay and Ned as "different" and in need of special education identification. In doing so, Laura consistently positioned Jay and Ned as outside the range of "normal" in her classroom. Further, she seemed to im-

plicitly support the other students' exclusion of Jay and Ned ("That's why I told my aide, I said, 'I'm just gonna plunk you right here.' The problem is both, neither one of those kids can work with anybody. And nobody, at this point in the year, it's like, 'I'm not gonna work with that child. He'll destroy my project.'")

The evidence Laura cited for Jay in particular seemed more related to her evaluation of his social interactions, "behaviors," and family history than to a learning disability. I wondered about this because the disproportionate representation of minority students in special education programs has been well documented (Artiles, 1998; Artiles et al., 1997). In a brief review of explanations of disproportionality, Artiles et al. (1998) identified theories ranging from "minority children's innate deficits to discriminatory professional practices" and including "social deviance variables" (pp. 543–544). The authors concluded that more consideration of sociocultural factors, student perspectives, and family context was needed within the research on student identification and placement. What factors, I wondered, were contributing to Laura's identification of Jay as different?

4

"He Was Immediate.
He Was Like *Immediate.*"

During the next 11 days of instruction, Laura and her class engaged in three cycles of guided inquiry. Within the GIsML orientation, each cycle has four phases: engage, investigate, constructing/revising explanations, and reporting. These phases are visited recursively as the students create and deepen their understanding of phenomena through different cycles of inquiry. The engagement phase is typified by the teacher's introduction of the problem context to be explored in a manner that invites students' interest. The investigation phase is typified by either first-hand (direct experimentation, manipulation, or observation) or second-hand (textual) investigation. Constructing and revising explanations typically takes places in pairs or small groups and might involve close interaction with the teacher. Reporting or "public sharing" involves students presenting their claims to their classmates and responding to questions as the learning community attempts to integrate and make sense of a range of claims about the same phenomenon. Discursive practices are thus important sites for learning within each phase as students attempt to make their thinking visible to others.

This chapter depicts Laura and her students as they participated in the engagement and investigation phases from the first cycle of inquiry. Laura first engaged the class in the problem context, the CDS, and then the students worked in pairs to build their own CDS.

Jay wears a bright purple t-shirt and stonewashed blue jeans, and Ned wears similarly styled jeans with a lemon-yellow sweatshirt. As the children move about the room turning in their math assignments and preparing

40

for science, the boys stand out as two spots of intense color among the patchwork of grays, blacks, blues, and whites worn by their classmates. When the students take their seats, Jay and Ned stand out for another reason: They are the only two children who sit without tablemates. Jay's desk has been moved near the door, and Ned's desk is in the back. A line drawn straight back from Jay's desk would hit Ned's, although it would have to pass through two tables of children first. One is a table of two girls and the other is a table of four children, two girls and two boys. Danny's seat has also been moved: He now sits in the back, not far from Ned, with his full-time teacher's aide at a table of two desks (see Fig. 4.1).

Laura stands at the front of the room. "This weekend, I sort of came up with another puzzle that I wanted to show you guys. Remember we started out with Grandma's mystery powder as a puzzle that we needed you to help me solve? Um, I have another puzzle that I was interested in having you work

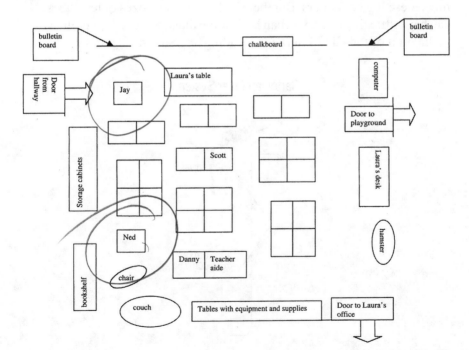

FIG. 4.1.   Seating Chart 2. Jay's fifth-grade classroom, October.

on. And this puzzle is called, it has a special name." Laura holds an assembled CDS in her hands and lifts it up for the students to see. "OK, this is called a Cartesian Diver System. I need you guys to pay attention. Theresa, could you look up here please? Now I'll bring this around so that everybody can see this." I am on the far side of the room, on Laura's left as she faces the class, trying to set up the video camera as quickly as possible. It is the first day of Laura's inquiry, and somehow we have gotten our signals crossed about her starting time so she is ready and I am not. Laura crosses to the back of the room and pauses briefly while I set up and test the camera and microphones.

Two minutes later Laura begins again. "Um, as I was saying, this is called a Cartesian Diver. And that's the name that we have for this, this system. And I want to bring it around so you can look at it a little bit. If you'll notice there's some things inside." Laura is holding the CDS in her hands and walking slowly around the room as she speaks. "There's a rubber band around the top. This stuff on the top is called rubber sheeting." After she passes Jay, he turns and gestures to Ned excitedly. They are both grinning. Laura continues walking. "What I'm holding on to here, this is called a test tube, these big containers. But there's also different sizes of test tubes. You can have little tiny ones, you can have some that are much bigger than this." A diagram of the CDS Laura was holding appears in Figure 4.2.[1]

Cartesian Diver System

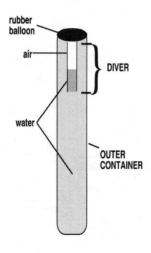

FIG. 4.2.

[1]This graphic was created by Shirley Magnusson and the GIsML research team and was used in several versions of text created by the GIsML research team to support students' second-hand investigations.

Laura's actions here, introducing the CDS as a puzzle, are part of the engagement phase of her floating and sinking inquiry. The purpose behind Laura's introduction of the CDS as a problem context is to spark students' thinking about weight, volume, and density. When Laura applies pressure with her finger to the rubber sheeting, additional water is going to be forced into the diver (the diver is an inverted test tube). This water will then compress the air in the diver and increase the weight of the diver, while not changing the volume of the diver or the total weight of the system. The CDS is a rich context because the same object (the diver) floats and sinks, which leads to additional investigations that address the nature of the materials and forces in the system that give rise to the phenomenon. It is also a context that captivates students, and has the potential to lead to many additional investigations of related concepts (see further discussion in K. M. Collins et al., 1998).

"Now this looks like kind of an interesting puzzle all by itself." Laura stops walking and stands near the back left corner of the room, holding the CDS up for the children to look at. "But something very interesting happens with this. And I want to show this to you. Can everybody see from where you're at?" Several students, including Jay and Ned, respond negatively. "OK," Laura continues, "why don't I have, could I have you folks just walk over here a little closer?" Laura gestures to the students on the far side of the room, including Jay and Ned, and they get up and cluster about her. Laura looks around the room, glancing behind her. "Can you guys see from where you're at? I want you all to see the test tube clearly. Can you see, Molly?" This time all the answers are affirmative. "OK, I'm just going to put a little pressure with my thumb on the top of this and I want you to see what happens." Laura's thumb is poised over the rubber sheeting. Before she presses down, there is a brief discussion about the components of the system—Maria wants to know whether the liquid is Sprite or water. Laura confirms that the liquid is water, and then presses on the rubber sheeting. As she does so, water is forced into the small test tube (the diver), compressing the air at the top and causing the diver to sink. The students all speak at once:

"Oh!"
"Oh, cool!"
"It just went down!"
"It's gonna go back up."
"It's an elevator, cool!"
"Going down!"
"It went up again."

"Why does it do that?"
"I thought it would just sink."

The excitement in the room is palpable as Laura raises her thumb and the diver returns to its original position. For several minutes, the students are mesmerized by Laura's manipulation of the system, and she turns to give each one a close look. When she turns toward Jay, he reaches out to manipulate the diver himself, and Laura holds it for it him. Jay presses down on the rubber sheeting, watching the operation of the system carefully. "That's an air bubble, isn't it?" he asks. No one replies.

"OK," Laura says, "why don't you all go back to your seats?" As they do so, she steps forward to stand in front of a long table loaded with the equipment for the inquiry.

"OK, class could I have you looking back here please instead of up to the front of the room? All the stuff is back here that I need to talk to you about. Now, um, Maria, and I think it was Ned, both of them, while we were over there when I was showing you what happens, when I pressed down, both of you guys said, 'Why is it doing that?' Well, that's the puzzle that I need you to help me solve."

Jay's hand shoots straight up into the air. He is kneeling backwards on his chair, facing Laura in the back of the room. "I know, I know, I know," he chants softly.

"Jay?" He is the first student recognized by Laura.

"Pressure. It's pressure," Jay announces confidently.

"Pressure?" Laura repeats. "Molly?"

"Pressure from your thumb pushes the air," Jay continues.

"Lack of air." Molly announces, overlapping the last part of Jay's explanation. Molly is one of the two girls sitting at the table of four that separates Jay and Ned.

"Lack of air? What do you mean Molly?" Laura uses revoicing to prompt Molly further.

I was operating the video camera at this point and I moved the camera to follow the speaker, which highlighted for me the overlapping nature of Molly and Jay's speech. Was Jay speaking out of turn, or did Molly interrupt him? Laura's repetition of Jay's contribution as a question, "Pressure?" was a discursive move called revoicing. Studies of classroom discourse have suggested that revoicing is often used to elicit further information from a student, to clarify a student's answer, to connect a student's response to those of other students, or to relate a student's response to sub-

stantive content area understandings (K. M. Collins et al., 1998; O'Connor & Michaels, 1993, 1996).

Jay's response to Laura's revoicing of his contribution indicated that he interpreted Laura's revoicing move as a request for more information. He responded by elaborating his initial response in the form of a claim, "Pressure from your thumb pushes the air." However, Laura followed her revoicing of Jay's answer by quickly calling on Molly, so that Jay and Molly overlapped each other's talk. In her interaction with Molly, Laura then used revoicing differently than with Jay, combining it with a follow-up question to elicit more information from Molly, "Lack of air? What do you mean Molly?"

This sequence of interactions illustrates how the same discursive move was used to provide different types of opportunities for these two students to participate in the classroom conversation. Laura, Jay, and Molly thus worked together to create an interaction that shaped Jay's participation as inappropriate: Jay spoke when it was no longer his officially sanctioned turn.

As Molly responds to Laura, Jay murmurs, "Uh-huh" under his breath, apparently indicating disagreement with her answer. "Like, if there's no air in the vial, everything sinks. But if there is air, it floats," Molly explains.

"Interesting. Maria?" Laura turns to call on another student, and Jay and Molly begin a whispered exchange, debating their relative explanations. As Maria answers, Ned slides off of his chair in the back of the room onto the couch. He still appears attentive, however, and watches Laura and the diver system carefully.

"Did you say it's just regular water?" Maria sounds doubtful.

"Just regular water." Laura confirms, maintaining eye contact with Maria.

"Maybe, like, um, is there, is the whole thing filled?" As Maria asks her second question, Jay's hand shoots up into the air again.

"Yup. Carl?"

Carl observes, "It goes down to a certain spot and then it stops and goes back up."

"Well, it stops at the bottom 'cause it just hits the bottom. And then it comes back up. I mean, that's just as far as it can go," Laura explains. Jay's hand is still up in the air, his right arm behind his head, holding his left arm straight up by the elbow. His left shoulder is raised higher than his right: He is holding his arm up as high as possible. Laura calls on another student, "Larry?"

"I think it's because when you push it down, like the water squeezes the air so it can't hold it up," Larry offers.

"The water squeezes the air?" Laura prompts.

"Yeah," Larry continues, "it squeezes the air and it can't hold it up. Because my mother used to tell me that about holding my breath."

"Like you're holding your breath. Interesting. Jessica?" As Jessica volunteers her answer, Jay's hand is still straight up in the air; now his left arm is behind his head, holding up his right arm by the elbow. After Jessica's turn, Laura introduces the term *claim* to the class, and Jay keeps his arm in the air during her explanation. "Well, now you guys are really coming up with some interesting ideas. And I want to give these ideas a name 'cause we're gonna be using this word off and on over the next couple of weeks. These are called claims. A claim is something that you are going to give as an explanation for why something is happening. In other words, you are claiming that the reason this goes down, this is a different size test tube in here, um, the reason this goes down is because, and you've all stated very different kinds of explanations about why you think this is behaving the way that it's behaving."

Driver and her colleagues (Driver, Asoko, Leach, Mortimer, & Scott, 1994) and Lemke (1990) both argued that one goal of science education is to enculturate students into scientific ways of knowing, and stressed that scientific practices need to be made meaningful for individuals. Lemke's approach focused on the ways in which scientific ways of knowing were reflected in the discourse of science, whereas Driver and her colleagues stressed the importance of students' participation in scientific activities. Informed by social constructivist theory, both scholars argued that students' negotiation and appropriation of the practices and tools of scientific inquiry, both physical as well as linguistic and conceptual, requires thoughtful guidance on the part of the teacher.

From this perspective, Laura's choice here was to introduce a tool reflective of the discourse of the scientific community, the claim. Laura not only introduced the tool but explained its meaning in direct connection to the activity the students were already involved in. In this way the students were introduced to the tool and its use relative to their own participation in classroom scientific inquiry. In her debriefing after this lesson, Laura reflected that her introduction of claim as a conceptual tool at this point in the instruction was deliberate and reflected her desire for the students to employ this term throughout the subsequent investigation (see discussion in K. M. Collins et al., 1998).

Laura calls on several more children, and, after 2 minutes, she recognizes Jay with a gesture and a nod.

"You know how, um, when you put, when you washing dishes, and you put a cup under water?" Jay begins. In order to face Laura where she stands in the back of the room, he is turned backwards in his chair, kneeling on its seat.

"Hm-mm."

"And then, when it, um, it sinks, and then it pops back up. Isn't that pressure from the air? The um, the water comes up, and pushes it right back. The water comes up with it, the water comes up and the cup, the cup comes up. Isn't that like, um, like the pressure from the air? That's what I'm thinking, the pressure from the air," Jay nods vigorously as he makes this last statement.

"That's what you're thinking, the pressure." Laura acknowledges. "Um, I know you guys have a lot that, that you want to talk about. But, I'm gonna give you a chance to do that but I wanna, because I'm gonna ask each of you to make one of these divers this morning. Because if you have your own, then you'll be able to look at it, and think about the reason that it's behaving the way it is. These two I made, and it'd be very difficult for you to understand how the system is working unless you, you make it yourself."

Before distributing the materials, Laura describes the system to the students, and clarifies by drawing a diagram on the board. She emphasizes that the large test tube should be filled completely with water, and introduces the notion of a sensitive system. "The easier it is to, to put, push down and have the diver move, that means that it's a very sensitive system. In other words it reacts very quickly to pressure on here," Laura indicates the rubber sheeting on the diagram. "What you guys want to try to make is a system that is very, very sensitive, so that when you push down it's not gonna take much pressure to get the diver to go down. And the, the more sensitive the system, then the, the easier it's gonna be for you to watch what's going on with your, with your diver. To make the system sensitive, you wanna have your test tube, the one inside, floating so that it's as close to that top part as you possibly can get it." Laura then explains the equipment distribution procedures to the class, and warns them to be cautious with the glass test tubes and beakers. Jay raises his hand while she is speaking and she pauses to recognize him. "Jay?"

"Um, I'm just curious," Jay begins, "if you put two divers in there, two or three divers in there, will it still float to the bottom?"

"You mean inside of this tube?" Laura indicates the large, outer test tube.

"Yeah."

"This one's a little bit skinny to do that, to fit more than one in there, but you could, we could maybe get some material that was thicker and we could try it with more than one. OK? Just to see what would happen. 'Cause that would be an interesting thing to look at." Laura turns and addresses another student, who asks whether the diver systems will have to be taken apart at the end of the class period. "The sheeting needs to be taken off at the end of the class period." Laura explains that another class will be using the equipment in the afternoon. "This stuff has to be dried off before we get to, um, sixth hour today. So I'm gonna ask you to put it over on some paper towels that I'll set up. Um, are there any questions about the materials that you'll be using? Jay?"

"OK, um, like the sheeting, what do you mean take it off?"

"Yeah, we have to empty everything out at the end." Laura repeats.

"Oh, OK."

"While you're looking at it, you don't take it off. OK?" Laura clarifies, "You wanna get, you know, look at your diver. Um," Laura pauses and starts to turn away from Jay, and he speaks again.

"I got one more question."

"Yes?" Laura turns to face Jay again.

"If you turn it upside down and you push the, um, sheet, will it go up?" Jay is apparently talking about inverting the whole CDS. Unbeknownst to him, the class is scheduled to construct an "Australian" CDS the following day, which will involve a similar type of inversion.

"No," another student responds before Laura does.

"If you turn it upside down?" Jay repeats.

"Oh, that's a good point." Laura begins. "Um, when you're holding your divers, keep it so that the bottom, of the, uh, diver is this way in the beaker," Laura demonstrates that the diver, the small test tube, should be inverted within the large test tube. "Because you don't, you don't want to put your diver in that way," she holds a small test tube right side up.

"I know," Jay responds, "I'm talking about if you were to have the diver and you were to turn it upside down, up in the air, and pushed the rubber in, would it go up?" Again he seems to be describing the inversion of the whole system, not of the diver itself.

"No," another student calls out.

"That's an interesting question, too. We'll have to see if we can make a diver that does that." Laura advises the class that when they have finished making their CDS she wants them to do some writing, "The things I'm gonna ask you to do some writing about when you're finished with your divers, I'm gonna ask you to describe how you made it, first of all. So you're gonna be asked to describe what you did to construct your diver, maybe draw a picture to help out with the illustration. I'm gonna ask you to describe what happens when you press down, which means you're gonna have to do some real good observing about the different parts of the diver and what's going on as the diver is diving and as it's going back up. Try to be very careful about looking at what's happening, with all of the different things that are going on in here. And thirdly, I'm gonna ask you to come up with a claim about why you think this is happening. So those are some things you should be talking about with your partner when you're constructing the diver."[2]

Laura distributes the equipment, one set (including a container of water, two large test tubes, a small test tube, a small vial, an eyedropper, a beaker, two pieces of rubber sheeting, and two rubber bands) for each pair of students. Jay and Ned work at Ned's desk in the back of the room. Jay constructs a working CDS almost immediately—he is the first student in the room to make one that works—and begins manipulating it with enthusiasm. He then assists Ned in finishing his system, helps him to attach the rubber sheeting, and advises him on how to reconstruct the system when it doesn't work: "Don't fill the diver all the way up, fill it like halfway."

When Laura visits Jay and Ned during her rounds through the classroom, she is able to talk with them about the operation of their systems because they have completed building them so quickly. This is the only pair she is able to do this with: Her interactions with the other groups center around making the CDS. She approaches the pair at Ned's desk and watches Ned pushing down on his system. His system is not sensitive and he has to push very hard. "OK, look at these two systems, guys. Look at them a minute." Laura kneels on the floor next to Ned's desk and picks up the boys' systems. She holds them side-by-side, one in each hand. "Take a look at them a minute."

Jay points to the top of Ned's system, where the rubber sheeting is indented into the outer test tube, "His is like down and mine is like flat."

"Look under the sheeting." Both boys lift up the edges of the rubber sheeting hanging down over the side of their systems. "Now push down." Laura continues. Both boys push down on the top of the rubber sheeting. "Do you notice anything happening with the water? When you push down, look at the water."

"It has air in it," Jay points out the air in his system with his left hand while pressing with his right.

Laura goes on, "OK. What is happening when it goes down? Why is it going down when you push your finger on it?"

"Mine's going down easier," Jay notes.

---

[2] Laura's whole-class demonstration and discussion of the CDS, the engagement phase of this cycle of inquiry, lasted 24 minutes and 49 seconds. During this time Jay initiated six exchanges with Laura, which took a total of 5 minutes and 7 seconds to complete.

20% of the time goes to Jay—

"Probably because yours is more sensitive," Laura acknowledges.

Jay reaches over and presses Ned's system, "He has to push down real hard."

Laura puts Ned's CDS down in a beaker and holds Jay's in one hand while manipulating it with her other hand, "OK. Now you guys just watch it. Watch all the parts of it. Look at it. See the diver here. Do you see anything happening?"

"It's going up and squishing," Ned offers.

"What happens?" Laura glances at Ned.

"The bubble just kind of squishes up like this," Ned holds his hands out and moves them toward each other, as though squeezing something between his palms.

"So how do you think it's doing that?" Laura prompts.

"Because of the pressure of the water. When this goes down," Ned points to the diver within the system, "the pressure of the water goes up." Ned raises his arms in the air for emphasis. "It's squishing the air bubble like this," Ned explains by moving his hands together in a squeezing motion again.

"Pressure, pressure," Jay starts. Laura looks at him and he continues. "When you press your finger the pressure squishes the air bubble. And then the pressure from the water makes it come back up." Jay makes a "thumbs-up" sign and moves his fist quickly through the air.

Ned starts to speak again as Laura stands up and says, "I'm going to ask you to write this down so you and Jay have to come up with a reason why this is happening." As she walks away, Jay and Ned pick up their systems again.

Later, Laura sits down to "debrief" or reflect on her teaching with Shirley Magnusson, Annemarie Palincsar, Danielle Ford, and me. Laura tells us, "I was pressing Jay and Ned a little bit over there. 'Well, what, what do you mean by pressure. What's happening with all of the things that you see going on?' And then Ned did say something about 'Well the bubble, is, is going away as it goes down. And so the pressure must be forcing the water to go in and have the bubble go away.' And, and I thought, OK." Laura pauses briefly and chuckles, "Now where do I go? But, um, you know, so they were really, and interestingly enough, the two kids who never get anything done, I mean, they're the last ones to finish their work, they're, they're completely disoriented, did their divers first."

Shirley wonders whether Jay was really first, having observed another pair. Laura assures her, "He was immediate. He was like *immediate*."

Annemarie adds, "I was stunned. I thought he was holding your system."

"And it was sensitive, too." Laura continues. "'Jay!' Then I said, 'Can you do it again?' He was like, 'OK.'" For several minutes we discuss which children never completed a CDS, and Laura wonders out loud about what impact that will have on the next day's instruction. Then she brings up Jay again, "Um, the comment from, I don't know if it was Jay? Or somebody said, 'Well, could you make one that's upside down?'"

Shirley confirms, "That was Jay. Very interesting."

"I thought that was, see and he will, and that's the thing about that child, is he just, he'll come up with this stuff. Like, 'Oh, OK, I know there's somethin' there' but then he's just, he's really EI [emotionally impaired] and can't sort it all out. But I mean he's obviously enthusiastic."

As our debriefing conversation draws to a close, Shirley comments on how willing the students were to keep talking rather than jump right into the materials. "Oh, they're very willing to talk." Laura chuckles, "Yeah they'll discuss 'til the end of time. There was one instance, it was when I needed to talk to Jay, when he kind of laughed a little bit at what somebody had said, or giggled or something. I've been real, I mean we as a group have been very conscious of, you know, what people say here is important, you know, and we need to all listen and be courteous."

I was puzzled by Laura's continued emphasis on Jay as emotionally impaired ("he's really EI [emotionally impaired] and can't sort it all out") because not only did Jay's participation seem appropriate to me, it seemed desirable within an inquiry designed to take place within a learning community. In her writing about learning communities, Rogoff (1994) argued that through taking up the discourse practices of their community, students transform their participation in the community and the opportunities for knowledge construction available for community members. Accordingly, the GIsML orientation to teaching emphasized making thinking visible through discourse and other forms of representation. Jay's willingness to verbalize his developing thoughts about the CDS was therefore characteristic of the kind of interaction that should be supported in guided inquiry instruction. Again I wondered about the intersection of Laura's classroom practices, which did not emphasize dialogic activity, and GIsML instruction.

Further, Laura had encouraged the students to come up with a claim about the CDS. Jay was certainly able to "sort it all out" when, drawing on Laura's prompting of Ned, he articulated the claim, "When you press your finger the pressure squishes the air bubble. And then the pressure from the water makes it come back up." As noted earlier, Jay and Ned were the only pair to fully articulate a claim about the behavior of the diver, as other groups were largely concentrated on building working systems. Although the language of Jay's claim needs some clarification—what he means by "pressure from the water makes it come back up"—conceptually it is an excellent beginning. He and Ned have identified the area of change within the CDS (i.e., the "squish[ed] air bubble") and have connected that change to the behavior of the diver.

While acknowledging Jay's talent in building the CDS, Laura continued to position him outside the class community by emphasizing that he did not adhere to the classroom practice of listening to each other ("what people say here is important, you know, and we need to all listen and be courteous"). This surprised me because I did not note any time at which Jay was not listening, or as Laura claimed, when he laughed at another student. I decided to watch carefully to see how he responded to others as the inquiry continued to unfold.

5

"Where's the Evidence?"

The students are sitting in their seats working individually when I arrive at 7:45 the next morning. As I set up the video camera and microphones there is a buzz of expectation in room, and the students sitting at tables begin whispering excitedly to each other. Laura asks the "passer-outers" to return the papers students wrote the day before. Laura stands at the chalkboard, facing the class, and provides them with an overview of the day's activity: They are going to use their writing on these papers to create, with their partner, a "report" (a poster) representing their current thinking about the operation of the CDS. The students will then share these reports, and their findings, with each other. Laura's description lasts 26 minutes, and although Jay raises his hand several times, he is not called on and remains silent while Laura talks. Five other students do raise their hands and are acknowledged. Laura's description of how to write the reports lasts nearly 30 minutes.

Laura begins walking slowly through the room as she speaks, pausing near Jay's desk so that she is standing between him and the rest of the class. Jay peers around from behind Laura, leaning sideways in his chair and listening with his hands folded between his knees. "When scientists do their investigations, many times they share their results with their colleagues or other people who are also scientists. So you guys, your colleagues are sitting right in this room. These are all people who shared the same experience yesterday. And, in reading through your things last night, it's amazing how many different ideas came out of that one experience. Now, if we get all those ideas out for everybody to think about and talk about, then the way you're thinking about something may get even bigger or grander than where you are right now. So, what is, what this is supposed to help you do is to take what you're thinking about and add other people's ideas to that so your thinking becomes even better than it was before … That's part of the class this year, is that we all want to be able to learn from each other … That's not something that we usually do in class. But it's, you'll learn a lot from each other. You may not realize it but everything people say goes in your mind and rolls around in there and adds to your thinking. So the more we can listen to each other think out loud, probably the better off we'll all be."

Laura moves to the front of the room and describes the "role as a listener" that students are "taking on." She emphasizes that they must do more than "sit politely and listen." They must listen for specific things and question what they don't understand. As she speaks, she creates a list on a piece of poster paper, held to the board with magnets, of what students should listen for when their classmates are speaking:

- What is the claim or explanation?
- Is it clear?
- Is there evidence?
- Is the evidence accurate?

Laura stresses the importance of evidence. "Now, when someone comes up and gives an explanation about why the diver works. Is that all they have? Or are they saying, 'Well, I believe this, because this is what happened yesterday in my system.' And evidence can be their drawing or a written explanation about things that happened yesterday."

Next Laura starts another list on a second piece of poster paper, which she titles "Format." "I'm going to ask you to do three things on your reports today. And what I'm gonna call this is the format. Format is a word that you use to tell what form your report is gonna be in. OK, what's the order of things, and what kinds of things that you include."

Format:
- Description of what happened
- Claim about why this happened
- Evidence

Laura again emphasizes the importance of evidence, telling the students to "Use some examples from what you remember yesterday or from what you have on your papers that would help explain your claim, or helps support [it]. Give evidence about why this happens."

Laura reminds the class that they need to be aware of the time, "I'm gonna give you, we'll start out with about 15 minutes to come up with your report. And that should be plenty of time." Jay stands up at his desk and stretches, and the rest of the students remain seated. Jay continues standing alone for the next 19 seconds while Laura continues talking, "Anybody have any questions? Jessica?"

"Are you gonna put us in groups?"

"You're gonna be with your partner ... You and your partner from yesterday. So, if I could have passer-outers, Brian and Daryl, you could make sure each pair, person will have a marker." At that, the rest of the students get up and begin moving about the room.

As in the previous day's interaction with Molly and Laura in which he ended up speaking out of turn, Jay again seemed to be "out of step" with the rest of the class. Scholars working primarily from the perspectives of ethnography of communication and interactional sociolinguistics have documented patterns in the discursive interactions of children and teachers that portray classroom life as defined by its rhythms, its patterns of activity and stillness, of quiet and of interaction, that set it apart from other contexts and forms of learning. For example, Erickson (1996) drew on the constructs of contextualization cues and conversation inferencing to document the ways in which the patterns of classroom interaction resemble the patterns of a musical performance in their rhythms and cadence. It is this cadence, according to Erickson, that acts as a cue to participants, signaling them when to enter the discourse or when an activity is changing.

Contextualization cues are the semiotic signs that relate what is said to contextual knowledge of the activity engaged in (Gumperz, 1982), or, in Gumperz's (1992) own words, "verbal signs that are indexically associated with specific classes of communicative activity types and thus signal the frame of context for the interpretation of constituent messages" (p. 307). Examples of contextualization cues include intonation, stress, pitch, rhythm, volume, register, and code switching. Goffman (1959) emphasized that physical movements, such as gesture or bodily orientation, be considered contextualization cues as well. Gumperz (1992) identified this process of determining the speaker's intent through "reading" contextualization cues, and thus constructing intersubjectivity regarding the speech activity at hand, as conversational inferencing.

This body of work suggests that interactional moments during which Jay seemed "out of step," such this one when he stood up while everyone else remained seated, be considered as moments when he misinterpreted Laura's contextualization cues. In the first example, Laura's use of revoicing for a variety of purposes might be at least partly responsible. In the second example, I could not identify a change in cadence, tone, volume, or any specific "cue" that signaled when to stand up and when to remain sitting. Of course, another possible interpretation of Jay's actions here includes that he was deliberately challenging Laura's authority by standing when the rest of the class was sitting. These different interpretations of Jay's actions result in very different understandings of who Jay is.

There is a lot of excitement as well as anticipation in the room as markers and sheets of paper are passed around and students move about freely, examining each other's reports. Jay and Ned work on the floor near Ned's desk in the back of the room. Ned begins writing immediately and Jay reminds him to "write what happened, not what we did." Jay looks up to the front of the board at Laura's list several times as Ned begins writing, carefully copying his writing from the previous day's paper onto their poster paper. Jay gets a second sheet of poster paper, and Ned holds the first sheet up so that Jay can copy it onto the second sheet. When they are finished, Jay compares their sheets to Laura's and tells Ned they still need evidence. Ned suggests a picture and begins drawing one while Jay turns to examine the reports of two children working near them. He then reports back to Ned to label their drawing. When Ned is done drawing, Jay picks up the marker and begins labeling the drawing. Laura circulates around the room but does not interact with Jay or Ned during this time.

Twenty minutes after they started working together, Laura signals for the children to go back to their seats. Jay stays near Ned's desk, still labeling their drawing.

"Um, I sense that there's a lot of excitement. A lot of you want to share some of your ideas. Jay, if you could go sit at your own seat."

"OK." Jay takes his report and paper and goes back to his seat.

"Thank you," Laura acknowledges.

"But we're still doing it!" Ned whispers loudly as Jay walks away.

When everyone is settled, Laura reminds them of their roles as listener, "You're gonna listen for their explanation, which is probably gonna be number two.... First of all you'll describe what happened. Then hopefully they'll have an explanation about why it happened. That's what you guys should be listening for. Think about whether that explanation is clear to you. Do you understand what they're talking about or do you need to ask them some questions in order to help you understand? Then, do they present some evidence that helps support their ideas. Are they showing some evidence that would help make their explanation really something that 'Yup, that's definitely true because they've really convinced me.' Evidence is used to convince people that your idea is the one that, that's correct. Or your idea is the one that we should really focus on. So that's where you want to get to the evidence piece. Now, I need to have a volunteer group that would like to go first?"

Ned whispers to Jay, across the two tables that separate them, and raises his arm at the same time, "Let's go first!"

Jay is unsure, shakes his head and whispers back, "We need to do number three. We didn't put any evidence."

"Oh, we can do it when we get up there," Ned assures him, but Jay shakes his head.

"Um, Carl and Kevin." Laura walks to the back of the room and sits on an empty desk.

Two boys, Carl and Kevin, move to the front of the room and hang their poster on the board, moving to stand on either side of it. Kevin has dark blond hair and blue-gray eyes, which usually reflect his mischievous, ready-for-anything demeanor. However, as he prepares to share with his classmates he folds his hands behind him and leans against the chalkboard, gazing down at the floor in front of him. Unlike his partner, Carl faces his classmates and Laura directly, his straight dark hair falling over his forehead, and he appears eager to begin. He talks quickly, reading off their poster, "It says 'I think the diver goes up and down when you pushed it because when it's pressed the pressure forces it down and when you take your finger off the air in the diver rises and makes it submerge.'" He turns to face his classmates, and points to several drawings on his poster as he continues, "And then we have how it is when your finger's on it, the pressure, this is how it is when it's off. And we have the how you make it, we have water in a beaker and poured it into a test tube and the test tube's filled with water. And then you get a diver, put it upside down and put it in here. Put rubber over that and then get a rubber band and put the rubber band over it and then push it down."

"OK. Does anybody have a question about their explanation? Anything that you would like them to make a little clearer?" Laura looks around the room, and calls on Jessica.

"I think sorta, um, on the bottom part where it's like 1, 2, 3, 4, 5 and stuff like that, it's kinda how you did it. I like the drawings." Jessica compliments the pair on their series of drawings depicting different steps in making the CDS.

"That's how they made it. I think the blue part, where they have that part colored in, is, is the what happens. Is that correct Carl?" Carl states his agreement, and Laura calls on Jay, who is the only student with his hand raised.

Jay has been listening intently, leaning forward in his seat and reading the poster in a whisper to himself. When Laura calls on him, he speaks loudly and clearly, "Where's the evidence?"

The room is silent for 6 seconds. No one shuffles their feet or papers and no one whispers to their partner. We are all waiting. Carl breaks the silence by turning to his partner, "Kevin?" The room erupts into laughter.

Kevin grins sheepishly, "Believe me, I don't know." As the laughter subsides, he adds, "We didn't have enough time."

"Well, let's go back to your, to your um, claim. Up at the top. It says, 'I think the diver went up and down when you pushed it because when you press it the pressure forces it down, and when you take your finger off the air in the diver rises and makes it submerge.' OK. Um, does anybody have a question about any of that. Anything that you're not quite clear on?" No one does, and Laura continues, "Can I ask you a couple questions? You know me, I always ask questions. Um, it says, 'When you press it, the pressure forces it down.' Can you explain that a little bit further? I'm not sure what you mean by that."

"There, there was a little bit of air at the top, and when you press it, it gets squished. It's like too much weight or something," Carl explains.

The next few exchanges focus on the drawings on their poster and whether the drawing shows the "little bit of air" Carl described. Jay comments that he likes their drawing, echoing Jessica's earlier compliment. Laura responds, "Would there be anything that people might feel would, they would want to have seen up there that is missing from this diagram?"

"Evidence," Jay states firmly, bringing up his initial point again.

"We talked about the evidence, yeah. But what else. Would you want to add something, Kevin?"

"Evidence," Kevin repeats.

"The evidence. Carl, would you want to add anything to your drawing to make it clearer?"

"I think we just, we were trying to state the facts of what we think. We don't have enough evidence," Carl agrees with Kevin and Jay.

"Not enough evidence," Laura repeats softly, then continues on a louder voice, "Um, one thing I might suggest, 'cause I know we talked about this, is, you were pointing out where the air was inside the tube?" Carl and Kevin nod. "It might have helped if you drew a little arrow or something and said 'air,' like this is what the air is and this is where the water is and this is where the tube is, so that we know exactly what parts you're talking about." Jay does not volunteer again.

Both when advising the students how to write their report ("Use some examples from what you remember yesterday or from what you have on your papers that would help explain your claim, or helps support [it]. Give evidence about why this happens.") and when telling them what they should, in their roles as listeners, look for in each other's reports ("Then, do they present some evidence that helps support their ideas. Are they show- ing some evidence that would help make their explanation really something that 'Yup, that's definitely true because they've really convinced me.' Evi- dence is used to convince people that your idea is the one that, that's cor- rect."), Laura stressed the importance of providing evidence for a claim. In doing so, she was explicitly introducing the conventions for interactions during this phase of the inquiry within the classroom community. Laura was also introducing the construct of evidence as important to the commu- nity of scientists, and describing how scientists use evidence to evaluate other scientists' work. Here, Laura's instructions to the class reflected the principles of the GIsML orientation to teaching in that she attempted to en- gage students in knowledge-building practices that mirrored those of scien- tists (Magnusson and Palincsar, 1995).

Jay's concern that he and Ned had not included evidence on their poster ("We didn't put any evidence.") as well as his question ("Where's the evidence?") reflected Laura's instructions to the class. However, when Carl and Kevin were unable to identify their evidence, Laura di- rected the attention of the class elsewhere rather than sustaining the line of inquiry into the boys' evidence. By redirecting the class's attention ("Well, let's go back to your, to your um, claim. Up at the top. It says, 'I think the diver went up and down when you pushed it because when you press it the pressure forces it down, and when you take your finger off the air in the diver rises and makes it submerge.' OK. Um, does anybody have a question about any of that. Anything that you're not quite clear on?") to the boys' claim, Laura may have intended to guide them in thinking about what kind of evidence would support the claim. However, the way in which she redirected the class's attention did not make any links, through either concepts or terminology, to Jay's question. Further, the marker "Well," followed by "let's go" signaled a shift away from Jay's question toward another focus. She did not acknowledge that the issue of evidence had been raised until several turns later when, after Jay had reintroduced lack of evidence as an issue, she responded, "We talked about the evidence, yeah. But what else?" Again Laura's response attempted to redirect attention away from Jay's contribution.

Laura's responses to Jay positioned him outside the circle of discourse in this exchange. Jay appeared to be trying to find a way to enter the conversation appropriately, and followed Laura's earlier guidance about looking for evidence. When Laura responded by attempting to exclude his contribution, Jay sought another way to contribute appropriately. Echoing Jessica's earlier comment, which had been responded to by Laura in manner that elicited further discussion on the topic ("That's how they made it. I think the blue part, where they have that part colored in, is, is the what happens. Is that correct Carl?"), Jay commented that he liked the boys' drawing. This was a bid to reposition himself. Again, Laura's response did not acknowledge Jay's contribution but redirected the conversation to what was missing from the drawing ("Would there be anything that people might feel would, they would want to have seen up there that is missing from this diagram?"). Again Jay was positioned as one whose contributions were not central to the class conversation. Interestingly, Carl and Kevin continued to acknowledge Jay's question about evidence after Laura attempted to redirect the class's attention.

This sharing session illustrated the complexity of guiding a whole-class discussion of one pair of students' work. The burden of this complexity was increased, in Laura's case, by the discrepancy between her everyday classroom practices and the dialogic practices she was attempting here. Laura herself acknowledged this when introducing this phase of the inquiry to the students, "So, what is, what this is supposed to help you do is to take what you're thinking about and add other people's ideas to that so your thinking becomes even better than it was before ... That's part of the class this year, is that we all want to be able to learn from each other.... That's not something that we usually do in class." I wondered how this tension would play out during the rest of the inquiry, and whether Jay would continue to contribute to the class conversation.

"I asked the folks who shared yesterday to come up, while you guys were finishing your math, and just give me a little review of what they were claiming yesterday as their ideas about why the diver was behaving the way that it was." Laura indicates a sheet of poster paper hanging next to her on which she has written "Class Claims." Laura reviews the claims and emphasizes that they represent the class's ideas. "This is where the sharing of ideas comes into play. We're going to list everything down so that we can look at it as a group."

Class Claims
1. Water pressure caused by your finger makes the diver go down.
2. Lack of air in the diver helps it go down.

Laura reminds the students that good audience behavior "means you're not fiddlin' with toys at your desks, or pencils, or equipment. Um, you're listening to what's being presented and if you have a question about what's being presented you need to make sure that you ask ... So don't be afraid to ask questions of your classmates. But you need to remember to do it in a polite way. Even if you maybe disagree with them you can disagree without being mean ... Remember to respect each person's thinking."

Jay has retrieved his poster from the pile in the back of the room and sits with it on his desk, watching Laura intently. Two girls, Terri and Maria, share first, and Jay leans forward in his seat, listening to the discussion but not volunteering. When there is some confusion in the girls' documentation, Laura invites them to step to the back of the room to examine a CDS. As the girls examine Laura's CDS, Jay gets up and follows them to the back of the room. His own poster clasped in his hands, Jay peers carefully at the system as Laura holds it up for the girls. Ned then gets up to have a look, too. The rest of the children remain seated.

Shortly after this, 18 minutes into the girls' sharing, Ned volunteers for the first time and asserts that their documentation is actually incorrect. He asserts that, "When they first came up and they said the air was at the bottom of the diver and the water was at the top. There's no way 'cause air rises and water goes down. So it wouldn't push the diver down because the air brings it up."

Maria appears frustrated that her initial error is drawing sustained attention, and Laura tells Ned that the error is "straightened out now." Jay then volunteers for the first time, and is called on by Laura.

"How do you know that, um, the water can't crash, I mean, how do you know the air can't crash into the water and make it go back up?" Jay looks at Laura and smiles expectantly.

"Scott?" Laura calls on another student.

Scott's question leads to a reexamination of the girls' second set of drawings, and Maria acknowledges a second error in documentation. Laura then asks Terri and Maria whether they have anything to add to the class claims. The girls are unable to articulate a connection between their presentation, which has focused on air being at the top of the diver, and the claims. Jay raises his hand for the second time, and when Laura recognizes him, he tries to build a connection between the girls' presentation and the current list of claims. He stands up at his desk and points to the class claims list, "On number two, for the class claims, um, lack of air in the diver." Jay pauses and turns to Laura in the back of the room, "Can I see that diver again?"

"Well, " Laura begins, moving toward the front of the room, "why don't we get back to that?" She walks past Jay as she finishes her sentence, placing a hand on his shoulder as she passes.

"Because it, the diver," Jay tries to explain, pointing to the board, as several other children also begin talking. However, Laura's back is to him now as she stands at the board, leaning over to talk to Maria and Terri. "We're gonna put a third one up here for ya, OK?" she tells Maria, her hand poised to write on the list of class claims.

"Can I finish now?" Jay calls out, still standing behind his desk.

"So what were you saying?" Laura reads off of the girls' poster, "Since the air's on top—" Maria stands next to Laura and reads the rest of the poster to her as Laura writes. Jay sits down.

To answer Jay's Question?

As in the previous day's sharing, Jay seemed to be trying to find constructive ways to contribute to the discourse. His first contribution, a question, was directly related to the girls' claim and to the issue of evidence ("How do you know that, um, the water can't crash, I mean, how do you know the air can't crash into the water and make it go back up?"). However, he was once again excluded through the lack of response to his contribution when Laura immediately called on another child. The second time that Jay tried to enter the discourse, his contribution was similarly appropriate. Here he tried to connect the girls' claim to those of the class, but when he faltered and needed to see the CDS again, he lost the floor and was not responded to again.

The ways in which Laura positioned Jay as an outsider to the main work of the class were subtle yet effective. During both days of public sharing for the first cycle of inquiry, Jay's contributions were excluded from the "official" conversation. The cognitive demands on Laura at this time were great, and my belief is that she did not exclude Jay intentionally, but rather because her expectations for his contributions were so low, she did not listen and respond to him fully. Laura had already identified Jay as "learning disabled or emotionally impaired," and this identification seemed to serve as a lens through which she interpreted his contributions and their poten-

tial to further the classroom conversation. During the second cycle of inves-
tigation, Jay continued to try to find ways to make himself heard by
imitating the participation strategies of others who were successful, as he
had done with Jessica.

6

"Jay Just Amazes Me During This, He Really Does."

"OK, there you go. It's sensitive!" Jay pushes up on the rubber sheeting of his newly completed "Australian" CDS, in which the entire system is inverted. To operate this system, one pushes up on the rubber sheeting while the diver floats at the top (what used to be the bottom) of the inverted test tube. As in the regular CDS, this causes the water to enter the diver, compress the air therein, and begin to sink the diver. Exploration of the Australian CDS marks the beginning of the students' second cycle of investigation, in which they typically explore the same phenomena in a different context to refine their understanding of it. Jay holds his system up for Laura, who is leaning over his desk to watch Jay and Ned working, to examine.

"Well, you had to push pretty hard, didn't you? It still works, you can watch what happens. But when you push that hard that means," Laura tries to explain to Jay that his system is not actually sensitive. She takes the system from his hands and holds it in front of him, demonstrating how hard she has to push to operate it. As she pushes up, he peers intently at the diver.

"It was gettin' in! The air is going up there!" Jay points to the air within the diver as the water compresses it. Although he had articulated ideas about pressure previously, the second cycle, with a slightly different and less sensitive system, seemed to support his observation and description of different details of its operation.

"Well, when you do your writing you're gonna want to record that. Talk about exactly what happens when you press, what did you see going on?" Laura turns away from the system to look at Jay.

"The air, and the water going up." Jay points to the water moving up into the diver and compressing the air.

"OK, and where do you suppose that water's comin' from?"

"Over here." Jay indicates the water in the test tube.

"And what's causing it to go in?" Laura is still holding and operating the system while Jay examines it.

"Um, when it moves, when it goes down," Jay points to the diver sinking slowly within the test tube, "the water goes up into the thing [the diver] and moves the air out the way."

Laura checks her understanding of Jay's response, "So you think it's because the diver's moving that, that water's going in there?"

"Hm-mm. It has to be." Jay nods vigorously, and grins, glancing quickly at the camera. He seems very proud of himself.

Laura lets the system return to its resting state and then pushes up very slowly on the rubber sheeting. She tells Jay to watch the diver as she does this, is it moving? Jay notes that the diver is not moving. Laura then asks whether he can see water rising into the diver. Yes, he observes that "a little bit" of water is entering the diver. "So," Laura asks, "do you think you could say that *because* the diver's moving, water goes in?"

Jay looks up at Laura and then at the system, "Hmmm, yeah," he shakes his head quickly. "No, no, I couldn't say that."

Laura then repeats her initial question about where the water is coming from and how it is entering the diver. This time Jay articulates a slightly different answer: "The water, some water's already up in the diver." He looks up at Laura and she nods. Jay continues, "And then when it moves down, some water, I think some water comes, like, up, or it's already givin' it a head start." Again Laura asks Jay to examine the movement of the diver as she pushes up on the rubber sheeting very slowly, and again Jay observes that the diver is not moving.

"Now what makes that diver start to sink?" Laura asks, continuing to push up slowly on the rubber sheeting.

"It's getting heavier."

"How's it getting heavier?"

"By the water."

"OK, the water going in?" Laura checks her understanding of Jay's assertion, and when he nods, she continues by repeating her initial question, "So where's the water coming from and why's it going in?"

"The water's coming from the test tube." Jay points again to the water in the test tube, and looks at Laura. She nods, and he asks, "And how is it comin' in?"

"Yup." Laura nods encouragingly, *"Why* is it going in?"

"I don't know how it's going in," Jay shakes his head slightly.

"What's different between now and now?" Laura pushes and releases the rubber sheeting, operating the system repeatedly, so that her motion becomes Jay's focal point, "Now and now? Now, what have I done?"

"You have pushed it, and then probably pressure pushed it up, and pushed it in there."

"OK, so when I pushed it, you're calling that pressure?" Again Laura checks her understanding of Jay's description. When he nods his agreement, she continues, "So where's that pressure go?"

"It goes into the water, in there, and it, um the water makes it, I mean the pressure makes the water go up."

"And then because the water is going up," Laura's final intonation here rises, as though she is asking a question.

"It gets heavier and it goes down," Jay completes Laura's statement. Together they have constructed a clear and concise claim that accounts for all of the components of the system's operation.

"Do you think you can write that down?" Laura hands Jay the system and takes a step back, about to walk away.

"I don't know," Jay says quietly, looking down at the system in his hands and then at the paper on his desk.

"On your paper, look," Laura points to the paper on Jay's desk. "Talk about all the things we were just discussing, OK? Talk about what the water does when you push on it, talk about the water on the outside of the test tube. And then at the bottom where it says 'Why?' try to, in words." She pauses and looks up from the paper, meeting Jay's gaze. "I know this is hard for you but try, in words, to describe why you think that's going on. What is happening with the pressure and the water inside the test tube? OK?" Jay looks down at his blank paper without responding, and Laura moves on to assist another student.

This interaction and the previous one with Ned in the first cycle of inquiry illustrate the central role of "guiding" in guided inquiry (GIsML) instruction. In contrast with previous models of inquiry instruction, which emphasized the "hands-on" aspects of inquiry learning, GIsML is informed by a social constructivist perspective that places importance on the roles of the teacher, the semiotic tools, the activity, and the other participants in mediating learning.

In this example, the Australian CDS as a physical tool worked with specific forms of discourse, expressed through Laura's questions, to facilitate and me-

Scaffolding —

diate Jay's understanding. *This kind of interaction, in which aspects of an activity out of a learner's range are controlled by a more knowledgeable other, is often referred to as scaffolding (Wood et al., 1976). One of the features of scaffolding is that a learner's attention is focused on specific aspects of the activity or problem. In this case, Laura used the CDS, her own language, and Jay's forms of expression to focus Jay's attention on the changes within the system and to build intersubjectivity between Jay and herself.*

Jay first constructed his understanding of the CDS through his intuitive, kinesthetic understanding of the world, as evidenced by his rapid and repeated constructions of working systems. Laura then carefully and skillfully scaffolded his expression of this understanding through oral language. However, she stopped short of scaffolding Jay's translation of these orally expressed understandings into written language. This might have been due to time and instructional constraints—at the time she walked away from him, Laura had already spent close to 6 minutes talking alone with Jay and there were 26 other students in the classroom. It might also have been influenced by her perception of Jay as a "nonwriter" who would or could not complete the writing ("I know this is hard for you but try, in words, to describe why you think that's going on"). The end result was that, although Jay physically demonstrated his understanding of the CDS and orally articulated a claim about its operation, at this point his claim remained undocumented in the way that "counted"—that is, his graded assignment remained blank. Later, a research assistant transcribed Jay's spoken thoughts for him.[1]

Simply telling a writer to document what he or she has expressed orally, as Laura did with Jay, may be enough for a student who is motivated to write, who has an awareness of the socially situated rules governing the form of the writing to be produced, and whose ontological history does not include being considered a "nonwriter" in school. However, for those students who struggle with writing because they prefer another mode of expression in which they are gifted, as in Jay's preference for oral communication, it is definitely not enough.

Writing research informed by sociocultural and sociocognitive theory has explored ways of guiding students' appropriation of written expression as a socially situated semiotic tool and demonstrated that such guidance,

---

[1]In our GIsML study of the students identified as having special needs, written expression was a common area of difficulty for our targeted students and this kind of limited scaffolding of the students' writing was common. In our subsequent GIsML study of the learning and participation of students having special needs, we found that "scribing," assisting students in documenting their orally expressed thoughts in their science journals, led to a gradual appropriation of science journal writing by the students (Palincsar, Collins, et al., 1998; Palincsar et al., 2000, Palincsar et al., 1999).

through genre instruction (Hicks, 1996, 1997) and cognitive strategy in-
struction in writing (J. Collins, 1998; J. L. Collins & Collins, 1997; K. M.
Collins & Collins, 1996; Englert, 1992; Englert & Raphael, 1989; Englert,
Raphael, & Anderson, 1992; Englert, Raphael, Anderson, Anthony, &
Stevens, 1991), results in students' appropriation of writing as a tool for
meaning making. The key features of this research are (a) its emphasis on
scaffolding students' expression of understanding through written lan-
guage, and (b) its illustration of the importance of making the cognitive
processes involved in composing visible for students.

Daryl and Brian hang their poster at the front of the room as Laura reminds the listeners of their role, echoing her directions from the first cycle
of investigations, "The rest of the folks in the class today, um, as we start
sharing I wanna again encourage you to question your classmates about
what they're thinking so you make sure you understand what exactly it is
they're um, trying to get across to you. And if you saw something different
or if you saw something the same, um, you know it might be important to
share some of these ideas with everybody."

Jay sits at Ned's desk with their poster resting between them. This time
the boys have worked to create a single poster between them, although they
have each documented a separate claim (and even used differently colored
markers) on the single poster. Jay leans forward in his chair, his attention focused on the boys at the front of the room.

Brian explains to the class that he and Daryl think putting pressure on the
rubber sheeting causes water to enter the diver, which changes the weight of
the diver and causes it to sink. "It [the diver] has got air in it and it has some
water in it. Then when you put your, and the rubber was like flat. Then
when you put your finger on it, it pushed the rubber down and the water that
took up the space of the, um, rubber went up into the vial and it took the vial
down. 'Cause it had more weight and it weighed it down." Jay's hand shoots
up as Brian finishes speaking. "And then when you took your finger off, the
water took the space of the rubber thing and it went back up. Jay?"

"Um, so you, are you saying that when you push the thing, the pressure
made the water go up in the, in the diver and it had, and then it had air in it."
Jay speaks out clearly from his seat at Ned's desk, "And when you pushed
the rubber thing, the water goes up into it and it, um, like squeezes the air out
and makes it heavy. Is that what you're saying?"

"Yeah," Brian nods.

Laura turns to Jay, "Do you agree with that, Jay?"

"Yeah," Jay leans back in his chair.

Shirley Magnusson, one of the researchers in the classroom, then asks Brian, "I didn't hear you, I didn't hear you say anything about the air. I heard Jay say something about the air in there and I didn't hear you say anything about air."

Brian explains, "It's like, it takes up, when the water goes it takes up the space of the air and then it brings it down. Like where there was air, the water goes inside of it and like crunches up the air kinda more, I guess."

Laura looks around the classroom, "Anybody else have a question that they might wanna ask about the understanding of their ideas here? How is that similar or different to our class claims that we have up there? Does it agree or disagree with any of those?" The current list of class claims, posted at the front of the room, reads:

1. Water pressure caused by your finger makes the diver go down.
2. Lack of air in the diver helps it go down.
3. Since the air is on top of the diver it floats back up.
4. Air gets compressed or squished. Water fills in so the diver is heavier and it falls.

Jay raises his hand as Brian reads the list of claims out loud. After reading the claims, Brian says that he is not sure about how his claim compares to those posted. Then he calls on Jay, who is the only student with his hand raised, once more.

Jay leans forward again, excited, "Number four, um, it comes with number four because you're saying that the air, the water goes into the air and number four is saying that, um, the air gets compressed by the water."

"Yeah, that's the same thing," Brian agrees, "I agree with what he's saying."

Shirley asks Brian to restate the claim in his own words, and Laura walks up to the front of the board and writes Brian's claim on the list as he restates it to her. She then asks him to read it to the class, "When you put pressure on the rubber, it pushes water into the vial, squishing the air. This weighs it down. This drops it down. When you take your finger off it gives the air more room and it floats up."

The class claps for Brian and Daryl as the bell rings, signaling the end of the reporting session. When we sit down in the empty classroom, Laura comments, "Jay just amazes me during this, he really does. His thinking. He's just with, he's just with everybody's thoughts. I mean he's thinking about what they're saying and he is responding and trying to internalize it, and 'Does that compare with what mine is? Yeah, now I want to share mine because I think mine is similar or whatever.' But, he was like, embellishing it a little bit further with terminology from his explanation and then they picked up on some of it."

Jay's participation in this sharing session was a turning point for him in this inquiry: This was the first time Laura acknowledged Jay's ability without reference to his "disability." It marked the advent of Jay's ability to gain access to the floor in ways recognized as socially appropriate by Laura. This appeared to be facilitated by his increased understanding of the CDS as constructed through his previous one-on-one interaction with Laura as well as a result of the ways in which he introduced his ideas.

Throughout the rest of the second cycle of inquiry, Jay continued to employ several discursive tools that facilitated his participation. Jay used the phrase "so are you saying" to enter the classroom conversation five different times. Each time his use of this phrase was successful in that it led to the opportunity for him to voice his thoughts and ask a follow-up question. In addition, Jay started explicitly referencing the ideas of other students as a way of introducing his own ideas, using the phrase "like [name] said." Jay used this strategy four times during this phase of instruction. Jay asked questions about the evidence with the phrases "could you show us" and "can you explain" five different times during this phase of the inquiry.

Jay used these sentence starters as revoicing strategies to join the conversation and to introduce his own ideas in support of (or as conflicting with) the ideas already voiced. By using these strategies, Jay became a central participant in the second cycle of reporting, initiating 24 turns during the sharing of four pairs of students (100 minutes of sharing, not including Jay's own sharing with Ned). In much the same way as O'Connor and Michaels (1993, 1996) described teachers using revoicing to realign students' participation status in the classroom, Jay used revoicing to realign his own participation status.

There was some evidence in the discourse of Shirley Magnusson and Laura Bozek that Jay appropriated these strategies through his interactions with them during the first cycle of inquiry. Laura and Shirley used all three of these strategies to elicit further explanation from the students, although sometimes in slightly different forms (note, e.g., Jay's repeated use of "So are you saying ... " after Laura's questions to him, such as, "So you think it's because the diver's moving ... "). Further, Jay used these strategies to introduce his own thinking for consideration by the class, where the adults used them to elicit more talk from the students.

It was particularly interesting that Jay demonstrated this kind of appropriation and transformation of these discursive tools to such an extensive degree, whereas other students did not. Jay's demonstrated strength in this area was consistent with his description of himself as learning best through discussion and his belief in the importance of sharing ideas with others (see chap. 2).

Jay comes to school the next morning eager to share, and he is wearing an outfit he later tells me is his favorite because he looks his best in it—black corduroys and a black-and-white flannel shirt, neatly tucked in. The boys stand proudly at the front of the room, Ned on the left side of their poster and Jay on the right, and they take turns reading their poster to the class.

1. I press the budum [button] and it goes down when I let go of the budum it goes up. [written by Ned]
1. When I barly touch the rubber sheeting the diver goes fast. And if I push down even harder it goes even faster. [written by Jay]
2. When you press hard and quik and it Forses water ~~and~~ it goes arund the tube pushes the diver and it goes down. [written by Ned]
2. The pressure from my finger goes into the water and to the diver. ~~the diver gets heavy~~ and the diver gets to heavy the pressure makes it drop and the wather risses the air up and it to have and it fors it to drop [written by Jay]

After they each read their claim, they turn the poster over to show a diagram that Ned has drawn on the back. The diagram depicts water going around the diver, forcing it down, which is consistent with his claim but not with Jay's.

Jay and Ned discuss the role of the air in enabling the action of the diver in response to a question asked by Shirley Magnusson. Then Brian poses another question: "Um, where does like, you know how you said you push the rubber thing and pressure like pulls it down? Where does the rubber go, in the water, and the water goes inside the diver, well where does, like, what takes up the space of the water that went in the diver? What takes the space of the water that went into the diver?"

"I think I might be able to answer that," Ned begins.

"What takes the space of the water in the diver?" Jay repeats Brian's question.

"When I was—" Ned starts to answer.

"And then when I let up," Jay begins less than a second after Ned, overlapping his talk, then stops.

Ned continues, "Because when you let go the diver goes up, and the air was squished, and since it got small the water that was compressing it goes out. And since there's no water compressing it so the air just comes back down where it originally was before you pressed it."

"So he means that when you push on the top the water goes into the vial, into the diver, and then there's lots of room to put the air in, and if you take off your hand then, um, the air comes back in because the water just drops back out. And it has, the air comes back," Jay explains.

Ned continues, starting before Jay has finished, "The water comes out because, because nobody's pressing the bottom and it's not, it's not compressing the air, so the air comes back down to what it was before you pressed on the rubber sheet."

Although they appear ready to share longer—Ned even offers to review the diagram for the class—no more questions are forthcoming.

Although this was the only reporting session in which the partners shared the responsibility of responding to the listeners' questions in terms of floor time, closer examination from the perspective of interactional sociolinguistics suggests that they are as much competing as collaborating.

Goffman (1981) proposed consideration of the ways in which participants' interactions construct their continued opportunities for and ways of participating, and he termed this the participation framework of the interaction. One aspect of a participation framework is footing, or the role of a participant relative to an utterance or to another participant.

Jay's first response, "What takes the space of the water in the diver?" was a repeat of Brian's question, and, because a response, not a question, was expected, Ned was able to begin a response and get the floor. This created a participation framework between Ned and Brian that excluded Jay. Jay's next turn at talk, a revoicing of Ned's statement, and animation of Ned, "So he means that … " could be read as a deliberate attempt to change his footing relative to Brian's question. By animating Ned and referring to Brian as "you," Jay bid to reposition himself as a central figure in this interaction, to change his footing. Animating Ned aligned him socially with Ned and conceptually with Ned's assertion. In addition, by addressing the statement directly to Brian and addressing him as "you," Jay aligned himself socially with Brian. Jay's turn here was thus a bid to enter the discursive stream.

Ned thwarted this attempt, however. When Jay paused slightly, "And it has," (pause indicated by the comma after "has"), Ned took the floor. Further, Ned made no effort to respond to Jay and directed his contribution only to Brian, addressing Brian as "you" and effectively creating a participant framework that excluded his partner, Jay.

This brief glimpse at the participation framework constructed here shows Jay once again attempting to position himself to enter the discourse. However, his moves were not validated through a response and he did not successfully enter at that time—one might even say his entrance was blocked by Ned's interruption—and the conversation remained essentially between Brian and Ned. The significance of this interaction lies in its demonstration of the sometimes subtle ways that other students blocked Jay's full participation in the activities of the classroom.

7

"It Will Be Very, Very Difficult for Him to Learn How to Function in the Class."

"During our investigation over the last week and a half, we've been looking at sinking and floating through an investigation of the diver, the Cartesian diver. We generated some explanations about why the diver was sinking and why it was floating." Laura begins by standing at the overhead projector, then walks slowly toward back of the room as she speaks. It is the first day of the third cycle of inquiry.

Jay is in his seat, dressed in a black-and-white knit shirt with a collar and black jeans, watching Laura intently. As Laura speaks, he raises his left arm slowly, then catches his left wrist with his right hand and holds his arm, bent, behind his head, ready to volunteer.

"Let's just as a class come up with some of the ideas that we thought about, that were claims that we came up with together." Laura moves back over to the overhead projector, picks up a marker, and uncaps it.

Jay watches Laura uncap the marker and uncoils his arm quickly. Laura glances at him, "Jay?"

"How, um, how it goes down and how the water, um, like, pushes it. And how—"

"OK, we talked about," Laura bends over and begins writing on the overhead projector, "the water, and, what were you going to say?"

Jay is watching the words as they appear on the screen, and turns to face Laura again. "About how does it sink and all that."

"How does it?" Laura has stopped writing.

"By the water."

"Excuse me?" The class is silent, no one is shifting in their seats, no hands are raised, no feet are shuffling. They, like Laura, watch Jay and listen for his answer.

"Um, OK," Jay takes a deep breath, inhaling audibly. He says softly, "Do I have to do this?"

"You don't have to, no. I can go on to someone else."

"OK. You said how does it drop?" Jay speaks quickly, and more loudly.

"*Why.*"

"*Why* does it drop?"

"Yeah, the explanation."

"Because the water, the water goes into the, into the diver and it makes it, when the water makes the diver too heavy, the diver drops."

Laura begins writing again, then pauses, "I'm trying to remember your words." She reads what she has written, "Water goes into the diver, when the water makes the diver," Laura pauses and turn to look at Jay again, "How did you say it again?"

"I said, the water goes into the diver, and when the diver, I mean, and when the water makes the diver too heavy, it drops," Jay explains.

"OK." Laura adds Jay's words to her writing on the overhead, so that the completed statement reads, "Water goes into the diver, when the water makes the diver too heavy it drops." She then asks the class for other claims. Jay volunteers again almost immediately, and keeps his arm raised throughout this discussion, but is not called on again. After 8 minutes Laura has created the following list on the overhead:

> Water goes into the diver, when the water makes the diver too heavy, it drops.
> Air helps the diver go to the top.
> Fish float because water is in the fish.
> Weight of the air. Air doesn't weigh anything.

When Laura finishes writing the last claims on the overhead she straightens up and looks over at Jay, who still has his hand raised. His arm trembles slightly and he opens and closes his hand as he watches Laura, waiting to be called on. "Jay?"

Jay points to list on the screen, and begins, "Um, you know what Maria said, about the air?" He lowers his hand and clasps it together with his other one. While still looking at the screen, he reads Maria's claim, "Um, 'Air helps the diver go to the top?'" He pauses and looks directly at Laura, "But, um, see, you know how the water goes up into the vial and makes it go down? But when you let your finger off it, it makes the water, I mean the diver, goes down?" Jay looks around the room but no response is forthcoming. He turns back to Laura, speaking more slowly and pronouncing his words carefully, "Well, there's not as much wheat, *weight*, as it is when you push it, because the water, the water makes it go down because the water pushes itself up *into* the diver and makes it drop." Jay nods once emphatically as he finishes, his face breaking into a proud grin, and raises his eyebrows expectantly.

"OK, I think that's kinda what we had said before," Laura nods in Jay's direction and then turns back to face the rest of the class.

"Yeah." Jay agrees with Laura but his face falls, and the excitement that had fueled his careful speech drains quickly away.

"OK," Laura addresses the class again, "were there any other ideas that you, 'cause I know that when we were discussing things there were still some people talking about things that maybe you were unclear of that you'd want to try to investigate further, any ideas that came up that you wanted to spend a little bit more time thinking about?" Jay's hand shoots up into the air before Laura finishes. "Maria?"

Maria, "Well, um, I don't know but, doesn't air weigh something?"

"So that would be something that you'd want to investigate?" Laura writes Maria's question on the overhead.

"Yeah. Because if the air doesn't weigh anything, how could it pull the diver up?" Maria explains. "Because the air is at the top, and that's how the diver gets up there, by the air pulling it up."

"I think it's pressure from the water," Jay says quietly, his arm still raised.

"Other questions that you have that you didn't feel were really answered yet for you, that you'd really like to think about further? Jay?"

"I have three. Can it work with mixtures? Can it work with other liquids? Can it work with bigger test tubes? I saw you have a big test tube back there," Jay glances at the materials in the back of the room as he finishes.

Laura adds Jay's question to her list, and the conversation continues for several more minutes. Laura then uses these questions to introduce the idea of second-hand investigations. "Sometimes people use information from other folks to give them help in trying to sort out questions that they might have. So, if someone else had done a lot of work in investigating Cartesian divers, do you think it might be interesting to read what they found out? To see if that would help you make sense of, you know, what you guys found out? If you went to that other source of writing and did some reading, that is called a second-hand investigation. Because you're looking at other people's work other than your own, and getting information from it." Standing at the front of the room, Laura explains that now the students are going to "get information from an expert." Each student is given a copy of the text, and Laura asks them to predict what the text will be about by reading the title, "What Is Matter?"[1]

Someone calls out "matter," while Jay raises his hand, whispering, "I can tell you." Laura calls on Maria, and she answers, "Like what your desk is made of." Laura asks the class whether they learned that in fourth grade and several answer yes. Next, she calls on Jay.

"Can I tell you 'what is matter?'" he asks, excited.

"Let's hold that thought, OK," Laura tells him. She calls on two more students, who offer "liquids and metals," and "what things are made of." Next Laura asks the children to listen to her read the first paragraph and to think about any questions they need to ask to "clear up their ideas about the article." She then reads the first paragraph, "'You see and touch hundreds of things every day. And while most of these things differ from one another, they share one important quality. They are all forms of matter. The universe is made of matter and energy. Matter is the part of the universe you can see and touch. Matter is what the earth is made of and matter is what you are made of.'" Laura walks slowly around the room as she reads, finishing near Jay's desk. "OK, what would you say, can you come up with a question that maybe you would ask somebody to see if they understood the article?"

Maria volunteers, "What is matter?" She pauses a moment, then adds, "It does sort of tell you but it doesn't tell you."

When Laura acknowledges him, Jay observes, "I thought, I learned this in second grade, I thought that matter was anything that took up space."

"Well, would that go along with what we're reading about here?"

"I don't know." Jay looks down at the paper on his desk and picks it up, "Sort of, yeah."

"Which part, what makes you say yeah?" Laura prompts.

Jay holds the text out in front of him, and runs his index finger along a line as he reads, "because it says anything that you can, I mean, 'matter is part of the universe you can touch.'"

"So that would fit along with that definition, too. Let's read a little further."

---

[1]This text was written by Shirley Magnusson, Annemarie Palincsar, and Danielle Ford, and later revised in collaboration with the GIsML research team.

After the second-hand investigation, the students conduct an additional first-hand investigation that involves testing a range of materials to see whether they sink or float. Each pair of students then writes their data on sheets of poster paper hung on the board. After they finish, Laura stands near this lists and tells the children, "You came up with a lot of data and now we have to make sense of it … Our job is to collectively try to sort through all of this wonderful information that we have up here. Let's start with claims." For the next several minutes students articulate claims about floating and sinking and Laura writes them on a sheet of poster paper on the board.

Christine offers the first claim, "I remember the other day somebody mentioned that all wood floats and the wood that we had, all of it floated."

"OK," Laura writes, "All wood floats" on the list. "Other ideas? Larry?"

"Not all wood floats. Like old wood, that sinks," Larry says emphatically.

"Can you give an experience that you had with that being the case?" Laura prompts.

"At the beach, I rolled some old wood into the water and it sunk."

"So that's some important evidence for this claim right here." Laura taps the paper next to where she has written Christine's claim. "What about some other claims related to materials we had yesterday?" There is a brief discussion of mass as a factor, then Laura calls on Jay.

"Because some things are heavier than others, and um, certain wood can float and stuff but wood is heavier than some things and some things are heavier than wood and it has to be light or like flat to float," Jay is sitting sideways at his desk so he can face Laura at the board, and leans forward with his hands in his lap. He looks up at Laura while he speaks.

"So you think shape might have something to do with it?" Laura asks, and Jay shrugs and smiles slightly in response to Laura's question.

"That's a possibility," Laura acknowledges, and writes "Shape makes things float or sink."

Maria then suggests that volume has something to do with it but she's not sure what, "Like, the volume has to with, um, like, I saw on a science show or something they put a piece of bread on the water and it floated but when they crunched up it sunk."

"That's interesting. So when it's crunched up it sinks and when it's flat it floats?" Maria nods and Laura continues, "So you're saying that the amount of space it takes up might have something to do with it?"

"Yeah," Maria nods again.

"Jay?"

Again called on

Jay turns backwards in his seat and looks at Maria, then back at Laura, "Maria, are you saying that what kind of shape it is, like is it flat?"

"Well, that was part of what she was saying, too." Laura answers for Maria. "Whether it was 'cause it was flat or a ball, she was talking about, or if was because it was bigger when it was flat and smaller when it was in a ball. There must be some reason why one of those would sink and one would float. That would be something that we would want to investigate."

Without raising his hand, Carl calls out, "I know why that happens."

"Why?" Laura turns to him.

"Because there's more stuff to float, on. Like, if you, well, I don't know a real good example but if you put a piece of paper on the water, it's flat, it will float for an amount of time and then sink. But if you crunch it up it will just sink down because all the mass is in one space."

There is a brief discussion in which Laura tells the class that weight doesn't change when a piece of paper or slice of bread is "crunched up," and then calls on Jay. Jay turns to Carl, "It doesn't matter if aluminum foil is crunched up or spread out it still floats." Carl is writing in his notebook and doesn't look up.

"Boy, you guys are really coming up with some good questions. If we could hold on to those questions a little bit, because those are some things I think would be worth investigating, let's go back to what we've got up here." Laura tells the students that, through their claims, they've identified four factors—size, shape, material, and heaviness—and now their job is to determine from the data they've collected which of those factors influence whether an object sinks or floats.

"Let's do one together here.... Let's say your group was in charge of organizing the data according to size. These are the cylinders, and you've got the large and the small. So you'd probably want to separate them into two categories? Large and small, right? To see if size was a factor in whether things sunk or floated."

Jay mutters, "No, size was not a factor," and slumps back in his chair.

Laura lists each large item, and then each small item vertically on a sheet of poster paper and then divides the paper into two columns, sinks and floats. As she calls out each item the students respond with "sunk" or "floated" and Laura records it on the sheet of poster paper. Many of the children appear disengaged: Matthew lays across his desk and several others simply lay their heads down; Molly and her tablemate carry on an animated, whispered discussion; Kevin and Carl, tablemates, don't look up from writing in their notebooks; Ned leans back and rests his head against the bookshelf next to his desk. After 4 minutes, Laura asks, "So what can we say about size?" Jay raises his hand immediately but is not called on. Maria offers a long reiteration of her argument for volume, the "size of the volume," which Laura summarizes by saying that the students' data do not support an argument for size as a factor.

"So, what I think I'd like you guys to do, so that we can do this quickly," Laura's volume increases and the children begin shifting in their seats, sensing an immanent change in the activity, "is assign certain people to sort out the facts.... Set it up so you have a 'sink' and a 'float.'" Laura waves a hand over Jay and the three girls sitting closest to him, "Let me have you four work together ... You guys sort things out by shape, so look at the spheres, cylinders, and cubes and see if there's a relationship there." She breaks the rest of the class into groups of four to six children and each group is assigned one aspect of the objects (size, shape, material, and weight).

Jay gets up from his desk and goes over to the table of two desks where his group is meeting, situated right next to the chalkboard and the table Laura uses as a desk, and stands with his hands in pockets. One of the girls in the group, Cynthia, has the sheet of poster paper on her desk, and sits with a marker poised in her hand. Her tablemate, Cheryl, sits next to her. Kim walks over with a chair and sits opposite Cynthia at her desk. Jay brings a chair over to the opposite side of Cheryl's desk, so that he is sitting beside Kim with his back to the chalkboard.

Kim begins by telling Cynthia to write down the names of all of the objects the class tested. Cynthia tries to get the marker to write, pressing down firmly and scribbling it quickly across the paper repeatedly, but it is apparently dried up.

"Can I try?" Jay asks, leaning over to Cynthia. Cynthia doesn't look up but keeps scribbling. Jay repeats his request, slightly louder, "Can I try the writing?"

Carl, who as been standing at Laura's table, presumably getting a sheet of poster paper, leans over to Jay, "If she can't do it, you can't either!"

"Shut up!" Jay responds, but turns to give Carl a quick grin.

Laura looks up from assisting a group in the back of the room, "We don't talk like that in here," she says firmly, looking at Jay, who looks down at his lap. Carl returns to his seat.

Kim reaches into the basket on Laura's table and hands Cynthia a new marker. Cynthia writes down each of the objects and its corresponding size, shape, and material as Kim reads the names off the board to her. Cheryl sits quietly. Jay tries three times to tell Kim and Cynthia that they are not completing the assignment correctly: "Mrs. Bozek said for us to organize it by shape." "You're supposed to do shapes." "Do it by shape." He is not responded to, and after the third attempt, he leans back in his chair and is silent.

Laura approaches the group then, and sees that they have not categorized the items by shape. She reminds them that they are "sorting things out by shape. So, do all cylinders float, or sink? What does the data say?"

Jay leans forward to Kim, "See. I toldja."

"Well, why didn't you help?" Kim responds.

Laura turns quickly to Jay, "We don't talk like that in here!" and points toward the classroom door.

The jangle of the holiday bells Laura has hung in the narrow window of the door punctuate its closing. From my seat across the room, I can see Jay's eyes and nose through the thick, tempered glass as he strains to see past the bows and bells into the classroom. His fingertips clasp the window frame on either side of his face. For several minutes he solemnly watches the conversation continue without him. Then he turns away.

Anderson et al. (1997) described three different foci that competed for students' attention in small-group interactions like Jay's with Cheryl, Cynthia, and Kim: interpersonal relationships, scientific activity, and task requirements. Here, as in the case they presented, students' attention to interpersonal relationships subverted their opportunities for engagement in scientific activity and learning. In addition, in this case the children's opportunity to complete the task appropriately was also thwarted.

In the children's (and Laura's) attentions to the social, interpersonal aspects of this interaction at the expense of attention to the scientific activity and the requirements of the task itself, it was possible to observe how Jay was made different. His demonstration of "emotional impairment" was constructed through the interaction so that he was, in a sense, "set up" by his classmates, Carl, Kim, and Cynthia, for recognition by Laura as different. He, of course, contributed to this by responding "Shut up" and "I toldja!"

In much the same way as McDermott (1993) identified learning disability as an interactional possibility in the case of his case study student, Adam, here emotional impairment and difference were interactional possibilities for Jay:

"Where is LD?" Behaviorally, the answer is clear. It is all over the classroom as an interactional possibility. Everyone stands in some relation to it. Everyone is part of the choreography that produces moments for its public appearance. LD is distributed across persons, across the moment, as part of the contextual work members do in the different scenes. Neither Adam, nor his disability, can be separated from the contexts in which they emerge. (p. 291)

As McDermott's work suggests, Jay's exclusion here was made possible by the constraints and affordances of the activity itself, the discursive interactions between the children, and the social histories of these children within this classroom community.

Consideration of this illuminated a pattern evident throughout the inquiry: With the exception of the scaffolding interactions with Laura noted earlier, in each of the activity contexts, Jay's ideas were not responded to—taken up, extended, or questioned—in the ways that he valued and responded to the ideas expressed by others. He consistently was the one who had to do the work of appropriation. Further, he was made most "different" in the interactions that relied on writing as a tool. As my work with Jay and this classroom community progressed, I became more aware of how deeply these issues of social capital, interpersonal relationships, and activity affected the learning opportunities afforded different students, and how they worked to create moments where Jay was made visible as emotionally impaired or learning disabled.

Notebook clasped to her chest, Laura has only a few moments to talk before she must attend a meeting. Standing near the door, she turns to Annemarie and Shirley and describes the children's confusion with the assignment and points to Jay's group as an example, "They were starting to correct their poster but Jay was being a little bit difficult."

I am across the room, standing behind the camera, and I feel compelled to share my observations and interpretations of events with Laura. At this point I make the decision to get involved in this research, and to try to influence Laura's perceptions of who Jay is and what he is capable of. I leave the camera rolling, and step around it to join Laura as I begin, "He was frustrated because he had um, he had told them what you said and they weren't listening to what he had to say. So that's why when you came over and repeated what he had been trying to say, that's why he was like, 'Well, I told you.' He was kinda frustrated with what they were doing."

Laura begins talking before I am finished, "He, he doesn't know how to do that in an appropriate way, though. They were probably ignoring him because they didn't like his tone or they didn't like how he was directing their activities. It's a real issue with kids like that, who have emotional, you know, things going on, they can't get their point across in a way that's productive to the group."

Laura's comments placed the responsibility for the failed activity of the small group, and Jay's subsequent exclusion from the group, squarely on

*Jay. Identifying him as having "emotional things going on" that interfered
with his ability to communicate "in a way that's productive to the group"
allowed her to locate the problem within Jay and not within the interaction.
If the problem lay within Jay, why was it not visible in the other instructional contexts, particularly public sharing, where Laura herself described
Jay's participation as "amazing?"*

*Public sharing and the small-group work described were both speech
events; that is, talk was necessary to complete the action in both activities
(Hymes, 1974). However, the type of talk called for and the response necessary
to validate that talk differed. One difference between the sharing sessions,
where Jay was an active participant as listener although the ideas he introduced were not responded to, and the small-group sessions, where he was first
discursively and then also physically excluded, was in the participation structures (the norms of interaction) of these two speech events (Philips, 1972).*

*As Laura repeatedly emphasized in her explanations to the children,
public sharing in this classroom community was defined as a speech event
in which everyone was supposed to talk and share ideas and question each
other "to learn from each other." Jay did not necessarily need his peers to
respond to the substantive content of his speech to participate successfully
in this structure; he only needed to participate in ways recognized as socially acceptable by Laura so that he could gain access to the floor. Jay's
successful participation was thus mediated by his appropriation of the
three linguistic tools discussed earlier, which supported his entry into the
discourse and allowed him demonstrate the ways in which he was successfully meeting the goals of the activity; that is, learning from his peers.*

*However, small-group activity had a different participation structure.
Unlike the norm for public sharing, the norms for small-group work were
not suggested explicitly by Laura and seemed to emerge from students'
prior relationships with each other and implicit understandings of
small-group work. This allowed Kim to take over, in collaboration with
Cynthia, and exclude Jay and Cheryl from the group activity. Cheryl accepted a silenced role and was allowed to remain part of group, but Jay
sought out ways to be included. In this speech event, the response of his
peers was necessary for Jay's participation to be ratified. However, rather
than responding to him in ways that validated his participation, Jay's peers
responded to him in ways that framed his behavior as inappropriate and set
him up for exclusion (e.g., Carl's teasing and Kim's first ignoring him and
then claiming he didn't help). Again, the participants and the activity thus
coconstructed Jay as different.*

I quickly search for a way to link my perceptions of Jay's participation with Laura's descriptions of him. What portrait of him could include both of our perspectives? "Do you think, what I was thinking about, um, because I've noticed this, this not being listened to happen with him a few times, do you think he's still getting enculturated into uh, sort of the ways of this classroom community?"[2]

Laura straightens and looks directly at me. When she speaks, her voice is firm and she appears to be growing angry or frustrated, "I'm not sure if he's capable of being enculturated. He has, he has so much goin' on. Um, I mean, his background is, his mother, when she had him, abandoned him immediately because the man she was going to marry didn't want a child and so she said, 'I'm outta here. Mom, you have to take care of him.' So his grandmother has raised him. And the grandmother just recently got married. They used to live in Andover City up until this year … They go on these religious retreats for weeks at a time and so Jay is left with all these different relatives while they're gone … They're in the process of building a house, so they're living with this family with about 12 kids. Grandma and Grandpa are sometimes there, sometimes not there. I mean his, his life is a mess. And so I just don't know if he's capable right now, it will be very, very difficult for him to learn how to function in the class. I mean, the conversation I had with him out there was, because his grandparents were coming every day after school for about two weeks. I asked her to do that and she did. Just a personal report and get his work. And during those two weeks he got everything turned in. He was a different Jay. And I told him out in the hall, I said, 'I want to see that Jay.' I said, 'He's buried in there someplace and we need to bring him out.' I said, 'I know that you participated so nicely in the science investigation, and I just, you know, I know it's there Jay but you have to bring it out.' And so, that was the conversation I had with him…. When I asked him to talk in the hall I think he thought I was gonna yell at him again. But I just said again we have to help you learn how to say what you mean without hurting people's feelings. I said, 'Kim's feelings were hurt because you yelled at her.' You said, 'That's what I said!' in a really you know nasty tone of voice. And nobody is going to listen to that. I don't know if any of this is eventually going to sink in or not. But that has been constant with him. Since the beginning. And if it's not sinking in yet, I don't know."

---

[2]In hindsight I regret using the phrase "getting enculturated," which placed the onus back on Jay for his exclusion. I was searching for a way to both honor and challenge Laura's interpretation by providing an alternative one, but my choice was not effective, perhaps because it supported Laura's portrayal of Jay as an outsider.

I am taken by surprise by the length and intensity of Laura's description of Jay and his family, and by the difference in our interpretations of the small-group interactions. I try to think of counter-evidence. "But I do see it in the large group. For example, today, he said 'It's the shape, it's flat,' and then a few minutes later Maria, um, was explaining something and Jay raised his hand and he said 'Are you saying it's the shape, Maria?' So you know, I do see, in the large group, when he gets the floor and he has the opportunity to speak and he's listened to, I see him expressing himself really appropriately."

Annemarie starts to say something but Laura appears to be growing more agitated and interrupts, "It's the nonstructured time, when it's, you know what I mean, and that's when he usually does break down when I give him a task and I'm not, you know, looking necessarily at him.... If it's large group instruction usually it's one person speaking at a time. So, you know, in terms of that kind of situation he does function but this kind of thing, he, that's when he's gonna go."

Annemarie begins a second time, "It strikes me that the onus on these children is twice as great as other children. I don't see other children appropriating the many, many ideas that Jay has introduced to this class, the way I see Jay appropriating their ideas. These children have to prove themselves in ways that are not expected of other children. It just breaks your heart."

Laura is unmoved by our attempts to point out the classroom community's role in shaping Jay's behavior and her interpretation of it. "But I mean, it's gonna be constant. Fortunately I think for him, I had a conversation with Carl and Kevin, and I said 'He's been having a rough couple of days.' I said, 'I don't know what's goin' on with him at home,' but, you know, I enlisted their help in terms of, 'When he gets like this, please, you guys don't feed on it. You guys are friends of his and you can say, 'Jay, not now. We'll talk about it at lunch,' or 'We'll talk about it at recess, but you need to sit down now.' And they were very responsive to that, they are kids that would be, you know, and he respects them. But it's every few weeks we have to go through this with Jay. And it's time for Grandma and Grandpa to start coming in after school. And the accountability, you know, that's real important for kids to have that accountability and he has nothing. There's no place for him to do his homework, there's kids all over the place, and they're rough kids. The family is an abused family and a dysfunctional family anyways. And there's cousins and aunts and uncles that are the same age." Laura laughs slightly, then continues, "But he's an interesting child. Very interesting."

Schiffrin (1996) analyzed the ways in which informants' narrative language choices revealed their conceptions of self and situated others to maintain that conception of self. Drawing on the work of sociologist Goffman (1959), she used the phrase "impression management" to describe the ways speakers use language to construct these images of themselves and of others. Throughout my conversations with her, Laura employed similar narrative strategies to create or "manage" impressions of herself and her teaching.

In this interaction, Laura created a narrative in which Jay was insensitive (hurting Kim's feelings) and she was sensitive (protecting Kim's feelings). Whereas I found her actions, especially her responses to Jay, at times incongruent with this sense of herself, Laura employed narrative impression management to preserve this sense of herself as a caring and sensitive teacher. Thus her conversation with Carl and Kevin, which could be seen as contributing to Jay's exclusion from the classroom community by marking him as "different" in the eyes of his classmates, appears in Laura's narrative as an attempt to help Jay manage his "problem." In the narrative where Laura is a caring and sensitive teacher, something must be wrong with Jay; therefore he must be emotionally impaired or learning disabled.

It was this conversation with Laura that motivated me to work further with Jay. This was not a project that I could choose not to do: In this moment, it chose me. Laura's descriptions of Jay's (in)abilities were so different from my own observations of his interactions, and from her own comments about him during earlier cycles of GIsML instruction, that I felt compelled to try to understand the dynamics that could lead to the construction of such "different Jay[s]." Informed by social constructivist approaches to understanding disability and ability, I wanted to interrupt the narrative Laura constructed about Jay with stories from his own perspective and from my observations of his ability, and I set about to do that. What I didn't account for was how difficult reconstructing her narrative of Jay would be for Laura, because it would require her to reexamine her narrative of self and because that self was so enmeshed with the historical, cultural, and institutional contexts in which she lived and worked.

8

"It's Like a Burst, a Burst of Fire."

I load the tape into the VCR, which hangs from the ceiling in the corner of Laura's classroom, and sit down next to Jay. I want to try to understand his interpretation of the guided inquiry interactions. How does Jay perceive what I view as the lack of uptake of his contributions by his peers and Laura, despite his repeated attempts to extend the conversation in substantive ways? What is his interpretation of the discursive moves that I see as contributing to his cognitive and social exclusion from classroom community?[1]

Laura has arranged for Jay to stay with me rather than go to art class, and she leaves us alone in the classroom. I explain to him that I want to try to understand his thinking about the inquiry, and that the videotape contains clips from three different activities. "After each clip we're just gonna just stop and I'm gonna ask you three questions. So, I'll tell you what they are now so you know now." I've given him a written copy of the questions, and we both look at it. "The first question I'm gonna ask you is what you were thinking during the activity. If you can remember, what you were thinking. The second thing

---

[1]My use of the word *substantive* derives from Schwab's (1964) distinction between substantive and syntactic forms of scientific knowledge. Schwab described substantive knowledge as the shared theories and constructs of science. Substantive structures undergo a constant process of revision as we learn more and are confronted by inconsistencies between our current substantive knowledge and our new data. Schwab described syntactic knowledge as understanding of the communicative and knowledge-building practices of scientists. Both, he asserted, were necessary for students' participation in inquiry (see K. M. Collins et al., 1998).

In their lack of substantive response to Jay's contributions, his classmates and Laura did not take up or respond to the scientific content of his observations and assertions. Further, there was often very little response to him at all. Lack of response thus worked to exclude Jay both cognitively and socially.

I'm going to ask you is, do you think the responses of the other people in the clip were helpful to your thinking? And the third thing I'm going to ask you is, whether you liked the activity in the clip or not. Whether you thought it was interesting to you or not, or helpful. So, here's the first clip."[2]

Together we watch Jay, Ned, and Laura talk about the CDS during the first cycle of investigating. Jay is eager to talk, and begins before the clip is over, "Yeah, I remember! I was, I was thinking about, um, the, the, I was thinking about the Cartesian diver." Jay repeats his thinking about pressure forcing water into the diver and making it sink, then emphasizes Ned's role in helping him figure that out. "I can't take all the credit, because Ned gave me, he came up with some ideas, too. So, so we was partners and we was doing like partners should be ... I mean, when we put our heads together, and our brains, we think of things that is, that's helpful for the lesson that we're doing." In addition to the opportunity to work with Ned, Jay tells me that the opportunity to build a CDS for himself was important. In other classes in school he has been shown demonstrations, but has never had a chance to make things for himself before, to "experience things."

The next clip depicts Ned and Jay reporting to the class. "Yeah, I was sharing with the class because, I was sharing my thoughts. And Ned, both of our thoughts." Jay talks about the importance of sharing because of the opportunity to get ideas from the questions people asked him, and the opportunity to share what he's thinking. He emphasizes that the process of verbalizing his thoughts, as a presenter and as a listener, helps him understand new phenomena. "Making the diver, that was something new to me. You know, so I had to discuss it in order to get it, you know, in order to get it into my head."

Jay adds that discussing is his favorite way to learn. When he discusses things, he can "take something old and then make something new. 'Cause it was like a good challenge. It's a good challenge, you know? When you ... combine something new and something old together you get new thoughts." His favorite part of the inquiry was, "When we like, sat down and discussed the diver, 'cause I learned something every time I did discuss it."

I ask Jay if he could say more about how he learns during a discussion, and he explains, "Like I, like from my old school, I had, I had a good teacher. She taught me a lot of things so when somebody else say something, I just like take what they're saying ... and remember what I, what I

---

[2]For details concerning my methodology here, see the discussion regarding stimulated recall and think-aloud protocols in the Appendix.

had learned from the year, and combine that. And when I think about it real hard it just comes out. It's like a burst, a burst of fire."

"A burst of fire, that's a neat comparison. Can you say more about that?"

"'Cause when you, you know how you really *gotta* say something?"

"Yeah."

"That's how I be thinking! 'Cause when, see, I can't hold, well, I can hold my peace, but, when it's so, it's so, it's so good that you know, I hafta, you know, hurry up and say it."

"I'm like that too. I like to say what's on my mind."

As the third clip begins playing, Jay recognizes it, "Oh, the sinking and floating." We are watching the small-group interaction before Jay was removed from the group. Jay looks at me, "I didn't get, I didn't get to explain in this one right here." We watch the rest of the clip in silence. When it finishes, Jay begins, "Well, I wasn't saying that much."

"No, you weren't," I agree.

"Everybody was blurting out so I gave them a chance to talk."

"Yeah."

"See she, well, it wasn't what *I* was thinking, it was what we was *supposed* to do."

"Right."

"I was thinking that, um, she said, we had shapes, right?"

"Uh-huh."

"Well, Kim, she was helping a lot, really. Because I didn't, I didn't get to express my feelings that much in, um, that group. So, she did, she had the brains in that group. I came up with some ideas but she had the brains in that group."

"How come you didn't get to express your feelings that much in that group?"

"Because I let every, everybody else express their, um, feelings."

"So that was your choice?"

"Yeah."

Jay says that the small-group activity was not as much fun as the rest of the floating and sinking program of study. When I ask him why, he explains, "Because, um, like, we had, had like, how can I say this? We didn't have discussion with the class, we just discussed it with groups. So nobody was asking questions or like that ... When we was discussing with the class when we had our, um, chart and that was kind of fun because we had people to ask us questions and then I could explain to them what I was thinking. It helps me think because like when we have a discussion, I'll like, I listen to everything and then I'll have something to say. And when I have something to say, when I have something to say I just express my feelings."

"How did you learn how to do that? Did you just, is that just part of your personality?"

"Yeah, I think so, because every time, it's like, I just be sittin' down listening and stuff. So, like in first grade, I was like the smartest in there."

"Mm-hm."

"In our classroom. And so, I just like, started, uh, listening to stuff, and then, so I started asking questions, and my teacher said I was like real smart, so."

"Your teacher said you were the smartest?"

"Uh-huh."

"Was that in Andover City? Or was that here?"

"That was in Axleton."

"That was in Axleton!" At that point, I only knew what Laura had told me—that Jay had moved to Axleton from Andover City at the beginning of the school year—so I am surprised to learn he had lived in Axleton previously.

"Uh-huh. 'Cause I had Mrs., it was this one Chinese lady."

I think of my friend and colleague in the Guided Inquiry Community of Teacher Practice, Faith Cleminson, who is from the Philippines, not China, and teaches first grade in Axleton. "Mrs. Cleminson?"

"Yeah."

"Whoa! She's my friend! I didn't know you knew her! And then you went to Andover City and then you came back?"

"Then I came to Agawam, then I went to Andover City and then I came back here."

"Wow! You've been in a lot of different schools. Which one was your favorite?"

"Well, I don't know. I came, well, I came to, uh, to Agawam when I was in first grade, and I stayed there until I was in third grade. Then I moved when I was in fourth. So I went to fourth, and now I'm here in fifth. I really like this school because of how we do stuff here. And we have, like better things than we had, than I had when I was in Agawam and Andover City. But I miss my friends. I had a lot of friends in Andover City."

Jay's articulation of his own approach to learning bore striking resemblance to the work of scholars of social constructivist theories. Jay's description of what we came to call his "burst of fire" strategy, "when somebody else say something, I just like take what they're saying … and remember what I had learned from the year, and combine that. And when I think about it real hard it just comes out. It's like a burst, a burst of fire," aptly summarized the dialectical relationship between individual cognition and social resources posited by social constructivist and sociocultural theories. The lack of uptake of his ideas did not seem to inhibit Jay's perception of his own learning; he emphasized the opportunities provided to him by the discourse of others rather than their lack of substantive response to his ideas. Jay reacted more strongly to the third clip, in which he "didn't get to explain" and Kim "had the brains," although he ultimately maintained that it was his choice to let the others talk.

In addition, the value Jay placed on discussion and the necessity of sharing one's thoughts with others resonated with the values guiding a learning community orientation to teaching and learning (Nieto, 1999; Rogoff, 1994). When a classroom is viewed as a learning community, emphasis is placed on the very dialectic Jay described, and on making one's thinking, tool use, and practices visible for others. Opportunities are provided for all students to participate and contribute to the dialectical construction of understanding in ways that draw on their strengths as learners and meaning-makers. The emphasis is not on simply "being nice" (Nieto, 1999), but on actively engaging with and responding to the ideas of others with the goal of constructing shared understanding.

Thus, one implication of adopting a classroom-as-learning-community perspective is that the role of response becomes of central importance. As asserted by Bakhtin (1981), response serves to activate thinking, to "create the ground for understanding" (p. 281). Bakhtin argued that understanding began with response, that "understanding and response are dialectically merged and mutually condition each other; one is impossible without the other" (p. 282). Jay acted on this principle each time he responded actively to the utterances of his classmates and Laura, and increased his own understanding as he did so (in his words, discussion helped him "get it into my head"). He also created opportunities for others in the community to increase their understanding; however, their lack of response to him and limited responses to each other (e.g., it must be noted how few of the students participated in the discourse) restricted the understanding the community was able to reach.

Although I was surprised to learn that Jay had gone to first grade in Axleton and that he had been in Faith Cleminson's class, I was not surprised when he articulated the powerful impact Faith's class had on him. Like Laura, Faith was a member of the GIsML Community of Teacher Practice and I had worked closely with her for 2 years. Through extensive observations in Faith's classroom, conducted 3 and 4 years after Jay was a member of her classroom community, I documented classroom practices that relied on an underlying structure of shared assumptions, goals, and practices. This structure seemed to support the idiosyncratic learning styles of individual students. Although there was always a tension between individual ways of constructing and expressing knowledge and the conventions that were recognized by the group, Faith strove to make this a productive tension.

Unfortunately, I did not have the opportunity to observe Jay's interactions within Faith's classroom community. However, prior to working with Jay, I conducted case studies of two students in Faith's classroom that illuminated her approach to creating and sustaining a learning community. These students each had idiosyncratic learning styles and were later referred for special education assessment. One, Robert, was subsequently identified as learning disabled. However, in the context of Faith's classroom learning community, both students were able to draw on their learning preferences as strengths. Because Faith "looped" with her first-grade class and moved with them to second grade, I was able to observe each of these students, Robert and Timothy, for 2 years. Rather than emphasize differences as deficits, these case studies demonstrated that Faith was able to sustain an environment in which individual differences were honored as valuable contributions to the community.[3]

Jay's own emphasis on the importance of Faith's classroom and its impact on his life in school reflected the affinity between his form of classroom participation and her model of learning. Jay and Faith shared a perspective on the importance of the classroom as a learning community, a perspective that was important in shaping Jay's sense of himself as a capable contributor to such a community.

---

[3]Summaries of the two cases from Faith's classroom and of the ways they inform an understanding of her development of a learning community appear next, with some discussion related to the ways in which community practices shaped ability and participation in her classroom.

Case 1   Robert was an outgoing, orally expressive, and very social child who struggled with print literacy. He entered first grade with little awareness of alphabetic principles, and he struggled to identify letter–sound relationships. He also had small motor difficulties, and the act of writing was a challenge for him. In Faith's classroom, he was able to work on his reading and his writing at his own pace, and to draw on his interest and first-hand knowledge of farming (especially tractors) to support his developing print literacy. He was also able to draw on the print literacy skills of other students, sometimes asking one of them to edit his writing or to help him use the computer's spell checker. In addition, Robert consistently drew on his own advanced oral skills to support and extend his written expressions. For example, when sharing his daily journal entries with the class, he extended his written entries through oral explanation of his ideas. The other students recognized Robert for his strengths in oralcy, and they often nominated him to serve as "spokesperson" or to lead the presentation of small-group work. In second grade, when Robert became a more fluent and independent reader, he wrote an invitation to me to come

(continued on next page)

Shortly after I conducted this stimulated recall interview with Jay, Faith and I meet to work on a conference paper, and I mention that I was working with a former student of hers, Jay. With a smile, Faith immediately recalls Jay and the first book he ever read, *Teeny Tiny*. Then her smile fades, and, her emotions present in her voice, she shares the following story:

> I'll tell you what I remember of Jay. When he came to my room, he was very hyperactive, up and down and very curious, actually. Touching everything. So, one of the assistant principals right away said, "He sounds like, from what I know, and what I've seen of him, he sounds like a crack baby." He says, "This is what you read about, this is how they behave." I don't think he was really listening to me.

---

[3] *(continued)*

and hear him read, and he asked that I bring a video camera to document his success. The class enthusiastically supported Robert's achievement and his reading of Dr. Seuss's *The Foot Book* for the camera, a book most of them were well beyond in terms of its complexity and length. Robert's story as a developing reader and writer illustrated the importance of the classroom community in defining what counts as a "disability." In contrast to an approach that would focus on Robert's "disability," Faith contributed to the formation of a classroom community where Robert was honored and respected for what he could do and assisted in learning what was difficult for him. However, at the end of second grade, Robert was referred for psychological testing by the school's reading specialist, who, despite Faith's repeated invitations, never observed him in the context of her classroom. Prior to entering third grade, Robert was tested by the school psychologist and identified as learning disabled. This has since led to a decline in his sense of his own capabilities and in his motivation to attend school (for additional discussions of Robert, see K. M. Collins, MacLean, Palincsar, & Magnusson, 2000).

Case 2   Timothy was a highly oral child who delighted in word play, and especially loved to create puns and jokes. He was also a big fan of comic books and often constructed his own, combining words and illustrations to create vivid stories featuring his classmates and his family. In Faith's classroom, Timothy drew on his interest and ability in comics to construct his daily journal entries and to document his interpretation of his observations during science investigations. At times, Timothy's ability to draw on the tools of narrative and metaphor in his oral and written expression led to some confusion in his communication with Faith, who drew on more conventional forms of representation. However, rather than suggest that Timothy's preferred means of constructing knowledge from the world were "wrong" or "deviant," Faith created opportunities that supported him in combining his own means of representation with those of the classroom community. One such opportunity was the construction of a book documenting the class's investigations into the nature of light. In constructing his page for this book, Timothy combined his own tools of narrative and metaphor with the agreed-on class claim about reflection. Another opportunity, which Timothy responded to in a similar manner, was provided by Faith's use of a daily journal in her guided inquiry investigation of sound. In his journal, Timothy drew on narrative and his love of comic-book-style drawing and dialogue to express his understanding of sound.

Like Robert, when Timothy entered third grade he was referred for psychological testing by his classroom teacher, who suspected a possible emotional or learning impairment due to Timothy's "unwillingness" to complete class assignments. However, Timothy's mother, an educator, as well as his guidance counselor, resisted this testing and instead referred Timothy's classroom teacher to Faith (for additional discussions of Timothy, see K. M. Collins, 1997).

It is telling that Robert, Timothy, and Jay were all referred for psychological assessment when they entered classrooms with different approaches to organizing learning. The experiences of these children suggest the importance of considering contextual as well as individual factors in shaping deficits, impairments, or disabilities.

I did have a referral, not written up and official but they call it TRC, Teacher Referral Committee, before you actually go into a formal committee. That's a way for them to weed or screen out some things … So I went to meeting, the psychologist was there, the special education consultant was there, the principal was there … And I presented this situation because they always encouraged us to, right away at the beginning of the year so you can get help, present students who are disruptive. And he was disruptive.

So anyway, I don't remember the details of the meeting but the one thing I remember was the suggestion that I would get one of these big empty boxes, and they even told me where I can get it, said they would help me get one, an empty box from a refrigerator, because it is tall enough, and make it into an "office" for Jay, as his "special place." That would "isolate him from the rest of the class so he wouldn't be so stimulated." Oh, they used all kinds of beautiful language "he's getting over stimulated" "maybe he's ADD." Already they are saying that, and this is in late September.

And I was thinking, while they were saying this, I was just dumbfounded. I was so much in shock that I don't even think I even resisted anything. They asked me to put Jay in a box! A teacher would not do that!…. What would that do with the rest of the class and their relationship with Jay? And vice versa? I don't want them to think Jay is a bad boy.

I have to say I lost a little bit of respect for the psychologist for suggesting that. He only saw Jay in the halls. He had not come in there and observed Jay in my room. There were times when he was OK. I just had to figure out how to calm him down … There were strengths of Jay, I never even got to say. I decided not to go back to them for more suggestions.

Faith continues to explain that she not only withdrew her "unofficial" (oral) referral of Jay, she found ways to work with him within her classroom community and did not, despite some degree of encouragement from the school psychologist, submit an official referral for him.

Faith's experience of feeling silenced in this meeting was unfortunately not unique. Applying a social constructionist lens, education scholar Mehan (1993) asked, "How are student identities produced? How does a student become a 'special education' or a 'regular education' student?" (p. 243). Mehan analyzed the interactions around the teaching, assessment, and labeling of students, paying particular attention to videotaped interactions of referral meetings such as the one Faith described. Mehan's analysis of the discourse within these referral meetings revealed that the teacher and parent became "lost voices," whereas the words of the psychologist were highly valued, and went unquestioned. Mehan argued that this was due to the technical language employed by the psychologist as "a clinically certified expert," a language not shared by the parents and the teacher and thus a language they were not in a position to question. There were echoes of Mehan's analysis in Faith's comments regarding her own silence, the role of the psychologist in the meeting, the use of "all kinds of beautiful language," and the decontextualized view of Jay that was constructed.

As we finish the stimulated recall interview, Jay suggests that I come back and interview him with Ned and Maria, because, he says, they were very helpful to his thinking during the floating and sinking unit. I agree to arrange this with Laura, who selects a time for us the following week.

The next week we meet during the same time of day, in Laura's classroom, and this time Laura has arranged for all three children to attend. Not wanting to call their attention to an interaction in which Jay was disciplined and excluded, I have cut the third clip from the tape. Maria and Ned are excited about the video and Jay seems really happy and proud in his role as "expert" in the interview—he sets up the chairs and puts the tape in the VCR and finds the remote while I set up the microphone and video camera, and he tells Ned and Maria, "She's gonna ask you questions. Wait 'till you see this!"

After the first clip, in which he makes the CDS with Jay, Ned is reluctant to say anything. Jay tells Ned how much he learned from him during that interaction and Ned shrugs, looks at me, and says, "Yeah, what he said." This, unfortunately, is the pattern of the rest of the interview: Jay points out, enthusiastically, specific interactions on the video where Ned or Maria asked a question or made a statement that "helped my thinking," whereas Ned and Maria seem puzzled by his comments. After several such moments, Jay finally asks them directly, "Well, what was *you* thinking?" but no responses are forthcoming.

After we view the second clip in which Jay and Ned are sharing with the class, Jay points out how Ned's explanation extended his own thinking. Ned turns to him, and chuckles, "To be honest, I didn't know what you were talking about there. About half the time, I had no idea what you were talking about."

Laura and I sit down alone after one of our regular GIsML community meetings. It has been several weeks since her guided inquiry investigation and I want to try to reflect on the instruction with her, to try to understand more fully her responses to Jay's participation. I have prepared transcripts of the same excerpts I showed Jay for us to read together, as well as transcripts of my stimulated recall interview with Jay. As we sit down together, Laura observes, "This whole process has been real helpful for Jay's self-worth." I ask her to elaborate, and she explains, "Well, a couple of things. Both the teaching, the guided inquiry lessons themselves, the idea of community in the classroom, the extra attention that Jay has gotten being sort of a case study of yours. All those things sort of rolled into one … You know, in the beginning of the year, he came in with like a bad-ass attitude that he was, that nobody was gonna mess with him. His role was to instigate things by messing with his neighbors or creating problems and he wasn't always focused on his learning ... He's a completely different Jay than this child at the beginning of the year who you would think oh, he's never gonna make it. I've even had conversations with other teachers about that. Jay wants to learn, and he wants to know why he's thinking the things that he's thinking, and it's important to him to think about other kids and what they're thinking. And I worry that's gonna be lost. Because he could so easily get caught up in a gang, or in being a bad-ass again, or, you know, going down that other path." Laura continues, attributing much of this change in Jay to the "climate" of her classroom. "My class has gotten to the point where they're pretty good about supporting each other, and listening to what people have to say, and commenting on somebody's ideas."

I share the transcripts from her teaching with Laura. As we examine Jay's interactions with her and with the whole class, Laura reflects on Jay's participation in the public sharing in particular. "I was pleasantly surprised by the fact that he was such an avid participant in those discussions. I mean he, he was a *leader* in terms of getting people to say what they're thinking ... It was interesting, coming from a kid like that, it seemed to make it OK for some of the other students who weren't all that successful in school to say 'Well, I can participate in this too. Shoot, Jay is doin' it, and he's not the smartest kid in the class.'"

As in their responses to Jay during the guided inquiry teaching, neither Maria, Ned, nor Laura engaged with the filmed and transcribed interactions by responding actively to the substantive content of the discourse and how it was being constructed. Maria absented herself by remaining mostly silent. Ned distanced himself from Jay both in the present moment and retroactively ("To be honest, I didn't know what you were talking about there. About half the time, I had no idea what you were talking about."). Ned's dismissive response and Maria's silences underscored for me the unwillingness or inability demonstrated by the rest of the class to engage substantively with Jay's contributions during the floating and sinking inquiry. Unwillingness to engage with Jay in metacognitively reflecting on the activity could perhaps have been due to his low status within the classroom community, a point I return to later. Inability to engage with him in metacognitive analysis may be attributed to Jay's apparent giftedness in this area.[4] Jay was consistently able to identify, analyze, and verbalize his thinking processes in a manner that is remarkable for any learner but most

---

[4]I am indebted to Carol Sue Englert for her comments regarding this interpretation of these data.

especially so for one who is 11 years old and has not received guidance in thinking metacognitively. It is possible that his classmates, Ned and Maria, simply did not possess the same skill.

As in her comments after he was physically excluded from the group, Laura used the occasion of reviewing the transcripts to restate her persistent low expectations for Jay regarding academic achievement and her high expectations that he would get into some sort of trouble ("he could so easily get caught up in a gang, or in being a bad-ass again"). Although Laura acknowledged Jay's participation as leader in terms of getting people to say what they were thinking, she didn't connect this to the students' development of substantive understanding within the problem space of the inquiry, but connected it instead to the social relationships within the classroom. In her view, Jay was not a leader because he helped students develop and express their ideas, but because he demonstrated that even a low-achieving student could participate, "coming from a kid like that, it seemed to make it OK for some of the other students who weren't all that successful in school to say 'Well, I can participate in this too. Shoot, Jay is doin' it, and he's not the smartest kid in the class.'"

The responses of Ned and Laura in particular to this stimulated recall event suggested to me an intimate relationship between the lack of response to Jay in the guided inquiry context, Laura's expectations for his achievement and behavior, and his positioning or social capital within that classroom community. If Jay were seen by the members of the classroom community through the same lens through which Laura viewed him (low academic capabilities, high probability of involvement in problem behavior) then it was likely, not surprising, that he would not be responded to in both large and small-group participant structures. Laura's teaching practices relative to Jay clearly communicated her expectations for him to the rest of the class, in both implicit (her own lack of substantive response to his utterances) and explicit ways (taking Carl and Kevin aside and asking for their help in managing Jay's behavior; placing him the hall during the small-group interaction). The community members seemed to be working together to exclude Jay.[5]

---

[5]My use of the term *social capital* derives from the work of sociologist Bourdieu (1977, 1990). Bourdieu posited a theory of *practice*, which asserted that social and cultural groups, through their engagement in shared practices, produce and reproduce their own organizational structures. Within this general theory of cultural organization, Bourdieu posited the existence of several forms of capital, social, cultural, economic, and symbolic. Social capital refers to the system of relationships among members of a community, which can be converted to economic capital. Within Laura's classroom community, high academic achievement and Laura's good favor can be considered a sort of economic capital. If Jay is perceived as not able to garner this form of economic capital, he will be excluded from the system of social relationships.

Despite what seemed to be a representative case of the mutually consti-tutive relation of teacher expectations, social relationships, and student achievement, I was wary of drawing conclusions prematurely. Although I had met with Jay and with Laura out of the classroom, I had not observed Laura's classroom instruction in several weeks. Further, in the same con-versation in which she expressed her low expectations for Jay at the begin-ning of the year, Laura asserted that her perceptions had changed and so had the interactional practices of her students, her "classroom climate." I concluded that it was important for me to work more with Jay and to con-duct further observations in Laura's classroom. I hoped that I would be better able to understand the relationship between Laura's teaching prac-tices, her expectations of Jay, and his role and positioning within the class-room community. With better understanding of this relationship, perhaps I could influence it, that is, work to reconstruct Laura's perceptions of who Jay was and what he was able to contribute.

→ Not Research!!

9

"You Got to Hear This!"

Jay and I are seated in a small room, approximately 10 feet long by 6 feet wide, down the hall from Laura's. A large table consumes most of the room, and Jay and I face each other across it. My pocket tape recorder rests on the table between us, its microphone aimed toward Jay. The room is used to sell breakfast and snacks out of in the mornings and as a sort of "time-out" and "extra help" room during the rest of the day. A poster taped to the painted cinder block wall above Jay's head reads "Practice Random Acts of Kindness." Above my head we are told "Everything I Need to Know I Learned in Kindergarten." There are no windows in this room, but if we leave the door open we can see through the windows in the exit doors across the hallway. Over the course of the next 5 months Jay and I will spend approximately 60 hours in this room together.

Today, I begin by sharing with Jay the transcripts from our earlier meetings, and I ask if he wants to change or add anything. At first he is concerned at this, and asks, "I don't want to change anything 'cause like, well, I thought I did good on the interview?"

"Oh, you did great!" I assure him, "This is just in case, it's been a couple weeks since we talked, just in case you thought of anything else that you wanted to add." Jay doesn't want to add anything, but says he will take the transcript home and read it over. We spend a few minutes reviewing his responses on the pre- and posttests, clarifying illegible items, and then I ask Jay what he thinks about us doing some writing together. I tell him that I'm interested how students and teachers use oral language and that his description of his own thinking has helped me learn about that. I said that I couldn't be in Axleton every day so I needed his help. If he wanted to work with me, his role would be to assist me in taking notes.

Next I show Jay my research journal, and the ways that I take notes in it. I tell him I try to write down all my thoughts in my journal, how sometimes I ask myself questions in it, and that I am careful to date each entry. We look at several pages of my journal, and Jay turns to a page in which I had sketched a Venn diagram. As he reads the page to himself, I explain that the circles represented what I was thinking about the process of learning and the influences of the classroom community, the ways of expressing meaning in science, and the strengths and interests of individuals. Jay reads a notation I made in the overlapping space of the circles, "Mediated by the teacher. Does that mean she's in the middle, like balancing?" I respond, "Yes, exactly."

Jay continues to look at the page, then looks at me, "I have an idea! I can write down my notes and you can write down your notes and then we can meet like every other week after school to share them. And we can have snacks!"

I agree that would be a great idea. I have two new matching journals in my bag (just in case) and I take them out now, and give Jay one. We spend a few moments setting up our journals, writing our names and each other's names and phone numbers in the front, and we agree to begin the following week, after school if it's OK with Jay's family and during recess if Jay is unable to stay after school. Jay offers to bring sandwiches but I assure him I'll take care of the snacks. That evening I phone Jay's uncle, who agrees that if working with me after school is something Jay would like to do and I take care of driving him home, it's OK with him.

Jay and I begin our next meeting by comparing our journals. Jay's first two journal entries describe plays that he watched at school and what he liked about them. After reading them to me, he asks if he can see my journal. My journal contains field notes from my observations in his class. Jay examines my field notes, and comments, "That's real good that you did that so I could like see what you think too."

"Good. Do you think you could try something like this during class sometime?" Jay had written his first two entries after school. I am hoping to reflect with him about the interactions in class, and his own documentation would be a great place to start.

"Yeah. I think it wouldn't be that hard."

"No, especially, I can write down what people say but I can't write down what you're thinking, so if you could especially write down what you think that would be helpful."

Jay leans back in his chair and tries to explain to me, "I'm not like, I'm a writer but when I don't put my head to somethin', I can't do a good job with it … 'Cause when I write I have to put my mind to it and think about it. I mean *think*. If can't do that, then I don't want to write about it."

"Do you think it would be easier if you had a small tape recorder like this one?" I point to the tape recorder on the table between us. My response is an effort to help Jay mediate his construction of text with oral language, the modality he appears most comfortable with.

"Oh, so then I could just talk into it?" Jay is enthusiastic.

"Yeah, to start. Then we could write it out from the tape together. Would that be easier?"

"Yeah! That'd be cool!" Jay is very enthusiastic about the tape recorder. Initially I get one for him on loan; later in our work, when he is using the recorder almost every day, he will ask for his own and we will drive to Radio Shack and get him one.

Before Jay begins taping I confer with Laura and she suggests that Jay's use of a tape recorder during class would be too distracting for the other children. When Jay and I meet again and I provide him with the tape recorder, two tapes, and extra batteries, we discuss Laura's concerns and decide that he will use the tape recorder at home to reflect on the school day. As the school year progresses, Jay will begin carrying the tape recorder in his Trapper Keeper notebook (along with the rest of his research materials), but he doesn't use it during class.

This agreement between Jay and me set in motion a pattern of classroom observations, after-school meetings, and collaborative work that continued for the next 9 months. Although I could not at this time have predicted the directions our work would go in, I did have some ideas of where I hoped it would lead.

My intentions for continued work with Jay were informed by a growing perspective among literacy scholars that "literacy" be considered as participation in the discourse shared by a members of a community engaged in socially and historically situated activity (Michaels & O'Connor, 1990). This perspective stems from theoretical arguments advanced by linguist and education scholar Gee, who regarded discourse as inclusive of factors beyond language, such as gesture, dress, and ways of interacting, that signal one's identity as a member of a specific community (Gee, 1991, 1996). Gee argued that every child "gets one discourse free" as a result of language acquisition within their home and family contexts. The discourses of the other communities the child subsequently participates in must then be learned, and it is the learning to control these secondary discourses that Gee (1991, 1996) termed literacy.

Informed by this perspective, I thought that Jay and I would begin by researching together the interactions of the classroom community and his participation in the different activity contexts within it. I hoped that this inquiry about his classroom community would eventually lead to our mutual inquiry and reflection about Jay's participation in the other communities of his life. In addition to furthering my own understanding of the dynamics I observed in the classroom, Jay's awareness and understanding of the norms and conventions for communicating within the different communities of his life would, I hoped, enable us to have conversations about the differences across communities. Further, I hoped that such inquiry would provide a starting place for conversations with Laura about ways of seeing Jay differently by broadening her awareness of who he was outside of her classroom.

However, this inquiry path reflected my own interests, not Jay's. Although we eventually would inquire together about other his participation in other communities, his church community in particular, Jay found ways of reshaping our immediate work to reflect his long-standing interest in insects. I was supportive of his attempts to do this because I was learning more about Jay through this inquiry. As we engaged more deeply in our entomology inquiry, I would come to see this as a unique opportunity to work with Jay as we both entered and took up the practices of a previously unfamiliar community. It was through inquiring together about entomology that we developed a relationship that subsequently supported inquiry and reflection about language practices in other contexts.

The day of our first meeting after Jay receives his recording equipment, he's so excited about sharing the tape with me that he brings it over to me at the beginning of the school day, while I'm setting up the videocamera. "You got to hear this!" he urges, waving the tape toward me and grinning.

I'm thrilled to see Jay so excited about our work. What insights about his classroom participation had he captured on the tape? "Should I play it now or when we meet later?" I ask, taking the tape.

Jay looks around the room, which is quickly filling with children. "Later, OK?"

After school, the first thing we do is listen to Jay's tape. We are sitting on opposite sides of a small table and we lean our heads together over the tape recorder as Jay voice fills the small room:

Hello. I am looking at creatures to see what makes them different. Right here we have a beetle and we have roly polys. Let's see what's the difference in them. Oh, the beetles are fat like the roly polys but fatter than 'em. And they don't roll into a ball. They don't have as many legs as the roly polys. The roly polys are like small. And plus they roll into a ball. They don't have as many eyes as them but they are interesting to look at. As you see, or as I see, they are going to get grass, and, food and water. OK, now I'm thinking, how is the beetle and roly polys different? They might come from different relatives ...Hold up, here's my cousin. Tell her your name ... OK, and we won't be hearin' from him anymore. I'll be coming with more information. Bye-bye.

Jay's voice is low and serious, reminiscent of a narrator on a wildlife show describing the actions of the animals on the screen. Later he begins interviewing his cousins and he slips into a sort of radio announcer or quiz show voice.

We begin discussing how to go from these verbalized thoughts to written text. We decide to enter the "important information" from his tape into the computer, organized by the location of his observations. (Harry, the entomologist we would later work with, would support this decision and call our locations "collection areas.")

Jay looks at me, "So, are you gonna be like typin' this?" He pauses and then adds, "because I can't type."

"You can type! I've *seen* you type!" I pretend to be shocked, teasing him a little.

Jay grins, "I can't type *fast*."

"Well, maybe that's one thing we could practice at. I'm thinking we could type it together."

"Yeah, we probably could." Jay bites into a slice of green apple, then starts chuckling, "But I know you be gettin' tired of me goin'," Jay motions as though typing with one finger, slowly hunting out each letter, then imitates me falling asleep, waiting for him. We both laugh. Then we begin entering the main ideas from the tape into the computer, taking turns.

We begin our next meeting with the printed text of Jay's tape. "I'm really excited about the insect ideas! Here's the notes printed out from what we took from the tape."

Jay flips through the printed pages, "How long did it go on for?"

"It went on for two pages. Remember we left out the part about the pizza and swimming because decided to focus on the insects?" Our printed text appears in Figure 9.1.

I explain to Jay that the observations he made were examples of the kinds of observations scientists who study insects make, and that then they might draw on their notes and the work of others to write a report about the insect they're studying. I show him a text about ladybugs as a sample: "This is something, an entomologist took some notes on ladybugs, and then typed

I. In the yard

    A. A Beetle and A Roly Poly: what's the difference?

        —Beetles are fat like the roly polys but fatter than them
        —Beetles don't roll into a ball
        —Beetles don't have as many legs as the roly polys
        —The Roly polys are small
        —Roly polys roll into a ball
        —They are going to get grass, and food, and water
        —They might be different because they come from different relatives
        —Roly polys have shorter legs
        —Roly polys have more legs than the beetles: beetles only have
          four legs

II. On the front porch

    A. Observing wasps and bees and mosquitoes

        —The front porch has a lot of wasps and bees and mosquitoes
        —In some ways wasps and bees can be harmful
        —The difference between the bees and the mosquitoes and the
          wasps is that one is bigger than the other
        —Wasps and bees are alike because both sting you
        —The mosquito doesn't quite sting you, he sucks your blood, he
          actually drinks blood from your body
        —Bees protect themselves by stinging, and so does the wasp

III. In the kitchen

    A. Observing lady bugs

        —Lady bugs are small and dotted
        —Lady bugs are not really harmful unless they fall in your food
        —Lady bugs are interesting to look at
        —Did you know that if the lady bug was large enough, the helmet
          would be harder than a football helmet?
        —How could a lady bugs shell be harder than a football helmet?
          Football helmets are just made out of elastic and hard plastic;
          theirs is made out of scientific stuff. That's what makes it harder.
          I have to find that out in the library.

FIG. 9.1.   Notes from Jay's recorded observations of the insects in his yard.

them up, and then he took those notes and made them into paragraphs, like we did with your eagle report. This report was based on his research."

Jay takes the article and begins reading to himself. I ask if he would read it out loud so I can follow along. He reads the first paragraph:

Did you ever see a little red and black beetle crawling along your window sill? It was probably a lady beetle or a lady bird beetle or just lady bug as some people call them. Most species of lady beetles are among our most beneficial insects as they consume huge numbers of plant feeding insects—mostly aphids. This fact and their attractive appearance have contributed to the generally good opinion of them held by most people. For instance, the French call them *les betes du bon Dieu* or creatures of the good God and *les vaches de la Vierge* or the cows of the Virgin. The Germans call them *Marienkafer* or Mary's beetles. (Fleming, no date, italics in original)

With the exception of the German and French, Jay reads the paragraph smoothly. We work through the rest of the text, each reading alternate paragraphs out loud. Jay interrupts frequently to comment on the text, both when I read and when he is reading (see Table 9.1). His comments demon-

TABLE 9.1

Text Reading and Spontaneous Comments

Text	Spontaneous Comments
There are probably as many as 4,000 species found worldwide …	*Jay:* Wow! That's a lot of species! *Kathleen:* Yeah, it sure is.
Adults of one common species, the Convergent Lady Beetle (Hippodamia convergens Guerin), spend the winter in protected hiding places such as logs, buildings, ground covering vegetation, and the like, where many hundreds of individuals may cluster together.	*Kathleen:* Wow! That would be awesome! Hundreds of ladybugs all clustered together? *Jay:* It wouldn't be awesome! Especially if they were all flying around your food! ((We both Laugh)) *Kathleen:* I think it'd be pretty cool. You might not wanna bring your food but it'd be cool to see. *Jay:* Yeah, it'd be cool to see.
They will also play dead when in danger	*Jay:* They do, a lot *Kathleen:* Really? ((Jay nods)) You noticed that? *Jay:* Yeah, cause I thought, I was, we thought my cousin killed one, and then she hit and then it wasn't dead. It was just standing there, and it looked like it was dead but later it flew away. *Kathleen:* Why was she trying to kill it? *Jay:* Cause it was going in her food.
Also, lady beetles probably produce a bad smelling odor...	*Jay:* It does? *Kathleen:* Hmm. Let's see what it says.
Lady beetles live in a variety of habitats. Trees, shrubs, fields, beaches, and even houses are good places to look for them.	*Jay:* I know that! ((We both start laughing because Jay's initial observations of ladybugs had been made in his aunt's kitchen.))

strate his efforts at making sense of the text by building connections to his first-hand observations and experiences with ladybugs.

After we finish the text I ask Jay, "If you want to really follow through on this investigation of bugs we could go to the insect lab and see how they do it."

"Oh, that'd be interesting. Really interesting!" Jay's beaming face expresses more excitement than his words. I tell him about my friend Harry, a doctoral candidate in zoology and ecology at the university who works in the entomology lab. We decide to make a list of questions in preparation for our visit to see Harry in the lab. Jay suggests three questions from the ladybug text, and we each write them in our journals:

1. Do scientists call them lady beetles? Why don't they just say ladybugs?
2. How can you tell if they (the ladybugs) are a woman or a man?
3. Did you know their wings are uneven? Why is that?

After we make our lists of question we begin picking up our papers and getting ready to work on a report Jay is writing on eagles for Laura's class. While I get the computer out, I comment to Jay, "When we were reading this [the ladybug text] you did a good job of connecting your observations to the reading."

Jay explains, getting more enthusiastic as he continues, "Yeah. I do that a lot. I do good at discussing stuff. I can comprehend good! It's like the burst of fire again. I mean, when you read something, it means that the book is really good. You don't do it just like every day. So, if the book is really good, you just like, can't keep quiet, even if you're reading to yourself." We both laugh and then he adds, "So you have to, like, make some kind of noise."

"Was that like with *Maniac Magee?*" Jay had told me previously that Jerry Spinnelli's book, *Maniac Magee,* was one of his favorites.

"Yeah!" Jay is enthusiastic, "I *couldn't* be quiet then!"

We both laugh a little and then I ask, "What did you like about it?"

"It was just like, how it explains, not explains but, uh, it gave you the kinda feelin' that you just wanted to keep on readin.' 'Cause it, when you read *Maniac Magee*, it goes, it goes, it like makes you wanna cry one moment, and it makes you wanna feel happy." Jay explains his response to the novel thoughtfully; although I haven't read the book in years and it's been several months since Jay read it, we begin a lively discussion about the story.

"What part made you wanna cry?" I ask.

"When like Grayson died." Jay looks solemn.

"Oh, my gosh! Wasn't that awful?" I tell Jay about the first time I read *Maniac Magee,* and my class came in after my planning period and found me at my desk in tears over this portion of the novel. "That was really sad. And then he went to the, um, after that didn't he run away and go to live in the cemetery? With those two little boys."

"Yeah. Yeah! He was just, he didn't actually want 'em, he was just runnin.'"

"And they came."

"Yeah. They were followin' 'im."

"What parts made you really happy?"

"When, like, um, at Christmas time, when he found his um, when he found a home at the Beale's house."

"Yeah. Remember when Grayson, didn't Grayson give him his glove?"

"Hm-mm."

"Yeah. I really liked that part."

"And he gave 'im a book. The first man that, I mean, *The Man Who Struck out Willie Mays.*"

"Yeah. He wrote it about Grayson. That was a good book! You're making me want to read it again."

My conversations and work with Jay during these sessions were important both for the ways in which they informed my understanding of Jay as a learner and for the support they provided for our developing relationship. As sociocultural theory would suggest, these were not unrelated: In asserting the dialectical and mutually transforming nature of social and individual cognitive processes, sociocultural theory called attention to the importance of relationships and the social interactions that occurred within the cultural context of development. It is these interactions that created the context in which appropriation and transformation could occur.

Drawing on Vygotsky's notion of the zone of proximal development, Erickson (1987) emphasized that one aspect of social interactions that created the context for learning was trust. Trust is necessary because learning involves risk, for both the learner and the teacher:

> *To learn is to entertain risk, since learning involves moving just past the edge of competence, what is already mastered, to the nearest region of incompetence, what has not yet been mastered ... Risk is also involved for the teacher. If the teacher engages a student with the genuine intention to foster the student's learning and the student then fails to learn what the teacher intended, the teacher is revealed as less than consummately competent pedagogically. (p. 345)*

Thus for both the learner and the teacher there is risk involved in learning: Both stand to be revealed as incompetent if the interaction is not successful. Erickson pointed out that identification as incompetent can have both local (within the classroom) and institutional (within the school) effects for the teacher and for the child. This is a point I return to later relative to Laura's identification of Jay as "impaired" or "disabled," and his increasing attempts to reposition himself.

What Erickson's assertions made visible in my interactions with Jay was the energy we put into building a trusting relationship. It was in the many seemingly small moments where Jay and I built this trust, such as in our discussion of Maniac Magee, *our negotiation of the typing responsibilities, and the development of our entomology inquiry. Our entomology inquiry provided a context in which neither one of us was an expert and thus supported the development of further trust between us. This trust provided a foundation for our learning as we each would later enter contexts where the other was more experienced and took on the role of teacher. In developing trust, we were creating a social context where it was safe to take the risks inherent in learning.*

In addition to building a social context supportive of risk and learning, we were learning about each other's ways of engaging with print literacy, prior understandings about ladybugs, and ways of making meaning more generally. Stone and Reid (1994) asserted that scholars of sociocultural theory have placed too little effort on discerning the active role of the learner, and the influence of the learner's prior understandings, in the process of appropriation and transformation. Drawing on sociocultural theory, Stone and Reid (1994) argued for consideration of learning, the process of appropriation and transformation, as a process of "coming to understand" (p. 73), a process that necessarily involved the tools, affordances, constraints, and relationships available in the learner's current context as well as the understandings and interests that the learner already held due to his unique ontological history. This relationship was particularly evident in Jay's response to the ladybug text as he connected his own experience with ladybugs to the assertions of the text.

Jay's reflections on his own process of meaning-making, of "coming to understand," as well as my observations of and interactions with him, illustrated that a preference for a specific kind of tool use can also be part of an individual's ontological history, which he brings to new learning contexts. In Jay's case, verbalizing his thoughts helped him reconstruct his current understandings in diverse teaching and learning interactions. During the guided inquiry investigation of sinking and floating, Jay's use of oral language to build understanding was evident in both small-group interactions (with Laura and with both Laura and Ned) and whole-class discussions (as a presenter and as a listener). It was also very evident in his interactions with the ladybug text; as he noted, "So, if the book is really good, you just like, can't keep quiet, even if you're reading to yourself." In the contexts where he was unable to draw on verbalization to mediate his thinking, as in the small-group work where he did not have a voice and the journal writing that he was asked to complete alone, Jay's participation and his construction of understanding were curtailed.

This is tutoring! Not Research!!

10

"So Who Wrote It?"

As suggested during the conversation I had with Jay about the ladybug text, we were also engaged at this time in revising a report he had been assigned about bald eagles. Writing was one way in which Jay was marked as different by Laura in her classroom, and it had a direct impact on his grades. Laura's perceptions of Jay's abilities as a writer were shaped by his classroom performance, in contexts where he was most often required to write alone and often as a form of assessment. In describing Jay's abilities in these contexts, Laura noted that, "He's not a good writer, but he'll write, just write-write-write-write, and not a period in the whole thing. You know, he can get things on paper, but it's not on there very well. He would much rather talk about it."

Informed by research regarding a sociocognitive, strategic approach to writing instruction (see review in Vaughn, Gersten, & Chard, 2000), I proposed to Laura that I begin to work with Jay on his writing. I hoped that by working closely with Jay on his writing, and by drawing on his skills in verbalizing his thinking, I could support him in constructing a text that would provide an alternative to Laura's labeling for him (i.e., "not a good writer"). Our work on this project began the day Jay gave an oral presentation in class.

The students are scheduled to present their research reports on endangered animals all week, and I call Laura one evening to confirm which day I should observe to see Jay's presentation. She responds, "Jay may not have a presentation. He typically does not complete work that he takes home." She tells me that although she has seen Jay taking notes, he hasn't turned in his report yet so she doesn't know if he'll be prepared to present. I suggest that perhaps Jay and I could work on his report together in our after-school sessions, and Laura advises, "You'll have to start by cleaning out his desk. He's really EI or LD and just not good at completing stuff."

Jay's is the second presentation. The first presentation has been a variation on a news and talk show format performed by three girls who take turns interviewing each other, reading from written scripts. They are lively and funny and the class is very entertained. My heart skips a beat when Laura calls on Jay. Will he have his presentation? Will the class respond as warmly?

Without speaking, Jay stands up at his desk in the back and walks slowly to the front of the room, a folded posterboard in his hands. As he unfolds the posterboard to reveal a three-sided, free-standing display, I glance over at Laura but can't read her expression. Jay has selected the bald eagle, and his poster is decorated with pictures and captions he photocopied from texts at the library and then cut out and pasted onto it. He proudly stands it up on the table in the front of the room and then stands behind it and grins at the class.

Jay begins by summarizing what he learned about the bald eagle, without reading from a text, "I did the animal the bald eagle. It's the national bird of the United States. It's endangered because of humans. Humans put DDT on the ground, and then it gets into water and the fish eat it." As he speaks, Jay points to various pictures on his poster. "When the birds eat the fish, their eggs get soft and break and the babies can't grow up. One unusual fact is that they mate for life. If their mate dies they don't mate anymore."

Students begin to raise their hands and Jay fields questions for the next 12 minutes. There are several questions about the pictures on the poster, and Jay explains each picture without reading the captions to the class. Two students ask for clarification about DDT, and Jay explains that it "gets inside like a disease" and "makes the eggs soft so the babies can't grow up." His presentation concludes when the bell rings for recess. On his way back to his seat, Jay calls out across the room to Laura, "What'd I get Mrs. B.? What'd I get? Mrs. B., did I pass? Did I get a D?" Laura does not respond.

After school that day, Jay and I begin to focus our attention on completing his eagle report. Over the course of 4 weeks of school (we do not meet over spring break, thus 6 weeks pass chronologically) we will spend approximately 8 hours writing, revising, and editing his report. We are, during the same time frame, continuing our entomology inquiry through the use of second-hand investigations.

We start with a blank form that Laura gave each of the students to organize their note taking, which she calls a "data sheet." This is a sheet of paper divided into 10 sections (5 on each side) and each section has a header (see Fig. 10.1). In addition, a grading rubric is provided that indicates points students

Replica of Laura's prewriting worksheet, side 1

Why is it an endangered species?	If you ruled the world, what would you do?	What's already being done?	Enemies	Life Cycle

Replica of Laura's prewriting worksheet, side 2

Adaptations	Myths, Legends, Unusual Facts	Appearance	Habitat	Food

FIG. 10.1.   Worksheet Laura developed to support students' completion of endangered species research reports.

will receive for including the content of each section. Although Jay's sheet is blank because he didn't use it to organize his notes, his presentation suggests that reading the sheet did provide some organization for his thoughts.

There are also directions on this sheet to write a poem about your animal. The first line and second line should each have two words, the third line, three words, the fourth line, four words, and the last line, one word. We brainstorm three different versions and Jay selects the one he likes best:

> Bald Eagle
> Bald head
> Eats slippery fish
> Flies in the air
> Bird

As we complete the data sheet together, Jay is able to respond from memory and provides information to complete each of the sections. However, some scaffolding is needed to help him interpret and use the sheet. Jay asks for clarification of the meaning of several of the headers, which I provide. I also ask questions to prompt him to extend several of his responses. While Jay fills out the sheet provided by Laura, I write in my journal, modeling the same kind of entries Jay makes. At the beginning Jay looks often at my writing; later, he notes that I am writing but concentrates on his own sheet. While writing, he often stops and asks how to spell a word or whether his spelling is correct. The following scene is representative of our interactions when filling out the data sheet:

"OK, we're almost done! Appearance." I am sitting next to Jay, and he has the sheet in front of him.

"What do you mean by appearance?" Jay looks up, pencil poised over the paper.

"Appearance means what it looks like. What does the eagle look like? Size, coloring."

"Oh, OK. It's white and it's black." Jay is still looking up, not writing.

"Where's the white part? People might not know that." I prompt, my own pen poised over my journal.

"On his head."

"So white head and?"

"And white wings, the underside, underneath his wings."

"OK." I write "white head" and pause, "And is its neck white?"

"Yeah." Jay begins to write, making a list under "Appearance." He looks up, "And their bottom, their body is black."

"OK." We are both writing. When Jay is finished I ask, "What color is their beak?"

"Orange, orange-yellow." Jay begins to write again, "How do you spell 'beak'?"

"B-e-a-k." I spell it out and write it on my paper as well, and then ask, "How about their claws?"

"Them's black too." Again Jay writes down his statement, and then checks it with me, "Is that the right 'too'?"

"Yup. When you want to say 'also,' it has two Os." I show him my page as well.

Appearance
—white head and neck
—white under wings
—the bottom part of their body is black
—their beak is yellow and orange
—claws are black too

After we have filled out the data sheet from Jay's memory, we read two articles about eagles together, and look for more information to add to our lists.

My interactions with Jay around his endangered species report were guided by an orientation called strategic writing instruction (J. L. Collins, 1998; K. M. Collins & Collins, 1996; Englert, 1992; Englert & Raphael, 1989; Englert et al., 1992; Englert et al., 1991). Strategic writing instruction has roots in sociocognitive and social constructivist theory and emphasizes the coconstruction of strategies with struggling writers through scaffolded dialogue. It brings together the explicit teaching of text structures and features with process and workshop approaches to teaching writing. Strategic writing instruction requires that teachers think carefully about both the cognitive processes and tools required by the task of producing academic text. It also requires that teachers work closely with students, assisting them to develop and coconstruct the strategy further to meet their own needs (see review in Vaughn et al., 2000).

The process of coauthoring with struggling writers and coconstructing writing strategies with them in the process is akin to the apprenticeship model of learning described by Lave and Wenger (1991). As Lave and Wenger made clear, apprenticeship relations involve sharing an understanding of the whole process and expected product, and also involve discourses unique to the forms of practice they are situated in. An apprentice is not expected to produce a product by stringing together seemingly unrelated skills practiced in isolation but is instead invited to participate, with guidance, in the entire process.

Although Laura often assigned writing as a form of assessment, such as asking students to produce written answers to the social studies questions after a class conversation, during the many hours I spent in her classroom I witnessed very little writing instruction. Laura's approach to teaching longer writing assignments, such as the endangered species report, was most closely aligned with a process model in that she emphasized the necessity of having multiple (a rough and a final) drafts. However, the writing conferences she had with students around their rough drafts were focused primarily on editing. Students then recopied their edited paper. Whereas shorter assignments, such as the journal entries during guided inquiry, were for the most part simply assigned with very little scaffolding, Laura provided some initial scaffolding of the longer assignments through note-taking guides, such as the data sheet Jay and I used. The students for whom writing came easily appeared to be well served by this "hands-off" approach.

What was missing here, for a student like Jay whose giftedness in spoken-language expression outstripped his skills in written language expression, was some guidance in going from his orally expressed thoughts to the data sheet, and then from the data sheet to a finished text. Jay needed to understand the entire process of producing an essay or report. What was the data sheet asking him to do? What does "a report" look like? How was completing the data sheet related to writing a report? What was missing was the apprenticeship, the guided practice, that would turn this data sheet from just a worksheet to be filled out to a thinking tool, a strategy to support the production of academic text, a "think-sheet" (J. L. Collins, 1998; K. M. Collins & Collins, 1996; Englert, 1992; Englert & Raphael, 1989; Englert et al., 1992; Englert et al., 1991; Vaughn et al., 2000).

Clearly the issue was not that Jay did not know the material, or that he hadn't done his homework in terms of learning about eagles. When given the opportunity to demonstrate his knowledge orally, he did so. Through our interactions around this sheet, Jay and I used it strategically to organize and support his writing. This is illustrative of the ways that the design of instructional contexts constructs ability and disability—Laura's approach to "teaching" writing constructed Jay as "not a good writer."

This phase of my work with Jay demonstrated the ways in which guided practice with a writing strategy results in the teacher and the student constructing the strategy together. This coconstruction was accomplished primarily through dialogue around Jay's writing as he practiced implementing the strategy. Together we developed a shared language for talking about the writing and the strategy, and in so doing developed a shared context and understanding of what it meant to produce "good" writing.

We have our data sheet and my notebook computer in front of us. I start a file for Jay, and ask, "OK. Let's look at your sheet. Where should we start?"

"With the first block. 'Why is my bird endangered?'"

"OK. So you think each block is like a paragraph?" Jay nods, and I continue, "How could we make that block into a sentence?"

"Easy." Jay starts typing, pronouncing the words slowly as he types. "My-bird-is-endangered-because-of-DDT." He pauses and looks at me, "What *is* DDT?"

I am surprised: Jay has been using DDT in his oral descriptions so it has not occurred to me that he doesn't know what it is. "It's a form of poison for insects, um, what's that word? For insect poison?" I am drawing a blank. "Let's check our notes." I turn to our stack of articles and the data sheet.

"I think it's a disease, it gets inside."

Suddenly the word I am searching for comes to mind, "Pesticide. DDT is a specific kind of pesticide."

"Oh, yeah. We did read that." Jay turns back to the computer, and types "pesticide," pausing to check its spelling. Then he asks, "Should we tell 'em what pesticide is?" This is the first time Jay has explicitly expressed interest in meeting the needs of a reader, something I tried to focus him on in my questions and prompts as we took notes.

"Sure. They might not know that." Jay continues typing, one letter at a time, pronouncing the words as he does so, "My-bird-is-endangered-be-cause-of-pesticide. Pesticide-is-poison-to-insects." He stops and turns to me, "OK. What's next? I think we should tell how the insects get into the bird." He answers his own question.

"OK." Something about having me there to talk to supports Jay in thinking through the organizational and composing processes. I am there to scaffold when he needs it but otherwise he is making the key decisions on his own.

Jay continues typing, "The-fish-eats, hold up," he pauses to correct his typing, "OK, the-insects-and-then," he stops and addresses me, "Can you type real fast?"

"No. You're doing great."

"the-e-a-g-l-e-eats-the fish. OK."

"What else is in that square?"

"And-when-they-go-to-have-a-baby-the-shell-breaks-open. OK."

"When the shell breaks open, what happens to the baby?" I prompt Jay to continue.

"It's dead?"

"Yeah. It dies. Do you think we should tell them that?" Again I encourage him to think of the reader, using a question he introduced earlier.

"Yeah. People might not know that." Jay borrows my phrase.

When Jay finishes this sentence I take a turn at the computer. Neither one of us is an accomplished typist so our work is slow. "OK. Next box, 'What is being done?' Tell me what to type."

Jay reads the notes, transforming them into sentences, and I type them into the computer. "The government said the farms cannot put DDT into the ground." He pauses, and peers at the screen, "You know, we didn't say DDT in the first paragraph. We just said pesticide."

"You're right. Do you want me to go back and put DDT in, like 'pesti-cide, comma, DDT?'"

"Yeah." Being able to read his own thoughts as typed text seems to encourage Jay to make these kinds of revisions and connections within his writing.

We continue this way, orally constructing the essay from the data sheet and sharing the typing responsibilities, until we have composed and entered the entire essay, as it appears in Figure 10.2.

Employing Laura's data sheet as a strategy for planning and producing text, Jay and I generated the first draft of his report. Our next step was to revise this draft. To support Jay in revising his report, I drew on my teaching experiences, sociocultural theory, and my experiences as a writer.

In my own teaching and classroom research, I found that many of my students were unfamiliar with the conventions of written academic English and did not possess strategies for planning at the levels of text and para-

---

May 6, 1998

My bird is endangered because of pesticide, DDT. pesticide is poison to insects The fish eats the insects and then the eagle eats the fish and when they go to have a baby the shell braks open and the baby dies.

The government said the farms cannot put DDT into the ground. The government made a law that people cannot kill eagles. So the people put transmitters on the tail of the bird to see if somebody hurt it or not. If someone hurts an eagle they have to pay a fine or go to jail.

If I ruled the world I would restore the fish so the eagke can eat.

Bald Eagle

Bald head

Eats slippery fish

Flies in the air

Bird

The eagle lays an egg and the egg hatches because the mom keeps it warm. The baby won't grow white head and tail feathers until four or five years old. The young eagle has to search for his own fish and some don't make it to be grown. If they do, they're lucky, and they can live up to forty more years. Eagles can have babies at fur or five years old but some "non-breeding" adults may not nest until they are eight years old.

They only have unusual facts they mate one time in ther hole life time and are only can lay up to two egg in there hole life s

Eagles will fight over food and they wait till samon is dead or near death after spawning. The eagles wait until the salmon are weak because trying to catch salmon before spawning wastes too much precious energy and body heat. The government thought that the eagles were killing salmon before they spawned, and paid $5 for each dead eagle. Over 350,000 were killed before this bounty was removed.

FIG. 10.2. First draft of Jay's eagle report.

graphs. To assist them, I worked with my students to develop several strate-gies that supported them in analyzing, identifying, and appropriating the linguistic features of published texts representative of the genre they wanted to produce.[1]

My approach was informed by sociocultural theory, most particularly Bakhtin's notions of social languages and speech genres. Similar to Gee's (1996) discussion of a discourse as a situated form of literacy involving the meaning-making practices of a particular social group, Bakhtin (1981) identified social languages as culturally and historically situated ways of using language shared by a particular community. Whereas social lan-guages were identified by the community who shared them, speech genres were specific forms of utterances differentiated by the social situations of their use (Bakhtin, 1986; Wertsch, 1991).

One of the central constructs of sociocultural theory was the dialecti-cal, mutually constitutive nature of social and individual cognition. Semiotic tools mediated this dialectical relationship, and, although this was thought to include both physical and psychological tools, language was by far the most studied form of mediation. Bakhtin's work was par-ticularly important here, especially his concepts of dialogicality and ventriloquation. Bakhtin's (1981) concept of dialogicality posited that a speaker appropriated his or her words from interaction with others, and the process of appropriation involved one of transformation. Thus speakers took up words from "other people's mouths, in other people's contexts, serving other people's intentions" and applied them to their own meaning-making (Bakhtin, 1981, p. 293). Bakhtin (1981) discussed this process of appropriating and breathing new meaning into words as ventriloquation.

Drawing on the work of Bakhtin as well as his experiences with struggling writers, J. L. Collins (1998) identified this process of appropriation and ventriloquation as "the copying strategy."[2] Wertsch described a similar reli-

---

[1]For example, we conducted genre studies in the form of close readings of the newspaper (*The Washington Post*) to determine how the characteristics of persuasive prose found in the letters to the editor differed from those of unbiased journalism found in the front-page news articles (Collins & Collins, 1996). A key feature of this genre study was the emphasis I placed on encouraging stu-dents to appropriate the features of the texts that they found effective, to "try on" the styles of dif-ferent writers.

[2]Collins identified copying as a "default" strategy; that is, one that we tend to rely on when confronted with unfamiliar writing tasks. Collins argued that while teachers often identified copy-ing as cheating, writers faced with a difficult or unfamiliar task often relied on it as a scaf-fold—appropriating the words of another, and, through the process of ventriloquation, completing a challenging writing task.

(continued on next page)

ance on copying as a scaffold in his discussion of the role of mimicry in Palincsar and Brown's program of research on reciprocal teaching (Palincsar, 1986; Palincsar & Brown, 1984; Palincsar, Brown, & Campione, 1993).[3] Both programs of research emphasized the importance of understanding the processes of appropriation and ventriloquation as different from behaviorist approaches to learning through imitation or modeling, and argued instead for the importance of facilitating students' guided practice with a tool—a question, a strategy, or a language structure to support their own meaning-making and meaning expression. In both cases, as well, learners were explicitly introduced to the tool to be appropriated in the process of participating in the whole activity—reading, listening, or writing—and not through isolated drill-and-practice approaches (see also Englert, 1992, regarding a sociocultural perspective on writing as holistic, social, and dialogic).

Informed by my experience as a teacher, writer, and scholar of sociocultural theory, I viewed copying and mimicry as potential scaffolds for Jay. In addition, Jay's skills at appropriating discursive tools in oral interactions, such as during the guided inquiry sharing sessions, and his demonstrated giftedness in metacognition, suggested that Jay would find these types of scaffolds compatible with his ability to identify features of oral and written texts. At this time, Jay and I were engaged in our entomology inquiry. The ladybug text we read repre-

---

[2]   *(continued)*

Having identified copying as a strategy struggling writers used to create scaffolds for themselves, Collins conducted a study with Cathy Fairbend in her eighth-grade English class to determine if this strategy could be explicitly supported by connecting reading with writing, with the goal of widening the repertoire of writing skills and styles possessed by Fairbend's students (J. L. Collins, 1998). Once a week for a semester the students engaged in a strategy Collins termed "I Wish I Could Write Like That." This involved reading short excerpts of exemplary text from works students were currently engaged in reading in class, then explicitly appropriating the style and structure used by the author while inserting their own words. Collins and Fairbend determined that students improved their control of syntax and paragraph structure at the end of the study.

I found myself drawing on this strategy I used in designing and planning this research: I spent many hours examining texts to identify the features of narrative inquiry. I examined texts that included a broad range of styles, including those that only represented the informants' words (cf. Patai, 1993), those that incorporated personal reflection (cf. Behar, 1993), those that seemed to draw only illustratively from narrative in the service of a larger argument (cf. Orenstein, 1994), and those that tried to incorporate a weaving together of literature, theory, and narrative (cf. Purcell-Gates, 1995; Taylor, 1991). I tried to garner from each of these approaches aspects of narrative research that would inform my own writing.

[3]Reciprocal teaching was developed to support the engagement of low-achieving readers with four cognitive tasks Palincsar and Brown identified as important to students' comprehension of text: summarizing, questioning, clarifying, and predicting. The participation framework of reciprocal teaching called for students to appropriate the role of the teacher and pose a series of questions, designed to reflect the four cognitive tasks, to the rest of their group (typically six to eight students). Initial participation had to be scaffolded: Teachers introduced questions and phrases and students borrowed, mimicked, or copied them to participate in the reciprocal teaching dialogue (much the same way that Jay borrowed phrases from Laura and Shirley to facilitate his participation in the public sharing conversation during GIsML instruction).   *(continued on next page)*

sented a real-world example of the genre of writing Laura had asked the stu-
dents to produce. In addition, Jay was interested in the topic represented in the
text and we had already spent considerable time with the text at the level of con-
tent. Drawing on the copying strategy, I helped Jay to revisit the ladybug text
and examine its form, and to draw from it ways he might revise his own text.

"OK, so we've got the title. 'The Good and Bad News About Eagles' and then, look at how they started this one, with a question." I point to the first line of the ladybug text we are reading, "Did you ever see a little red and black beetle crawling along your windowsill?" Jay and I are sitting with my computer and our papers surrounding us. Our first full draft (depicted in Fig. 10.2) is on the screen.

"They started out with a question." Jay notes. "And look, we put DDT two times. Look at it." Jay points to the screen and says this last part somewhat scornfully.

"That's OK." I'm not sure what he means, "What are you thinking?"

"These," Jay points to the first two paragraphs, "should be one sentence, I mean one paragraph, about DDT."

"OK, that's a good idea." We cut and paste the sentences together into a paragraph. "Now what about, I'm still concerned with the opening sentence. We could start it with a question, like they did."

"Did you know that my bird, did you know that eagles are endangered because of DDT?" Jay grins, proud of himself.

"I like that! Do you like it?"

"Hm-mm." Jays nods and then points to the screen and continues, "Could you put, 'Did you know that eagles are endangered because of DDT?' Then, 'DDT is a pesticide'?"

"Yes. That's a good idea."

We make those changes, and then I read it back to Jay, "Let's see how it would sound to someone who didn't know what we were doing. See how it sounds. 'Did you know that eagles are endangered because of DDT?' DDT is a pesticide which is poison to insects. The fish eats the insects and then the eagle eats the fish and when they go to have a baby the shell breaks open

---

[3]   *(continued)*

The success of reciprocal teaching dialogues in supporting elementary and middle school students' reading comprehension has been well documented (see Palincsar, 1986; Palincsar & Brown, 1984; Palincsar et al., 1993). Prior to participating in reciprocal teaching, students scored approximately 30% on independent measures of reading comprehension. After a minimum of 25 days of participating in reciprocal teaching dialogues conducted in small groups (six to eight students), 80% of the students achieved an "independent score of 75–80% correct on four of five consecutively administered measures of comprehension, assessing recall of text, ability to draw inferences, ability to state the gist of material read, and application of knowledge acquired from the text to a novel situation" (Palincsar et al., 1993, p. 45).

and the baby dies. The government said the farms cannot put DDT into the ground. The government made a law that people cannot kill eagles. So the people put transmitters on the tail of the bird to see if somebody hurt it or not. If someone hurts an eagle they have to pay a fine or go to jail."

Jay breaks in, "We should put if someone *hurts it* or kills it."

"OK, yeah, that's good." I agree and Jay makes the change on the computer.

We continue working our way through the draft in this manner. Using the ladybug article as a model, I ask Jay, "If we look at the ladybug paper, next they talked about the young, the pupae and the larvae and everything. Do you think that should come before the poem and the 'If I ruled the world?' section?"

"Yeah. 'Cause you know why?" Jay is grinning. He is having more fun with this writing than I've seen him have with writing in any other context thus far. The computer seems to help: Jay is excited about learning how to use this tool, and it relieves him from having to recopy the entire text by hand each time he wants to change something.

"No, why?"

"The poem and the 'If I ruled the world' should be at the end," Jay announces. "You don't see a poem in the middle of this report," he points to the ladybug paper.

"Yeah. I think that's a good idea. Do you know how to move a whole paragraph?" After Jay moves the poem, I focus his attention back on the paragraph we've left behind, "Let's look at that paragraph for a second. In the life cycle of eagle, mating comes before laying the egg. So do you think the mating sentence should come before the egg sentence?"

"So," Jay pauses and reads the first sentence of that paragraph to himself, softly, "The eagle lays an egg and the egg hatches because the mom keeps it warm." Then he reads the next paragraph, "They only have one unusual fact, they mate," he turns to me, "Yeah, yeah it should," and makes the change.

Our final draft of the report appears in Figure 10.3. Although there are still changes that could be made, I determined that we had reached a limit with this particular piece and that it was time to move on.

Had Laura's writing instruction been organized differently, Jay would not have appeared "learning disabled." In the context of composing his eagle report, what seemed most important to supporting Jay's writing were the oral interactions we had while writing. Talking to me about what might come next, whether the spelling of a word was correct, and what the reader might need to know supported Jay's production of text. Without this kind of interaction he was uninterested in producing a written draft of his report, although he had done the background work and was willing to present his ideas orally to the class.

Jay
May 20, 1998
science: endangered species report

The Good and Bad News
About Eagles

Did you know that eagles are endangered because of DDT? DDT is a pesticide which is poison to insects. The fish eats the insects and then the eagle eats the fish and when the eagles go to have a baby the shell breaks open and the baby dies. The government said the farms cannot put DDT into the ground. The government made a law that people cannot kill eagles. So the people put transmitters on the tail of the eagles to see if somebody hurts it or kills it. If someone hurts an eagle they have to pay a fine or go to jail. Thanks to the government eagles were recommended to be taken off the endangered species list in May of 1998.

They only have one unusual fact: they mate one time in their whole life time and only can lay up to two eggs in their whole life. The eagle lays an egg and the egg hatches because the mom keeps it warm. The baby won't grow white head and tail feathers until four or five years old. The young eagle has to search for his own fish and some don't make it to be grown. If they do, they're lucky, and they can live up to forty more years. Eagles can have babies at four or five years old but some "non-breeding" adults don't nest until they are eight years old.

Eagles will fight over food and they wait till salmon is dead or near death after spawning to catch it. The eagles wait until the salmon are weak because trying to catch salmon before spawning wastes too much precious energy and body heat. At one time, the government thought that the eagles were killing salmon before they spawned, and paid $5 for each dead eagle. Over 350,000 were killed before this bounty was removed.

About 600 nesting pairs of bald eagles live in Washington State. Many other eagles migrate there in the winter to eat salmon from the Skagit River, one of the most important wintering areas for bald eagles.

If I ruled the world I would restore the fish so the eagle can eat.

> Bald Eagle
> Bald head
> Eats slippery fish
> Flies in the air
> Bird

FIG. 10.3   Jay's revised and edited eagle report.

Considered along with our reading of the ladybug text, my writing with Jay illustrated that the role of orally mediated interaction in supporting Jay's expression of meaning through written text was consistent with his approach to constructing meaning from written text. In contexts where he was supported in using oral expression to mediate his understanding, Jay was a competent reader and writer, and appeared to enjoy both activities. Similarly, the guided inquiry contexts in which Jay was able to draw on oral mediation, public sharing, and his individual interactions with Laura, he was a successful participant. It was only those activities that relied on mediation by individual tools, such as writing alone, or where he was silenced, as in the small-group work, where his "disability" appeared.

Jay and I are in our workroom. I've printed our completed, edited eagle report and I've also brought several pictures of eagles that I printed off of the Internet and some heavy paper because a cover is part of Jay's grade for his report. Jay cuts out the pictures and, using a glue stick, fashions a cover for his report. I help him gather the various rough drafts we've written and advise him to staple them together. Jay has taken to wearing the remote microphone during our meetings together—he thinks it's cool—and he wears it down to Laura's room when he walks down there to turn in the report. It is clearly visible, hanging down the front of his shirt. As he makes his way down the hall, I am surprised to hear the following conversation, recorded through the remote microphone and amplified through the headphones:

Laura:	Hey, guy.
Jay:	Hey-ey. I got it!
Laura:	You got it done!
Jay:	Uh-huh. I gotta staple it.
Laura:	Oh, my gosh!
Jay:	These are the rough copies.
Laura:	These are the rough drafts? I bet you feel good about this. Wow. So what did you do to get this done? What did you have to go through?
Jay:	We did a lot!
Laura:	You did some, uh, research?
Jay:	Research, and we read things off the Internet. And she got some stuff from the library.
Laura:	So who wrote it? Did you write it?
Jay:	Yeah, I wrote it and I typed it out on her computer and she printed it out.

Laura:	Wow. That's a lot of work, isn't it?
Jay:	Mm-mm.
Laura:	Are you ready to turn that in?
Jay:	Uh-huh.
Laura:	OK. I'll read it over for you tonight.

So who wrote it? Did you write it? Maybe Laura didn't mean it the way it sounded. Maybe she only meant the congratulatory parts of her response to Jay. For me, Laura's response reflects the emphasis on the individual nature of ability (and disability) and achievement that pervades her teaching practices and her classroom culture. It is what impedes her classroom from becoming a learning community. For Jay, it is a step forward, toward acceptance and approval: When he returns to our little room, he is beaming. He tells me, "She thought it was awesome."

What

11

"Jay, We Gotta Find
You a Group."

Spring in this part of the world is characterized by mud—and rain, which leads to more mud. It's hard to remember, as I make my way back down the dirt road after dropping Jay off and listen to the thwump of mud in my tires, that this rain and mud are working together to create fertile ground in the fields around me. Sometimes the pace of change is not what we wish it to be.

Although my after-school collaboration with Jay was going well that spring—we were working on his eagle report, reading and discussing A Wrinkle in Time, *and continuing our second-hand investigation of various insects while planning a trip to the University entomology lab during the summer—my work with Laura was not. Laura's reaction to the eagle report, a blend of surprise, doubt, and congratulatory support, was just one example of the many ways in which she communicated her persistently low expectations for Jay. I tried to share what Jay and I were doing with her but she did not want to talk about it: She was always too busy. She seemed to welcome my weekly intrusions into her classroom to videotape, but dismissed my attempts to portray Jay, his abilities, and his family in more holistic ways in our conversations. I watched as Jay became more and more excluded within the classroom community, and as he began to respond to this exclusion in ways that ultimately confirmed Laura's portrayal of him as "different."*

The students sit in a U shape and Jay, Danny, Cheryl, Scott, Ned, Matthew, and Molly are outside the U, each a separate little island scattered around the margins of the classroom (see Fig. 11.1). It's reading time. Laura distributes the novel the students are engaged in reading, *The Whipping*

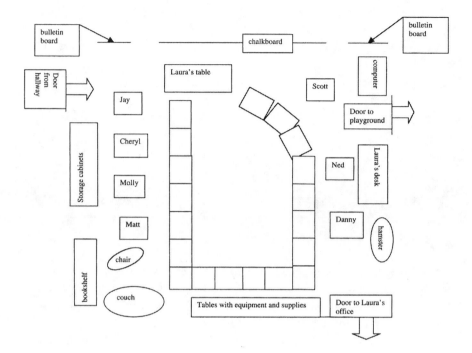

FIG. 11.1.   Seating Chart 3. Jay's fifth-grade classroom, March.

Boy, and passes out copies of a worksheet as well. The students are going to learn about similes.

Jay volunteers to read the directions at the top of the worksheet out loud, "A simile is the um, comparison of two alike things using the words 'like' or 'as.' *The Whipping Boy* is filled with such comparisons. Here are, here's a few examples."

"OK. Here *are* a few examples." Laura corrects Jay's reading as she walks to the back of the room. She pauses and reads from the worksheet, "'Your tongue hangs out like a red flag.' What are they comparing your tongue with?"

Jay turns around in his seat to look at Laura and the rest of the children, "A red flag."

Laura nods to the child sitting on her right, "Maria?"

"A red flag?" Maria repeats Jay's answer, although she sounds uncertain.

The class continues working through similar examples for 4 minutes, then Laura asks them to complete the rest of the first portion of the worksheet individually. This calls for the students to revisit chapters 1 through 8 of the novel, find examples of similes, and write the example with the page number on their worksheet.

Jay works quietly by himself, diligently finding similes and filling in his worksheet. Twice he raises his hand and Laura, who is walking around the perimeter of the room hanging students' social studies posters on the wall, walks over and reads what he has written.

After 9 minutes of working individually, Laura has some students share their responses. Then she tells the class, "OK. Take a few minutes to chat with a neighbor, and come up with some other similes that you can think of."

Jay stands up at his desk, and looks around the room. Jay stretches his arms above his head as he continues to look round the room. Then he picks up his paper and pencil, walks over to the other side of the room, and looks around from there. Jay then walks to the back of the room and gets a large hard-covered book from the shelf. With the book in one hand and his paper in the other, he settles himself into a big armchair near the couch in the back of the room. He places the book on his lap, puts his paper on the book, and, 1 minute and 35 seconds after Laura told the students to "chat with a neighbor," Jay begins to work alone.

Of the other students whose seats are on the periphery of the room, only Matthew has found a partner. Ned works alone at his desk, having completed a tour of the room similar to Jay's and not found a partner. Scott, Cheryl, and Molly each work alone at their desks: They didn't attempt to get partner. Matthew, also sitting outside the U, finds a partner in Roy. During the 6 minutes and 45 seconds that the class works in pairs, several students get up and talk to others, but no one approaches Jay, Molly, Cheryl, or Scott.

Jay does not have roller blades so he will be playing goalie. He emerges from the small office in the back of the classroom, swathed in protective hockey gear, which, with the exception of the hockey stick, looks to me like what a baseball catcher might wear: shin pads, chest plate, and helmet. It is Carl's equipment: He and Kevin have asked Jay to join in their game at recess. Jay bursts out the door with the boys, thrilled to be on their team, to be asked to play. In a long-awaited grudge match, they will be taking on the sixth graders today.

Laura stays in the classroom during recess and hangs rain forest mobiles students made from the ceiling. Several students—all girls—stay and help or talk quietly with each other. Twelve minutes into recess Laura realizes that Jay did not hand in his homework assignment. The classroom has a back door that leads outside, and she steps out of it now, "Jay! Jay! Come in here!" When Jay doesn't respond, Laura sends one of the girls out after him.

When Jay comes in—sweaty and flushed and carrying his (borrowed) hockey stick—Laura reminds him of the missing homework assignment, and tells him he must stay inside for recess because of it. She suggests that he call home and leave a message for himself. He walks to the phone at the front of the room. "Hi, Jay. This is yourself calling. Don't forget to bring your homework tomorrow so you can go out for recess." Jay walks back to his desk and sits down. He begins to unbuckle his shin guards, then leans over and rests his head on his desk. He does not do the missing assignment.

"What I'd like you to do today is get in your groups and think about a roller coaster ride, how you might design it. I'm gonna ask you to present your roller coaster ride tomorrow." Jay's hand has been up for several minutes and he sits sideways in his chair so that he can face Laura. When Laura says "groups" he lowers his arm and starts trying to signal Kevin, who sits across the on the side of the U facing Jay, by mouthing the words "you and me" repeatedly. Kevin appears to not understand him. Laura picks up a stack of poster paper and stands at the front of room near Jay, between him and the rest of the class. "Um, once you have your groups situated, come up and get your papers." The students stand at once and begin moving about, quickly merging into groups.

Jay gets up and stretches, looking around the room. He walks around to the far side of the U and goes over to Kevin. Kevin shakes his head "no" to Jay and points to his two partners. Jay walks back to the other side of the U and stands behind Roy and Carl, who are seated next to each other leaning over a sheet of poster paper. Jay leans over, apparently to try to join in. Matthew approaches and stands behind Roy and Carl.

Jay is not acknowledged by either Roy or Carl. Neither boy talks to him or moves over in a way that invites his participation or even viewing of their paper. He leaves and goes up to front of room. He stands at Laura's table, behind her. She walks away from him then comes back. Scott is also unable to find partner and stands behind the table next to Jay, waiting for Laura. Laura tells Scott, "How about Brian and Jim?" Scott walks very slowly over to them, and sits on periphery of the partners. Laura turns to Jay and says, "Jay, we gotta find you a group." They stand together for 20 seconds, looking at the room of children working. Laura points to Todd, working alone in the back of the room. Jay walks over, but when he approaches Todd shakes his head "no."

Poor Pedagogy & Management –

Laura watches this and approaches Carl, Roy, and Matthew as Jay walks around the U, passing near their group. Laura steps forward and physically places herself in the lines of vision of Carl, Roy, and Matthew. She reaches out and places one hand on Jay's shoulder, making him a part of the group by extension of her physical presence. Laura looks at the boys, "OK?" and walks away.

It has taken Jay 5 minutes and 21 seconds to be accepted into a group; 5 minutes and 21 seconds of work time that ends up being 21 minutes long. Even then, the extent of his acceptance is questionable. He stands on the edge of group, as does Matthew, peering over Carl and Roy's shoulders at what they are doing. Carl and Roy make no overt effort to include Jay or Matthew. After several minutes Jay and Matthew sit down on the edges of the group. Both Jay and Matthew kneel in their chairs with their forearms on their desks, trying to lean over and see the paper. Matthew finally gets up after 10 minutes and tells Laura no one is listening to him. Jay sits silently.

When the class leaves the room, I ask Laura, "What was the problem with Jay finding a partner?"

"People don't want to work with him because he fools around. And unfortunately they're starting to make those choices."

"He kept trying. I watched him and he sort of went to several different groups and then he came up to you—"

Laura interrupts, "They're starting to make some more informed decisions about that. You know, 'Now I want to do well and I don't want to get in trouble.' And, it is unfortunate but I don't know. Like Kevin, for instance, his parents don't want him anywhere near Jay. So, Kevin's like, 'No, I can't work with you.' I think they accepted him into the group once he got in there but I don't know how much input he's having. He gets along OK with Carl."

More and more frequently and in increasingly more explicit ways Jay was excluded from the classroom community. The social exclusion described in these scenes had dialectical consequences for Jay's academic performance and for his learning opportunities. For example, his time and energy to work on assignments, such as the simile worksheet, were diffused by the efforts he had to put into attempting to overcome his social exclusion. In the specific example of the simile worksheet, Jay did not complete the assignment within the given time. He kept it on his desk and began working on it after lunch, alone at his desk, while Laura read a chapter from a different novel to the class. This was a time when the other students were doing puzzles with each other, drawing, or just relaxing, a time when Jay could have been building social relationships had he been sitting near anyone (in the

U) and had he not had to complete his assignment. Jay's low achievement and social exclusion were thus dialectically forged.

Further, a clear pattern developed within the classroom community that suggested Jay was not the only student consistently excluded and that these instances of exclusion were influenced by the differential perceptions and expectations Laura held for different students. In addition to Jay, Laura marked each of the students who were excluded in conversations with me as different in some way. Scott was on medication for an emotional disability. Laura identified Ned as learning disabled and, although subsequent testing by the school psychologist confirmed this, his parents had him tested independently and those tests contradicted the school's results. Cheryl was hearing impaired. Matthew, a student of Korean descent, had been previously referred for special education assessment but had not been subsequently identified. After a conversation with Molly during lunch, in which Molly said she wanted to be a professional singer and therefore did not really need school, I asked Laura about her. Laura's response was reminiscent of her responses when I asked about Jay: She explained her own perceptions of Molly's home life, "One time early in the fall she sat here and a cockroach actually fell out of her clothing. I mean it's nasty, really nasty. They have no money. We can't change that. I mean I can have her functioning in here but I don't know."

One way of trying to understand how Laura's perceptions and expectations for these students influenced their social positioning and academic achievement is by looking at the classroom as a community with its own culture. McDermott argued that "culture" is not the property of individuals but is present in the ways in which people organize their lives together (McDermott, 1993; McDermott & Varenne, 1995, 1996). A community of individuals develops, expresses, and reproduces its culture through the routines and practices shared by its members. These routines and practices are shaped by the values of a community and determine who is marked as "different" (McDermott & Varenne, 1995).

Both her values and those of her students shaped the routines and practices of Laura's classroom community, its culture. Although culture is created through interaction, because of her position of authority in this community, Laura was able to strongly influence which routines and practices were followed. Each decision Laura made relative to Jay—when she repeatedly placed him (and the other "special" students) at the margins of the classroom physically, when she sent him into the hall, when she did not take up or respond actively to his attempts to participate, and when she

called him in publicly from recess to complete his missing assign-
ment—were all expressions of her values. Each of these actions communi-
cated her values to the other students in the class: Jay doesn't complete his
work, Jay's ways of participating in the classroom discourse are inappro-
priate, Jay should be excluded.

It's reading time again, and today's lesson is vocabulary. Each student in the class had been assigned one word from the book the class is reading, *The Whipping Boy*, for homework the night before. When called on today, they are to walk to the front of the room, say the word, read the sentence from the book that includes the word, read the definition of the word, and read a sentence of their own composing that demonstrates use of the word.

Laura is going in order of seating; because Jay's desk is alone near the door he will be called on first. He takes out his vocabulary assignments, places it on his desk, and looks around the room. Students are still shuffling papers. Jay gets up to blow his nose. Laura sits at an empty desk within the U, and calls on Jay, "Go up to the front please."

Standing at the trash basket, Jay turns to face her and speaks from behind a wad of tissues, "Me?"

"Yes."

"While I'm blowing my nose?" Jay is still speaking from behind a wad of tissues.

"Shall I come back to you or are you finished?" Laura's voice is firm.

"I'm finished." Jay throws out his tissues, picks up his paper, and walks to the front of the room. He speaks clearly, "Furious. 'He gave a furious shout.' Furious means a violent rage." Jay pauses and looks up from his paper at the class, and gives himself a drum roll, "Dat-da-da! I got furious when I took the test."

"When you took the test? The test gave you violent rage?" Laura laughs, and several students join her. Jay smiles and goes back to his seat.

Laura does practice math problems—the class is studying metric measurement—on the board while the students watch. Jay has him arms tucked up under his white t-shirt, hugging himself as he wiggles in seat. His eyes are trained on Laura, and he calls out the right answers at the appropriate times, as do several other students. This is apparently the expected mode of response because once the right answer has been called out Laura begins another problem.

After continuing this way for 14 minutes, Laura begins a problem with, "Let's try another one ... They said we have 3.75 meters and they're asking us to tell how many centimeters … Can anybody figure out what we might do?" Laura walks over to stand near Jay's desk, between Jay and the rest of the class. Jay, his arms still tucked under his shirt, leans over and tries to look around Laura to the board. As he leans over, he begins to lose his balance. A look of surprise and panic crosses his face as he struggles to regain his balance with arms trapped under his shirt. He loses this struggle, and falls out of his seat, to the floor. Jay gets up quickly and straightens his chair, looking sheepishly around the room as he takes his seat again. The class doesn't miss a beat; no one acknowledges discursively that this has happened although several students look toward Jay. He appears to be unhurt.

Later Laura comments on the incident, "That's 50 percent of the time. The other 50 percent is what you see. So it just depends on what happened in his life, or how confusing it was probably at home this morning, or did he get in an argument with somebody on the bus. I mean falling out of his chair this morning, the class handled it pretty well. Had they blown apart I would have had to say something to Jay but since they were willing to go right on, we just ignored it and went on."

Laura is standing at the front of the room, explaining a worksheet to the class. Jay gets up to sharpen his pencil while Laura is talking. He stands at the pencil sharpener and does an exaggerated stretch, yawning and extending his arms above his head. Jay waits there for 1 minute and 30 seconds when, still talking, Laura walks over and places a hand on his back. With one hand on his back and still talking, Laura guides Jay back to his seat. Before he sits down, Jay grins and looks at the class, shrugs, and lifts both of his hands, palms open, up in the air. The gesture seems designed to amuse the class, to pose the question, "What did I do?" And the gesture is not lost on Laura; she leans over and speaks to Jay quietly. When she walks away from his desk he immediately raises his hand, and sits there with it raised as Laura walks across the room. Laura leans over to help another student with the worksheet, and Jay stands up and sharpens his pencil.

Sitting at her table in the front of the room, Laura returns students' math homework, "When I call your name come up and get your paper, please." One by one, students go up and get their papers. Five students—Jay, Scott, Molly, Tina, and John—don't get papers returned. As Laura nears the bottom of the stack, Jay leans over and peers closely at the remaining papers. He sits back down.

When all the papers are passed out, Laura stands up, "All right if you could trade your papers with a neighbor." She looks down and begins pag-

Behavior issues

ing through the math book on the table, looking down. Jay watches Laura, then looks around room. His desk is bare.

Laura orally reviews the previous day's math lesson, walking once past Jay's desk to the back of the room as she does so. "Just a little review from yesterday, if you recall what we worked on yesterday was changing back to base units, like millimeters back to meters." Laura walks back up to the board and writes one example illustrating the numbers of places after the decimal associated with each prefix. "And we talked about, if it had the prefix 'milli' your number was going to look like this, with three places after the decimal point."

Jay is shifting in his seat and appears restless. Laura asks the students to mark each other's papers and begins to read answers from the book. Jay looks around room, then turns and watches Cheryl, the child behind him, mark Matthew's paper. After 2 minutes Jay turns around and rests his chin on his desk, staring at the bulletin board across from his seat. After another minute he bends down and looks at the bottom of his desk, then sits up and stretches one arm under his desk. He appears to be scraping at something with his hand. Jay then leans back in his chair and folds his arms across his chest, watching Laura. Laura is not watching him. Jay holds his chin in his right hand, his right elbow resting in his left hand. With a quick movement, he flicks a piece of gum from his right thumb into his mouth, and chews it rapidly several times. Jay looks over to see that Laura is still not looking at him, and takes the gum out of his mouth and examines it briefly, glancing around to discern whether the children near him are watching. Then he replaces the gum and continues chewing. He sits with his arms crossed on his chest, staring straight ahead at the bulletin board across from his desk, and chews his gum furiously.

Later the same day Jay would find his math homework crumpled in his desk. He had not, as he thought, turned it in. Shortly after this, with Annemarie's support, I bought him a Trapper Keeper notebook and we spent an enthusiastic afternoon setting it up. His aunt, with whom he was staying at the time, seemed surprised at the idea that he needed one and then bought her son and daughter, Jay's cousins, each one as well. Before doing so, she asked me to write a list of what to buy, including details like what kind of notebook paper, pens, and pencils would be best. Laura reported to me that after Jay got his Trapper, he carried it "Everywhere. It's never out of his sight!" and that he was much more organized in completing his assignments.

Jay clearly needed some help organizing his assignments according to the conventions of school. When I taught high school, I spent several weeks during the first part of the school year helping students set up their notebooks,

Collins comparing what she did as a teacher to Laura —

learn how to keep an assignment calendar, learn how to take notes, and so on. Thereafter, I would periodically check their notebooks with them. The structure of Laura's classroom activities did not provide this kind of scaffolding of personal organization. Exclusion from the activity, as in this example, or withholding of rewards, as in the recess example, were used as punishments for forgetfulness and disorganization (as were failing grades).

I am not suggesting that Laura, or any teacher, should have to buy supplies for a student. However, at 10 years old, needing some assistance with personal organization is not extraordinary. There were four other children who also missed math that day due to a lack of homework. (I remember weeping over a forgotten spelling assignment in fifth grade until my father drove me back to school to retrieve it. I quickly learned not to forget my assignments!) In addition to providing scaffolding of organization, the math activity could easily have been restructured to include these children in some way. If, for example, Laura had checked the homework to see who had completed it before passing it out, she could have set the five students to work on an alternative problem set.

Right

Jay began to respond to Laura in ways that seemed to oppose her authority, and in doing so he seemed to be trying to align himself with his classmates. The first sign I saw of this behavior was after his oral presentation about eagles, when he called across the room, "What'd I get Mrs. B? What'd I get? Mrs. B., did I pass? Did I get a D?" This was not typical behavior for him and at the time I was puzzled by it; in retrospect I saw it as the initial example of what would become repeated attempts to reposition himself within the classroom community by aligning himself with his peers. By calling out in this way, Jay publicly called attention to his successful completion of the assignment and challenged the identity Laura constructed for him as someone who doesn't complete his work.

As the school year progressed Jay found himself increasingly isolated, socially, physically, and discursively, from the classroom community: The whole class was complicit in his exclusion. Throughout the school year, one way that Jay was excluded was through the lack of substantive response to his utterances. In both large and small-group settings he was often either not responded to at all, or responded to negatively. His response to being excluded from the classroom community was to either become silent (during small-group interactions especially); to become more orally expressive; or to act in ways intended to challenge Laura's authority and align himself with his peers—the behavioral equivalent of talking out of turn—by sneaking gum, getting up to sharpen his pencil, blowing his nose repeatedly, and so on.

Thus sociocultural theory offers a view of identity and social positioning as dialectically produced through situated action and reaction. In resisting Laura's negative identification of him, Jay was attempting to reconstruct his identity within the classroom community. The more Jay was excluded by his peers, the more he attempted to reconstruct the negative identity Laura constructed for him as a positive one. What was at stake for him was his positive social image with his peers, so he worked to reposition himself and align himself with his peers. Laura risked much the same thing—her positive image in front of the class—so she had to respond to Jay's attempt to reconstruct himself in ways that continued to mark him as an outsider.

When I tried to address the ways in which she and Jay seemed to be coproducing the behavior that she identified as an indication that he was "emotionally impaired," Laura was unwilling to engage in this discussion. She argued that I was not aware of how "impaired" he was the rest of the time, when I wasn't there. She further located the source of Jay's "problem" as within Jay and his family, "So it just depends on what happened in his life, or how confusing it was probably at home this morning, or did he get in an argument with somebody on the bus." Finally, she realigned herself in collusion with the class to view Jay as an outsider: "I mean falling out of his chair this morning, the class handled it pretty well. Had they blown apart I would have had to say something to Jay but since they were willing to go right on, we just ignored it and went on."

Laura was right, I was not there all the time. However, it was clear to me when I was there that she had a role in shaping Jay's behavior. Something as seemingly simple as standing between him and the rest of the class, using her body to exclude him from the group, led to Jay's leaning over and falling—an event that seemed to confirm Laura's assessment of Jay. It was beginning to become clear to me how complicated her vision of Jay was by her expectations for him. Unfortunately, Jay's exclusion became even more explicit as we approached the end of the school year.

Tomorrow the class, with the exception of Jay and Kevin, will spend the day at a historical village that depicts life in this midwestern area of the country in the early 1900s. Today they are reading a text, prepared by the village, describing the things they will participate in and observe.

Laura reads the first paragraph of the text out loud, then calls on different student volunteers to each read a paragraph. There is little discussion of the content of the text until after the eighth paragraph, when the class turns the page to begin a section about recess. Laura explains, "At recess tomorrow obviously there won't be kickball, basketball and football and things like that." This provokes some response as students speculate over what games there would be at recess. Laura starts to describe the facilities at the village, but the students are still talking. "There's a nice large," Laura looks around the room, "Sh. There's a nice, a large, this page has a picture of students at recess," Laura turns the page of her copy of the text and holds up a page featuring a large picture of children playing Red Rover.

Jay, who has not been joining in the talk and has been watching Laura, turns the page of his own text, and exclaims, "I know how to play that game!"

Laura looks around the room, "Quiet please! There's a nice yard school-yard in the front where they played games. One common game that you guys have already played here was—"

A student calls out, "Red Rover."

"Red Rover. That was something that they played a lot of," Laura continues. "Um, some children used to bring homemade toys and games like jacks where you bounce a ball and pick up jacks."

"I know how to play that game," Jay repeats.

Laura raises her voice, "Let's read about homemade toys and games in this section."

Several students raise their hands to read at this point, including Jay. Laura looks around the room and as her glance slides away from Jay he says, "I got, I got something to say about that."

Laura turns and calls on Kevin.

"I got—" Jay tries again.

"Just a minute, Jay. We'll get back to you."

The class goes on to read about "punishments," such as "switches and dunce caps," but they never do get back Jay. Laura tells the students to read "with a partner," and Jay gets up to go stand near Kevin. None of the students appear to be reading; most are chatting and talking excitedly about what the trip tomorrow will bring. Jay walks away from Kevin and, on the way back to his desk, lingers near the door, looking out into the hall.

Because she wants to stay an extra hour at the village beyond when the buses would have to return, Laura has arranged for parents to do all of the driving. After the students leave the classroom, I ask Laura how she decided who gets to ride in each car. She responds, "I talked to the people yesterday whose parents were driving, and I said, 'Who do you want in your cars?' And they named off kids. And there were like 8 kids, and you can probably imagine who they were. Well, Jay and Kevin aren't going because they couldn't get rides home at that time of the day. But," Laura slowly counts off the other children who weren't wanted by their peers, glancing around her at their empty seats as she speaks, "Scott, Molly, Amy, Cheryl, Matthew, Ned, um, you know, nobody wants these kids in their group. So I just sort of assigned one to each group."

"When is the Chicago trip?" Laura and I are alone in the classroom. Three weeks before the end of the school year, it will be my last visit to her class before summer, although not my last visit to Axleton Middle School.

"The 29th." Laura walks over to a cabinet against the far wall of the classroom. Her back is to me as she reaches into the cabinet. She turns her head and says over her shoulder, "Jay's not going."

"Yeah."

Laura stops, and turns to face me, "Has he mentioned that to you?" She seems surprised that I know Jay's not going.

"Yeah, he did."

Jay had told me the week before, in the car on the way home from our after-school meeting. When we got into the car, he asked, "You know that saying about the stick? Why do I always get the short end of the stick?" I asked him what he meant and he was silent for a few moments; then he described the upcoming trip, and concluded by emphasizing the high cost, "Can you believe it cost that much to go to Chicago?"

Laura turns her back to me again and gets her purse out of the cabinet, "What's his, uh, feeling on that?" She walks over to the table at the front of the room, places her purse on it, and faces me.

"He's," I pause, trying to capture my reading of Jay's emotions, "he seems pretty disappointed. You know, at first—"

Laura interrupts, "His cousin's not going either, you know, the one across the hall."

"I think money is a factor," I suggest.

Laura assures me, "The Moselys have money."

"Oh, really?"

Laura nods, "And that's who they're staying with, so I don't know." She is moving things around on her desk, straightening up.

I ask Laura how much the trip is per person, and she tells me that it's $90, then continues, "Well, at this point, part of it too was that I had, you know," she pauses and looks directly at me. Her voice is firm when she goes on, "He can't go unless a parent goes with him. On a trip like that, I don't trust him out of my sight. And there's no way I can keep track of kids all over Chicago. So probably, since they knew it was two people, they chose not to. Plus it would have been an additional, with his cousin that's three, three amounts."

I don't respond immediately. I am growing angry at Laura's assertion that it was Jay's choice not to go: the cost and requiring him to bring a "parent" clearly put the trip out of reach for him and his cousin. Here again I see her expectations for him shaping his opportunities. Because I feel myself getting angry, I am silent, thinking of how to respond in a way that will not provoke further defensiveness.

After several seconds Laura continues, "This is the most I've ever had not going, Jay, Ned, Danny, Amy, Cheryl, Molly, but this particular group is very challenging, so. I'm countin' the days.... It has not been a fun year. They've been a real drain. That's unfortunate because I do have some really nice kids in here. A lot of my girls are really nice. But they're not all that bright. So you just work with them. They aren't that interested in learning." Laura is speaking softly now, and sounds tired and almost wistful. "A couple of years ago, you should have seen that class. Those people were like sponges. That was the last year that I taught the enriched reading group. Out of my class, usually I had about 25 kids in the enriched reading group, and they were from other people's classes. That year, 11 out of the 21 were from my homeroom. So I had, usually how we'd do it is I'd give them a diagnostic test, you know, with a grade level equivalent, and all of these kids were reading above eighth-grade level in comprehension and vocabulary. So it was just a remarkable, remarkable group of kids. I was sorry to see them go. This year was like, boom! Back to reality!"

12

"I'm the Boy Who Likes Bugs."

As the school year drew to a close, the tension in my relationship with Laura increased, and we developed a somewhat oppositional stance toward each other. Neither of us explicitly recognized or made reference to this tension, but it was present in my persistent attempts to portray Jay's "emotional impairment/learning disability" as coconstructed and in Laura's consistent responses that, through interrupting me, turning away, and refusing my invitations to meet outside of the classroom context, silenced my position. To acknowledge or listen to my interpretation meant seeing Jay differently, and to do this meant seeing herself and her classroom community differently.

As Erickson (1987) asserted, risk is involved in teaching and learning. When learning is less than successful, both parties stand to "lose face" or be revealed as less than competent. The consequences of failed teaching and learning interactions have effects at local and institutional levels for both teacher and child. Locating a problem within each of the excluded children and identifying this "problem"—emotional impairment, learning disability, poverty, hearing impairment, ethnicity, lack of family support—as the sole cause of their school failure allowed Laura to avoid these consequences and to avoid examination of the situated cultural values, as represented by the organizational, interactional, semiotic, and activity-related practices of her classroom, which made their perceived differences into deficits. Further, by locating the problem within each of the excluded children, Laura was not called on to rewrite her narrative of herself as a sensitive and successful teacher.

139

Laura's impulse to identify Jay as emotionally impaired and/or learning disabled reflected the deficit or medical model approach to understanding low achievement and school failure (see discussions in Trent, Artiles, & Englert, 1998; Gavelek & Palincsar, 1988; Poplin, 1988a, 1988b) Nearly a century ago, educator and philosopher John Dewey laid the foundation for social constructivist theorists who would later challenge reductionist approaches such as Laura's:

> The easy thing is to seize upon something in the nature of the child, or upon something in the developed consciousness of the adult, and insist upon that as the key to the whole problem. When this happens a really serious practical problem—that of interaction—is transformed into an unreal, and hence insoluble, theoretic problem. Instead of seeing the educative steadily and as a whole, we see conflicting terms. We get the case of the child vs. the curriculum; of the individual nature vs. social culture. Below all other divisions in pedagogic opinion lies this problem. (Dewey, 1902/1990, p. 182)

Inspired in part by these ideas of Dewey's, social constructivist theory emphasized the importance of examining the social nature of learning at three levels: (a) the level of the learner as a social being with a unique ontological history of interests, needs, and strengths; (b) the level of the interaction or relationship between the learner and others in the learning community; and (c) the level of the psychological processes, strategies, symbol systems, or activities being "taught," which must be viewed as cultural (i.e., social) tools that embody the habits of mind of particular communities of practice. Learning ability and disability were thus viewed as cooperatively produced through the interactions among learners, tools, activities, and social relationships (see also Gavelek & Palincsar, 1988, on contextualism and Poplin, 1995, on holism). This did not mean that differences did not exist among learners, but that these differences were made to matter in more or less salient ways by the learning task, tools, and interactions present in the learning context.

These issues were made particularly visible through Jay's attempts to participate in his fifth-grade classroom. At times the nature of the task and tools assigned, such as independent writing for assessment purposes, disabled Jay's display of learning so that he appeared learning disabled. Consider, for example, Jay's display of understanding about eagles when asked to give an oral report, to write a report individually, and to write a report with the assistance of collaboratively created writing strategies and a word processor. Guided by values that stressed individual achievement and competition for Laura's attention, the classroom activities provided little space *for the kind of dialogic discourse Jay thrived on. At other times Jay was able to successfully negotiate the requirements and structure of the learning task but his attempts to display or construct understanding were thwarted by the constraints of the social relationships within the classroom. This was demonstrated numerous times when Jay appropriated and employed discursive tools to participate in class conversations, and his attempts were silenced by lack of substantive response from his peers and Laura.*

An additional demonstration of the social nature of learning and display of ability and disability at the level of social relationships involved not only Jay but the other "identified" children. Laura's values and expectations regarding the potential of individual children to participate in and contribute to the learning activities, based on the various ways in which she identified them as "different," shaped their opportunities to construct and represent their understanding. The social positioning of these children within this classroom community was embodied through their physical positioning at the margins of the classroom. Although officially "included" by their assignment to Laura's classroom, they were excluded from true membership in the community. As Laura asserted, "Nobody wants these kids in their group. So I just sort of assigned one to each group." In Jay's case, this persistent exclusion and negative identification led to his attempts to reconstruct Laura's portrayal of him.

The close of the school year marked the end of my exploration of these issues in Laura's classroom, but the beginning of summer vacation provided an opportunity to work further with Jay in contexts where he was not excluded from the community of practice but rather was a vital and contributing member. Further, these contexts—composing blues poetry, conducting an entomology investigation, and attending church—were representative of his unique ontological history and interests. Working with Jay in contexts where his participation was supported by others and motivated by his own interests provided opportunities to understand more fully his capabilities and strengths and the ways that they had been limited in school settings. As we entered this phase of our work together, Jay and I also entered a new phase of our relationship, where he became more fully involved in research process and worked with me to collect and interpret data.

Although I am 15 minutes earlier than we had planned, when I park outside the main entrance of Axleton Middle School, I see Jay waiting inside the front door. He leans forward and opens the door for me as I approach, grinning his welcome. He is eager to leave and disappointed when I tell him we have to go to the main office first. The rest of his class is preparing to get on the bus for their trip to Chicago, and he wants to leave before they do. We go to the main office together, and, having arranged permission for this "private field trip" earlier with his principal, I am able to sign Jay out quickly.

Jay is wearing his black-and-white flannel shirt and black corduroys, and at 7:30 on this June morning it is hot and humid already. I put the air conditioning on as we pull out of the school's parking lot and Jay directs the vents toward his face, telling me, "I tried to look as nice as I could. I put my best outfit on, and I even put cologne on." I assure him that he looks and smells very nice, and tell him that I was so excited about his visit that I had trouble sleeping the night before. He replies that he had the same problem and was awake until after 1:00 a.m.

Our first stop is a breakfast cafe near the university, where Jay orders and eats pancakes, scrambled eggs, bacon, sausage, diced potatoes, and lemonade. He is thrilled that I tell him to order whatever he wants, although he is concerned about costs, and he checks with the waitress to make sure that refills are free before ordering another lemonade. During breakfast we plan the rest of our day, including a quick review of the questions he wants to ask Harry about entomology. We also discuss other parts of the campus he wants to visit, and develop a list that includes the law school, the school of education, the natural history museum, and the football stadium, where Jay dreams of one day playing.

We go to the stadium first. A high, black metal fence surrounds the stadium and today the main gates are locked. Through the fence we can see construction workers going in and out of the stadium and hypothesize that there must be an open gate somewhere. We walk slowly around the fence —I'm worried that if the construction workers need hard hats something dangerous lurks around the corner—and Jay waves at the workers and calls out through the fence, "She goes here. Can you let us in?" We get several glances and even a smile or two but no one rushes over to unlock the gate. We continue around the building and just as I am trying to think of who I can call to get us into the stadium—Are any of my former students who played football still on the team? Would they have access?—we walk up to the final gate, and it's open. We walk through a short tunnel that goes under the seats and the stadium unfolds before us. Jay is just awestruck. We sit down and he just basks in the moment, totally thrilled and absolutely beaming.

Our next stop is the law school library, where we are both happy to get into the air conditioning. Jay is noticeably impressed by the architecture and facilities. He sinks into deep purple armchair and asks, "How did you get to go to a school like this?" We rest for about 20 minutes and discuss the admission process, ways to get scholarship funding in addition to playing football, what college classes in different disciplines are like, and careers he might be interested in, which include entomology, law, football, and automobile repair. When I describe my own undergraduate course work as an English major, Jay is surprised to learn that in college, it is possible to choose classes that are small and discussion-oriented.

Next we visit the school of education and my office, where Jay uses the computer and we visit entomology sites on the Internet. Then we walk around campus, stopping for brief visits at the undergraduate library and the student theater, where we are treated to a brief peek at the play in progress, *Cyrano*. Many of the stone buildings on campus are covered in ivy, and as we continue to walk around Jay is impressed by this and reaches out to touch it, fingering the leaves to make sure it's "a living plant that can climb a building."

When we arrive at the natural history museum, where Harry's office is, we are a few minutes early. We decide to spend them in the gift shop because it is right across from Harry's office and seems to beckon to us, especially Jay. He is captivated by a display of shark teeth, and touches them carefully, exploring their points and polished surfaces with his fingers. Then he moves on to a row of little white cardboard boxes that each hold a small polished gemstone, and begins picking up each one and inspecting the way the light catches and reflects off its surface as he turns it in hands. Suddenly a jar of peacock feathers at the end of the counter catches his eye and he rushes over, exclaiming over how soft they are and insisting I touch one. My eyes meet those of the young woman at the cash register, and she seems more amused than concerned, so I join Jay. They are indeed very soft!

We go next to Harry's office, where he is seated at his desk but stands to meet us when he hears us in the hall. Jay, holding his back straight and his shoulders square, walks right up to Harry, extends his hand, and announces, "Hi, Harry! I'm the boy who likes bugs!"

Harry smiles and takes Jay's hand, "That's great! I'm Harry, and so do I!" Jay's face breaks into a grin. I know I've brought together two kindred spirits.

For the next 2 hours we tour the museum and the conversation is almost entirely between Harry and Jay. We begin on the second floor, the Hall of Evolution, and I am struck by the nature of Harry's interactions with Jay. Harry guides Jay through each exhibit, bending over or kneeling by his side and talking to him quietly. At each display, Harry asks Jay questions, first about what he sees and then about what he thinks it means. "Why would an animal that eats fish need teeth like that?" "Why do you think that dinosaur had a fin?" Jay responds readily, offering his interpretations without hesitation. Together they draw on all of the clues in each display and construct interpretations relating form and function for each creature. I am a step behind, my first instinct being to stop and read the information posted at each display, until I realize that their conversation is much more instructive.

Jay's desire to examine everything through touch persists here and Harry, who works in the museum as well as the entomology research lab, seems totally unperturbed by this and guides Jay in carefully touching the items that are within reach and not behind glass. I am reminded of Jay's reaching out to touch the CDS while Laura held it, before he built his own. Jay doesn't seem to hesitate to touch the items that intrigue him, regardless of the context and of whether others participating in that context are handling the objects. Touch seems to be part of his way of interacting and of learning, part of the way he focuses his attention on something. With the exception of the guided inquiry investigation, this was not something I had the opportunity to observe in his classroom learning.

We take a break to have lunch at a nearby Vietnamese restaurant, where Jay spots Annemarie dining with a colleague and we go over to say hello. During lunch Harry tells Jay about his dissertation research on mites. To study the life cycle of the mite he is interested in, Harry has to collect grasshoppers, because the mites live on the grasshoppers. Jay and I ask Harry questions about the process of collecting the grasshoppers and mites for his study. As we are leaving the restaurant we see Nancy Marano and Danielle Ford, my GIsML colleagues, whom Jay recognizes from their work in his classroom, so we stop at their table and say hello. I can tell Jay is pleased at running into so many people he knows at the university.

After lunch we return to Harry's office and he shares his research materials with us, showing Jay how he documents his fieldwork and observations with both words and illustrations. After this we go upstairs into the archives. Row after row of tall cabinets fill the center of the room, and counters with stools line its perimeter. Each cabinet is comprised of drawers, and each drawer contains specimens. The specimens are carefully pinned to the lining of the drawer, and each pin holds a tiny little tag identifying the specimen with its scientific name and the date and location where it was collected. Harry explains that the lining of the drawers contains a preservative, which prevents mites from eating the dead specimens.

The array of insects is incredible and Jay and I are both completely captivated. We examine several trays of insects, especially butterflies, moths, ladybugs, and cicadas. Once again Harry guides Jay (and me) through observations designed to point out form–function relationships, such as coloring and camouflage. Harry tells us that red and orange tones are meant to communicate to predators that an insect tastes awful or is poisonous. He tells us how birds actually learn to follow this scheme and that other insects that don't taste bad have evolved to "mimic" the coloring of those that do. Jay and I are both fascinated. Jay reaches out with his fingertips to stroke the velvety-looking back of a very large moth, and Harry tells him that the insects are very fragile because they are dried, and guides Jay to what can be gently touched without damage (e.g., the backs of the beetles, which are so shiny and hard they look lacquered) and what cannot (wings, especially those of butterflies and moths).

Although we examine insects from all over the world (I am particularly entranced by the trays of jewel-toned butterflies from South America), Harry has us spend the most time with trays of insects Jay might actually see at his home. Jay looks each tray over carefully and then identifies the insects he's seen in his observations. Each time he identifies an insect as familiar, Harry asks him a series of questions about where and how he observed the insect, and what inferences Jay might be able make about the insect's habitat, eating habits, life cycle, and predators from these observations.

Jay is unable to answer all of these questions, and Harry stresses the importance of noting the date, place, and location of collection for each specimen. He advises Jay to make this a habit in his own observations. I notice Jay examining the tiny, careful printing on each identification tag and his hesitancy in responding to Harry, so I suggest that perhaps he could use his little tape recorder for this purpose. Harry's response is enthusiastic, "That's what scientists do when they're collecting, use a tape recorder in the field and then make notes from the tape later." Harry stresses that with damsel and dragonflies, insects Jay's especially interested in, it's important to note their colors (especially the colors of their eyes) immediately because they lose their brilliant iridescence as they die and dry out.

Each time we observe a particular insect, Harry identifies it with both its scientific and common names. After we examine the insects in the archives for 2 hours, Harry brings Jay over to the counter around the edges of the room. There he sets up a microscope for Jay and mounts a selection of the insects Jay's identified as present in his yard on slides. Harry helps Jay focus the microscope and then uses a sharp pair of tweezers to point out the different structures on the specimens while Jay peers through the microscope. Harry again asks Jay questions about the forms he's observing and their possible functions. Jay is enthusiastic, and again responds with his interpretations freely. They are on their second insect when Jay leans over to

Harry in a conspiratorial way, and says in a low voice, "Why is science like another language?" Harry explains the need for a community of scientists interested in the same insect to communicate with each other and to have some agreement about what is being described. "It's all about specificity and communicating."

Jay is very excited about the possibility of collecting his own insects and we return to Harry's office to discuss getting started. Harry helps us locate a student collecting kit in a supply catalog, and gives Jay three really beautiful, hinged, wooden storage boxes from his own supply. The boxes have hook and eye closures and are lined with the same treated material that lines the storage trays in the archive. Harry invites us to return later in the summer to show him Jay's collection. As we are leaving, he reminds Jay that, "Without your field notes, your collection is useless."

13

"Do You Think I'm Proper?"

After our visit to the university, Jay and I meet again the following Monday, the first day of his last week of fifth grade. I'm there, at his invitation, to watch him "graduate" from the Drug Abuse Resistance Education (DARE) program, run by the local police department in cooperation with the school system. The students in Laura's class stand together at the edge of the left side of the stage, and as each one walks forward Laura announces their name. As they exit the stage, each student receives a DARE shirt and diploma. Jay wears his new university T-shirt, hanging nearly to his knees, and hangs back in the wings of the stage, waiting until last to march across the stage. He then walks to the center and waves and bows as the audience, having been asked to hold their applause, claps for all of Laura's students. Jay accepts their applause with a second bow and then gives a final wave and grin before leaving the stage.

After the ceremony, we meet to confirm our summer plans and to write thank-you notes for Harry. "My favorite part was going to the bug lab," Jay reflects as he munches on a chocolate chip cookie. A card for Harry sits on the table in front of him. Jay writes silently for several moments, then asks how to spell "studying." "I thought so," he responds when I tell him.

> Dear Harry I want toell [to tell] you that you one heck of a man studying bugs and insects and stuff. So I'm writing this letter because I [want to] say thank you for taking time off of work for me!
> by Jay

After he finishes writing, Jay leans back in his chair and finishes his cookie, reflecting, "I don't think they should have science like another lan-

147

guage. Well, I do and I don't. Because sometimes I get confused by the names. But I understand Harry's answer, because if someone is like from another country like China they have to know what you're talkin' about.''

"When we studied science in your class, when we did the Cartesian driver, did you think science had another language?" I ask.

"Yeah, but already knew some of the words like density and volume. I got this back." Jay slides his eagle report from his Trapper Keeper notebook toward me.

I read Laura's written comments out loud, "'Jay, This is an excellent example of using rough drafts to form a well-written paper. You should be proud of your hard work—it shows! I am very impressed. A+.' All right good for you!" Jay grins as I congratulate him. "What's the other sheet?" I ask, indicating a typed memo resting on Jay's notebook.

"Oh, that's just about next year, sixth grade," he hands it over to me.

"'Welcome to sixth grade,' I read out loud, 'Last year we transformed the sixth grade hall into a forest theme. This fall your child will join one of our teams of teachers and become part of our new theme, the Western Hemisphere.'"

Jay opens his eyes wide and rolls them toward the ceiling, "Oo-kay. The Western Hemisphere." He shakes his head and takes another bite of cookie.

I continue, "As such we will be transforming our halls and classrooms into the Western Hemisphere." I look up and, meeting Jay's eyes, we both laugh. "Our hemisphere will include many things, animals, buildings, people, insects, trees, etc. Over the summer, please collect, purchase, or borrow materials to help us." I look up again, "Well, maybe you could do something with insects?"

Jay looks down, shrugs noncommittally, and then asks, "Do you think I'm proper?"

"What do you mean?"

He tries to explain, "Do you think I *talk* proper? Like somebody, you know, how um, people in military school are, or something like that talk? I don't think I am."

"Why not? Did somebody tell you that you weren't proper?" Jay shakes head "no" to my question, and I continue, "Do you wanna be any different than you are?"

"No," Jay laughs a little, then adds, "Because, um, Kevin had written 'wanna,' and then Mrs. Bozek said, 'That's not a word.' And I was like 'it's not?' And then I said, 'Ain't is a word,' and Mrs. Bozek was like, 'Yeah.' And Kevin was like, 'No it's not.' And then Mrs. Bozek said, 'It's a *slang* word.'"

"What does proper mean, do you think?"

"I think proper English is when you don't say 'ain't' or 'I ain't got none' or somethin' like that. You say, 'I don't have any' or somethin' like that. When you talk real fancy, well, not fancy, but you talk different," Jay explains.

"Different than what?"

"Than other people. Like, 'cause some people say 'I don't have anything.' And some people say 'I ain't got nothin'.' See? That's like the difference."

I nod, and ask, "How would you describe your own way of talking?"

"I just, well, see if I talk to somebody I don't know, and I'm tryin' to make a good impression then I talk like, kinda different, but any other thing I don't talk different. If it's something important that I have to really do, and I have make a good impression, I mean, you know, like to get a job or somethin' like that, then I talk proper. And if I'm like at home, school, or church I just talk the way I talk."

Early in our relationship, Jay expressed a long-standing interest in poetry and in music, especially jazz. Informed by his interests and by his sensitivity to the relationships between language use and social contexts, I suggested composing blues poetry together as our next writing project, and he was immediately intrigued. Based on a series of poetry lessons I had conducted as a teacher, which my students had always had great fun with, we collaboratively composed 12-bar blues poetry.[1]

We begin by reading some poetry by Langston Hughes (1994). As he flips through the book of Hughes's poetry I've brought, Jay is immediately drawn to a poem entitled, "Mother to Son," and reads it out loud to me.

Mother to Son[2]

Well son I'll tell you:
Life for me ain't been no crystal stair.
It's had tacks in it,
And splinters,
And boards torn up,
And places with no carpet on the floor—
Bare.
But all the time

---

[1]My mother, a special educator, first developed the 12-bar blues writing lessons with her students, drawing from Greenfield's (1988) book of poetry, *Nathaniel Talking.* We then worked together and developed a project where her students, elementary Option I students in a rural classroom in upstate New York, composed poems and exchanged them, via the mail, with students in one of my classes, "average" 12th graders in a high school outside of Washington, DC.

[2]From *The Collected Poems of Langston Hughes* by Langston Hughes. Copyright 1994 by the Estate of Langston Hughes. Used by permission of Alfred A. Knopf, a division of Random House. Additional poems from this source appear on pages150 and 151 of this chapter.

I'se been a-climbin on,
And reachin' landin's
And turnin' corners,
And sometimes goin' in the dark
Where there ain't been no light.
So, boy, don't you turn back.
Don't you set down on the steps
'Cause you find it kinder hard.
Don't you fall now—
For I'se still goin', honey.
I'se still climbin',
And life for me ain't been no crystal stair.

Jay pauses after reading it, then reflects, "Just because something's hard don't give up. I like it," he stops, then adds, somewhat shyly, "I thought it was gonna be good because it has like, 'mother to son' in the title." Flipping through the book, he finds the section on blues poetry and suggests we read "Wide River."

I agree, and offer, "A hint for reading this, like with 'Mother to Son,' it's written like someone's talking. So pronounce the words like they're written."

"Yeah, I know," Jay nods. "I think it's kinda going back to slavery times, the way we talked. That makes it good, like it has more expression in it." He reads the poem to me:

Wide River

Ma baby lives across de river
An' I ain't got no boat.
She lives across the river
I ain't got no boat.
I ain't a good swimmer
An I don't know how to float.
Wide, wide river
'Twixt my love an' me.
I never knowed how
Wide a river can be.
Got to cross that river
An' git to ma baby somehow.
Cross that river,
Git to ma baby somehow—

> Cause if I don't see ma baby
> I'll lay down an' die right now.

"I like that one!" Jay announces when he's finished.

"Me too. Can't you just hear someone singing it?" I burst into song, and Jay bursts out laughing. Then he catches my improvised tune and we do a duet, half laughing and half singing our way through the poem. When we're done, I ask him, "Do you want to try writing some blues?"

"That'd be fun!" Jay is enthusiastic, but then adds, "I need the music to inspire me!" I take out an audiocassette recording of blues music and, while listening to several songs, we read Eloise Greenfield's (1988) description of 12-bar blues poetry. Then we return to Hughes and take turns reading verses of "Bound No'th Blues" to each other.

Bound No'th Blues

> Goin' down de road, Lawd,
> Goin' down de road.
> Down de road, Lawd,
> Way, way down de road.
> Got to find somebody
> To help me carry dis load.
> Road's in front o'me,
> Nothin' to do but walk.
> Road's in front o'me,
> Walk … and walk … and walk.
> I'd like to meet a good friend
> To come along an' talk.
> Hates to be lonely,
> Lawd, I hates to be sad.
> Says I hates to be lonely,
> Hates to be lonely an' sad.
> But every friend you find seems
> Like they try to do you bad.
> Road, road, road, O!
> Road, road … road … road, road!
> Road, road, road, O!
> On de No'thern road.
> These Mississippi towns ain't
> Fit fer a hoppin' toad.

"OK," I ask again, "Do you want to write one?"

Jay grins but looks down at the book, "I can't write *po-etry!*"

"Yes, you can! Of course you can!"

"I'll think of something and you write it down," he suggests.

"OK."

Jay looks down at the book again, "People still talk like this a little bit. Like, 'ain't got nothin'.'"

I have the pen poised over my journal, "Is that your first line?"

"Um, ain't got nothin', ain't got no food. Ain't got no food!" He jumps out of his seat and comes around the table to stand next to me, peering at the paper as I transcribe his words. Soon we've recorded the following verse:

> Ain't got no food.
> Ain't got no clothes.
> Ain't got no woman,
> So let me
> clean my toes.

After we share a laugh over the last line, I point out the rhyme scheme of our poem, "Look at the pattern of rhyme. You've got the rhythm down but look how this rhymes." I point back to 'Bound No'th Blues,' still open on the table. "Lawd, road, Lawd, road, somebody, load."

"It don't have to be exactly like that, do it?" Jay asks.

"Well, blues have a certain pattern. If we want to write blues we want to fall within that general pattern." We look again at Greenfield's description of the blues.

Jay offers, "Baby take me back." He pauses, then grins, "And I promise I won't slack!" He laughs again and his giggles are contagious.

After the laughter, I suggest, "Let's save 'And I promise I won't slack' for the third line 'cause that's where we want the rhyme with 'back.' So, baby take me back home with you? To be with you? Where I belong?"

"Where I belong." Jay leans over the table, watching me write.

"OK."

"And I ain't gonna slack!" he adds exuberantly. As I write the last line he looks up from the paper, "This is fun!"

We continue this way for the next 30 minutes, composing several stanzas. Jay corrects my writing several times, noting that, "You keep leavin' the g's on. We want it to have expression!"

Baby take me back
where I belong.
Baby take me back
where I belong.
And I promise
~~I won't go back.~~
I ain't gonna slack.
Baby take me back
where I belong.
Baby take me back
where I belong.
I'm ~~sitting~~ sittin' here ~~begging~~ beggin' you.
~~in the words of this song~~
And let me sing this song.
Splinters in my toes,
blisters on my hands.
Splinters on my toes,
blisters on my hands.
Been ~~playing~~ playin' all day,
tryin' to get in my band.

As our writing continues, Jay takes up the 12-bar blues format and corrects my suggestions when they differ in rhythm or rhyme from it. For example, after Jay plays with several rhymes for the word *shoes*, I offer, "How about I need a new pair of shoes?" to start the fourth stanza.

"Hold up. But we want to use shoes to rhyme it, right?" Jay asks.

"Yeah."

"So make that the second line." He whispers softly to himself, "Think, think, think."

"How 'bout my feet are sore, I need some new shoes?" I offer.

"I got the walkin' aroun' no-shoes blues!" Jay announces with a grin, "And I ain't got no money so I can't pay my dues!" Based on this inspiration, we compose the following two stanzas together:

My feet are so sore,
I need some new shoes.
My feet are so sore,
I need some new shoes.
I got the walkin' aroun'

> no-shoes blues!
> I'm beggin' my cousins,
> let me borrow your shoes.
> I'm beggin' my cousins,
> let me borrow your shoes.
> I ain't got no money,
> 'cause I paid my dues.

"Now sing it!" Jay announces proudly.

"Well, I don't know if I can sing it," I hesitate, and Jay jumps in.

"I can!" In a clear, strong voice, he sings a very "bluesy" version of our song. When he's through, I point out, "See you can write poetry!"

"No, I can't!" Jay denies his talent but smiles as he does so.

"You just did."

"I'm just, it's rhyming words. Well, I guess that still is poetry. It's not like *real* poetry."

"Why isn't it like real poetry? Look, Langston Hughes got a whole book of 'em! And he's a famous poet."

"You think I could be a famous poet?"

"Sure!"

"OK, let me sing it again!" This time Jay adds the beginning of another stanza at the end of our poem, "Baby talk to me, I need to hear your voice." I quickly write down this addition, then he continues, "Talkin' to you is like eating cake that's moist, naw that's not a good one."

"Talkin' to you is like breathing, I have no choice?" I offer.

"That's good!" Jay nods enthusiastically.

> Baby talk to me,
> I need to hear your voice.
> Baby talk to me,
> I need to hear your voice.
> Talkin' to you is like breathin',
> I have no choice.
> Please talk to me, baby.

Jay sings our song one more time in its entirety, dancing around our little room as he does so. He looks over to me as he finishes, "This was fun! I wish we did it earlier!"

*Four months after our first collaborative efforts, unprompted by me, Jay
taught his cousin, Tasheka, how to compose 12-bar blues song-poems. The
recording of their interaction in this activity (I was not present) offers an illustration of internalization as appropriation in the sense posited by
Wertsch (1998). In their discourse together, it was possible to discern Jay's
appropriation and transformations of the 12-bar blues format.*

Jay:	Hello, Kathy. This is Jay and
Tasheka:	Tasheka.
Jay:	Welcome to our basement, where we're ready to go. And a 1, 2, 3, and action! What we're going to be talking about to-day, we're going to talk about how to make up a blues song. You know what I'm sayin' Tasheka?
Tasheka:	Hmm-mmm.
Jay:	When we are making this song, you're not s'posed to, well, you can play around but sometimes you have to be serious. You know? Make a line, you know, and make it sad. ((sing-ing)) ding-ding-ding-ding
Tasheka:	Sad?
Jay:	Yeah. The blues are usually sad. You didn't know that? Did you?
Tasheka:	Not really.
Jay:	Like, ((singing))

<blockquote>

I been in my bed/
sick I count the days/
and in a little while/
I think I gonna be dead.
'Cause I got the blues/
The blue-wooo-wooos/
I think I got the blues.
</blockquote>

Tasheka:	I think it's s'posed to rhyme.
Jay:	Nu-huh. It's not. I just made it up.

Jay's instructions to Tasheka about the activity of composing a blues
song, "You can play around but sometimes you have to be serious," illustrated his understanding and transformation of an activity he initially engaged in with me. He then adopted the role (and discourse) of teacher and
tried to give directions to Tasheka, "Make a line, you know, and make it
sad." His role as teacher also included modeling of the composing process.
In addition, it was possible to identify his appropriation of what might be

termed "movie director talk" as he encouraged Tasheka to participate in
the performative aspects of the activity, "And a 1, 2, 3, and action!"

Jay and Tasheka then had a spirited discussion in which Tasheka dis-
puted Jay's authorship of the song. Jay again took up the role of a teacher
and attempted to scaffold Tasheka's participation by giving her a "beat,"
and starting her off, as she requested, with a word. Despite Jay's choice of
words, Tasheka made a valiant effort to compose a stanza:

Jay: I made up that song.
Tasheka: I don't think you did.
Jay: Yeah. We didn't do nothin' together right now. I'm just tryin'
           to teach you. OK. Talk into the thing-y. OK, let's go. And a 1,
           2, 3, 4. You want a beat or what? You gonna make up a song?
Tasheka: I don't have a song. Gimme a word to get started.
Jay: TOE JAM!
Tasheka: ((singing)) You're a toe jam, baby, yeah. If you don't wash
           me ((both children crack up))
Jay: You gotta feel it. You gotta be into it. Just make up somethin'.
Tasheka: I don't have anything.

Jay's advice, "You gotta feel it. You gotta be into it," seemed to capture
the unity of agent and semiotic tool posited by sociocultural theory. Wertsch
(1998) referred to this as an "irreducible tension" between agents and
mediational means and asserted that "the essence of examining agent and
cultural tools in mediated action is to examine them as they interact" (p.
25). In this view, individual and social development were inextricably
bound through semiotic tools. Thus, in this interaction, the rhythm and
rhyme of blues music, the 12-bar blues composition pattern, and the tape
recorder were different tools that mediated Jay and Tasheka's action and
interaction. Vygotsky (1981a) posited that forms of mediation such as these
were both products of their sociocultural context, and served to facilitate,
shape, and define the activity contexts in which they were applied. Certainly
that was the case in this example: Jay and Tasheka defined their activity together in relation to the tools they employed ("we're going to talk about
how to make up a blues song") and the tools then shaped their activity.

Although much of his work centered on explicating development of
speech as a semiotic tool, Vygotsky (1981b) viewed "various systems for
counting; mnemonic techniques; algebraic symbol systems; works of art;
writing; schemes; diagrams; maps and mechanical drawings; all sorts of
conventional signs; and so on" (p. 137) as forms of semiotic mediation.
Further, Vygotsky (1978) explored the representational uses of drawing

and gesture by young children. As we have seen with Jay and Tasheka, additional forms of semiotic mediation may include technological tools such as computers, calculators, and tape recorders, and artistic forms of expression such as dance and drama (Palincsar, 1998; Wells, 1999). The critical feature shared by these diverse forms of mediation is that they fundamentally shape the activity in which they are applied. Vygotsky (1981b) asserted that mediational means did not simply facilitate action that would have otherwise occurred in a more cumbersome fashion; rather mediational means created possibilities for action that would not have existed otherwise:

> *By being included in the process of behavior, the psychological tool alters the entire flow and structure of mental functions. It does this by determining the structure of a new instrumental act just as a technical tool alters the process of a natural adaptation by determining the flow of labor operations. (p. 137)*

Dewey's (1913) work on interest supported Vygotsky's consideration of tool use by suggesting ways of thinking about the unity of agents and material tools when employed in purposeful action. Here, Jay's use of the material tool of the tape recorder was particularly interesting. Through his use of the recorder to participate in composing a blues song and in our research project together, Jay demonstrated his genuine interest (McPhail, Pierson, Freeman, Goodman, & Ayappa, 2000) in both activities. The tape recorder became an extension of himself in the activity, a part of his identity as researcher and "blues man." He encouraged Tasheka to pick up these identities in part by encouraging her use of the tool: "I'm just tryin' to teach you. OK. Talk into the thing-y." As we moved into another area of Jay's interest, our entomology inquiry, his use of the tape recorder as an instrument of research, a way of being-in-the-activity, became even more salient.

14

"This Ain't Easy!"

In early July our insect collecting kit arrives and I take it out to Jay. First we stop at McDonald's, which has become our customary meeting place since school is out, and have a soda and plan our day. I show Jay the books I've purchased for us, an insect guide and the biography of Charles Henry Turner (Ross, 1997). The insect guide is a *Peterson First Guide*, designed for children and recommended by Harry (Leahy, 1987).

Jay examines the biography, noting "This looks like a good one. Might give us the feel of what it's like to be an entomologist." We decide to read a little of it then go to the park. We take turns reading the opening sections of the book, which situate the beginning of Charles Henry Turner's life historically and introduce his interest in insects.

When we get to the park we unpack the insect collecting kit and try to speculate what each item is for. I find the booklet of directions and start reading them out loud while Jay lays the equipment out on the picnic table. My first concern is safety: I want to make sure Jay knows how to handle the poison that comes with the kit properly. I find the section on "kill jars" and we sit down and read it together. The poison is ethyl acetate, which the directions assure us is a "humane and rapid method" for killing insects. After reviewing the safety precautions, we take turns reading the rest of the directions to each other. Then we spend several minutes figuring out how to assemble the net. Finally we're ready to begin and start walking toward the small, slow stream that runs through the park.

Jay stops and looks briefly at the directions again, which we've carried down with us, "I wanna see how do you do this." Jay studies the series of diagrams that depict how to maneuver the net, "OK, I got it. I got it." He swishes the net around for practice, "I know how to do it now. And," he looks around, "I see a whole buncha' dragonflies!" He grins and chases after one.

I spot one closer to us and try to be helpful, "There's one! Get it!"

"I found one right here!" Jay swings the net down, but the damselfly perched in the grass eludes him.

"Aw. I think this is gonna be tricky, huh?" Again, I'm trying to be helpful.

"Got it almost." Jay is not easily daunted and looks around for his next target. He spots a moth on the ground near him

I cheer him on, "Right there, right there, right there, yes!" Jay swishes the net over the moth, then lifts it up slowly. "Close the net!" I remind him.

Jay peers into his now-empty net. "I closed the net but it flew out."

"You sure?" I, too, bend over the net but it is indeed empty. "OK. Let's look for another one." I see the shadow of a moth pass over the edge of the water near us, "There it is! There it is! I see the shadow. It's blending in with grass!"

Jay swishes the net quickly through the air, "I got it!" He sounds as surprised as he does triumphant.

"Close the net! That was hard work!" I congratulate Jay, who is beaming. He clutches the net closed with one hand and holds the pole with the other as we walk back to our picnic table. He looks at the kill jars we've set out on the table.

"How we gonna put it in the jar?"

"Let me read the instructions," I reach for the booklet.

"We can't use our hands," Jay reminds me. "This is a butterfly."

We decide that tweezers are the right tool for the job and Jay reaches into the net cautiously while I hold one of our kill jars open. He aims for the body of the small yellow moth, urging, "C'mere buddy. Dang!" The moth flutters away from him but stays in the net. "This ain't easy!" He is able to grab the body gently with the tweezers on his third try and drops it into the jar, where we examine it together.

"Cute little one, isn't it? Did you see his mouth? Really interesting." I am peering at the creature we've trapped while Jay gathers up the net again.

"We might as well leave that one in the jar and go get another one."

"Is your grandma gonna be too grossed out?" I am worried about Jay's keeping the collection at his house—his brand new house.

"Naw, not if I keep it in the basement. Hey, we gotta make our notes!"

"That's right. Where we caught it, what's the name of this river?"

"You can write better than me," Jay urges, holding the pen and field notebook out to me.

"I don't think so. You do this one. We'll take turns." Jay makes the first entry into his field notebook, noting the time and place of the capture of the moth. Then he picks up the field guide and begins looking in our guidebook under butterflies and moths. "I found it! It is a moth."

"Can you tell what kind of moth?" The guidebook I've purchased describes the insects in detail but has few pictures. We're not able to determine what kind of moth we've captured because we haven't learned how to interpret the language of the book yet. We flip back and forth between diagrams of the insects' bodies, which label their parts, and the descriptions of each family of moth. After several moments trying to identify the moth, Jay notes, "This is so much harder than it looks." There are not enough details in the words or pictures for us to be sure of our identification.

"Look at his little head and his little eyes," I suggest.

"Hey, the magnifier!" Jay exclaims, suddenly remembering the small magnifying glass that came with our kit. With the magnifier we are able to make a much more detailed assessment of the moth but are still not sure of our identification.

After we pin it down, Jay asks, "OK, now we can catch another one. Do you wanna try?"

"OK!" I try for a butterfly first, and miss, "This is harder than it looks! Oh, there's one right in front of me!" I point out another small moth.

Jay cheers me on as I swish the net down, "Go Kathy! Go Kathy! Did you get it?" We peer into net I'm holding firmly closed. "Yes!"

After we place the moth in the kill jar, Jay takes a turn with the net and I point out a large dragonfly to him. "Oh, look at that one! Oh, you gotta get that one! There you go." I'm encouraging Jay as he moves in slowly, then suddenly brings the net down onto the rock where the dragonfly rests. Smack!

"Yes!" Jay announces triumphantly.

"You got him! You got him!" I run closer as Jay lifts the net up to reveal the dragonfly stuck to the metal rim of the net, "Oh no. You smashed him. Oh, man."

Jay looks up from examining the smashed dragonfly, "He was gonna die anyway."

"Yeah, but you don't want to ruin your specimen. We'll have to practice this. Next time try to aim an inch or two away from the rim of the net."

Jay's enthusiasm is undaunted and he removes the dragonfly to the kill jar, to make sure it's dead (it is) and we take turns examining it with the magnifying glass. "This is so cool," he announces, looking at the dragonfly,

"I could get used to this!" Then he looks up at me, "We shoulda' started this sooner!"

We leave the dragonfly in the kill jar and Jay takes the net closer to the water's edge. Without hesitating, he walks up and smoothly swishes the net through the air, snatching a damselfly in midflight and whipping the net back around to close it. I am amazed at the fluidity and deftness of his approach, "You didn't even need me! That was so awesome! You just walked right up and caught it! It didn't even take you any time!" I peer into the net, "And we didn't damage that one at all!"

Jay grins proudly, "I said, 'I'm gonna get this one,' and I did!"

I hold the net open while Jay removes the damselfly with tweezers and places it in one of our kill jars. I lean over to look more closely, "Aw man, he is so cool looking. Look at his eyes." The damselfly's large, bright eyes are starting to fade as it dies. "How sad."

"I'm sorry you had to die," Jay tells his specimen. Then he looks more closely, "Man, he's dying. He's almost dead."

"He's so pretty, all blue and green."

"Look it, he's got a big eye, and you can see it's green."

Jay picks up the Peterson guide we've been using and together we find a series of illustrations of darners, damselflies, and dragonflies (Leahy, 1987, pp. 20–23). We determine from the illustrations that this specimen is a damselfly. I look at two descriptions and read them to Jay, "I think it's either this one or that one. This one, spread winged damselfly, it says 'usually metallic green or bronze above and pale straw color below' and 'typically inhabits ponds and marshes'" (Leahy, 1987, p. 22).

"Yup, that's it cause it's green," Jay agrees, now taking the specimen out to mount it. While pinning it, he observes, "Oh, nope. It's black on the other side, with little red dots on it's side." We can't find these details in our book so again we're not sure of our identification. That doesn't bother Jay, who pours through the guidebook, then pauses and looks up at me, "Isn't this cool? We're getting good at this." He decides to pin the specimen on its side to show off all of its colors.

We walk back down to the water and Jay spots two damselflies flying together, stacked on top of the other as though in an embrace. Swish! He captures them both on one swift movement and shouts over to me, "Two at the same time! They was matin'!"

"But didn't Harry say they laid eggs in the water?" I'm pretty sure Harry said this, and I'm also pretty sure I'm not prepared to discuss insect mating.

"Yeah, he did. But I know they was matin'."

"Let's check the field guide," I suggest. We've walked back to our picnic table and as I pick up the guide Jay tries to remove one of the damselflies, who have now separated, with the tweezers. As he tries to get it in the jar, it gets out of the tweezers and flies away. Jay watches it fly away. "When I was puttin' it in, I let it go too fast." He looks at the remaining damselfly, "I think dragonflies and damselflies will be my specialty. And beetles, too. There's a lot of beetles near my house."

We kill and pin the damselfly, tentatively identifying it as a "bluet" and then decide it's time to pack up. Before we leave, Jay picks up the tape recorder and announces, "We had a good time trying catch these specimens, and then we caught 'em. The big one's [the first moth] wings is brown and clear with yellow dots," he pauses.

"On its thorax," I add.

"Yeah, and his stinger, isn't that the stinger?" Jay turns to me.

"The abdomen."

"On his abdomen. On his thorax is white and some of his hair is white too. He has a big spout and six arms. His eyes are yellow."

From the perspective of sociocultural theory, Jay and I were attempting to enter a new community of practice, the community of entomologists, together. After this initial insect-hunting adventure, we met weekly during the rest of the summer to hunt, collect, identify, and label insects. Both of us were new to entomology, but we held different areas of expertise and interest that helped us to form a mutually supportive partnership as we took up the tools and practices of entomology. This meant that there were no rigid apprentice–mentor roles in our relationship but rather shifting roles as we moved to support each other's "weaknesses" with our own strengths.

My interest in reading, as well as my own sociocultural background, led me to first "look up" what we were supposed to do in the texts. As we grew to rely more closely on the texts for insect identification, my strengths in print literacy enabled me to figure out the organizational features of the three insect texts we used, and I was then able to help Jay engage with them usefully. Similarly, Jay's agility with and interests in using the mechanical tools of entomology, particularly his ability to catch insects swiftly after that first day, made him an expert in the capture of our specimens.

As we moved to take up the tools of entomology we "tried on" aspects of the identity of entomologists. This was most evident in our use of three tools: (a) the discourse of entomology, where we comingled our own ways of seeing and describing with those of entomology in a manner that Hicks (1997) termed "hybrid discourses" and identified as typical of students learning previously unfamiliar academic genres; (b) the tape recorder, which Jay began using in a performative way and grew to employ in the service of our data collection, ultimately assuming responsibility for all of our taping; and (c) Jay's entomology journal, which he at first used reluctantly, recruiting his cousin to do the writing, then appropriated as his own and filled with his own writing.

The week after we begin collecting together, Jay greets me with a grin, an audiotape, and a nearly full collection box. When I listen to the tape, I realize Jay had taken his pocket tape recorder out into the field with him and used it to record his entire process of collecting, not just the field notes.

The slap of footsteps hitting the earth provide the background noise as Jay, breathing fast, talks into the tape recorder, "Argh! Can't get it. Wish I could get it. Go, Jay! Here I go! Come on down. I almost caught you. Almost caught it. Dang!"

"Hi, Kathy. I just caught a red dragonfly. I was chasin' it around and now I'm downstairs in the basement. And now I have my cousin workin' with me today. Say hi."

Tasheka says, "Hi."

"Tell her your name."

"Tasheka."

Jay explains, "And she's gonna help me catch dragonflies. I just caught a big one. And I caught two red ones by a hill near my house."

Tasheka adds, "We just found a green bug."

"I caught a big green one by the light post in the garden. I caught all these today. Eighteen bugs! Can you believe that? I mean you just got to look at this big one. You just got to. I can't wait 'till you come and see them. OK, this is Jay and Tasheka reporting. Over and out."

Jay and I sit at a picnic table, entomology books spread out over its surface and his collection between us. We are trying to identify his specimens. Jay reads from a description, "Shiny brown head."

I examine a damselfly with the tweezers and magnifying glass, "OK, brown head. Ours has that."

"The thorax is brown, spotted or striped with yellow or white."

"Hmm, ours is brown."

"The females have a yellow or brown spot on wing tip and a broad brown band or black spot near base." Jay looks up from the book and pokes at the amber-colored spot on the wing tip of our specimen. "So we found it. Platbenis lydia."

"Sounds like it. Check what it says for habitat."

"Slow streams and marshes. Yup, we found it!" Jay sings a little song, "I'm lucky. I'm smart. I am just *intelligent!*"

"We just caught a bug in Tasheka's kitchen," Jay says into the recorder.

"On the windowsill of my kitchen," Tasheka adds.

"It's a real bug too, like we read in that one book," Jay explains. After a pause, he adds, "And now we're gonna hear from our sponsor, Tasheka."

Tasheka speaks in high, squeaky voice, "I like the pretty colors and stuff."

Jay imitates a slow drawl, and asks Tasheka, "A pretty lady like you wouldn't mind sharing with us, what's the most difficult part of catching these bugs and killin'em?"

"Getting them out," Tasheka answers, still speaking in a high voice.

After a brief pause, Tasheka returns with her natural voice and says, "I just caught two. And we caught this ugly one but the inside was pretty."

Jay adds, "He had blue stuff on his booty. OK, now we gotta look it up."

Jay holds our tape recorder as we work in the park. It is Tasheka's first time working with us. Jay speaks directly into the recorder, "This is Kathleen, Jay, and Tasheka talking from our bug lab headquarters at the park. What we're doing is labeling 'em. Like 1, 2, 3, 4, 5. Now we're gonna hear from our sponsor, Kathleen."

"What does that mean, I'm a commercial?" I ask.

"No, not a commercial!" Jay makes a face, then continues, "Now we're gonna hear from our *reporter*, Kathy." He whispers to me, "Now you supposed to tell 'em what you're doing."

"OK. What we're doing is giving each of the bugs a number. Then we're gonna make a chart that corresponds to the numbers and on the chart we're going to put all of the information about the bug that we know."

"Look at side of great big one you can see his veins and stuff," Tasheka points to Jay's prize dragonfly, a *Panax Junius* with a wingspan of approximately 5 inches.

I peer into the box, "Oh, what is this grasshopper leg doing all by itself?"

Jay leans over, "That's not a grasshopper leg. Whose leg is it?"

After we figure out which specimen lost its leg, we set about the serious business of making labels. Jay nominates Tasheka to do all the writing.

"No, we'll share the writing responsibilities," I clarify.

"Like every other one?" Jay asks. "But she *likes* to write!"

We take turns making the labels, and after Jay makes his first one he shows it to me, "See, I told you I couldn't write."

"What's wrong with it?" I ask him.

"It's stupid. You can't read it."

I assure him, "I can read it. It's fine."

"But you the only one," he announces, showing the piece of paper to Tasheka, who responds by reading it out loud.

"See. Everyone can read it." Jay shrugs noncommittally, and when it's Tasheka's turn to make a label, she keeps going, making several.

Jay encourages Tasheka to continue and she writes for about 20 minutes. Then Jay decides he wants to write, too. "It's not OK for her to do *all* the writing. I do wanna write *some.*"

While Jay's writing, Tasheka asks, "Do we gotta add the scientific names?"

Jay answers quickly, "Yeah. 'Cause we might say damselflies and the other people might say who knows?"

In August, we return to the university to see Harry. Jay shows him his collection proudly, opening the two cases, which are now filled with specimens, with a flourish after he sets them on Harry's desk. Tasheka hangs back shyly, standing near me.

Harry looks inside, "So do you know what you got here?"

Jay points to different specimens, "These are dragonflies and these are damselflies." For the next several minutes Harry takes Jay through the collection, and they name each specimen with its scientific and common name together. Jay points to one and says, "Now this is really a *bug*!"

"That's a true bug, exactly right." Harry nods, "When an entomologist says a bug, this is what they're talking about. Do you know what makes a bug a bug?"

Jay responds quickly, "It bites, a bug is a bug because it bites or it has pinchers things on their mouth and that design on their back."

"SLURP!" Harry makes a sucking noise, trying to give Jay a hint.

"They suck?" Jay laughs. "Oh, yeah, sucking mouth parts."

"Yup," Harry laughs, too.

"And don't they have that thing on their back?" Jay asks.

"Yup. They have like half-wings. You can kinda see, it's clear for half of it and solid up here. These are called pennetipters. Penne means half, tipter means wing."

Jay turns to me, "I told you it was a real bug!"

"Yeah, you did," I agree.

Harry looks at the collection again, "What do the numbers mean?" Jay gets out his notebook, and explains the system we've developed with corresponding numbers.

"All right," Harry nods, "so let's see this notebook."

Jay opens up the first page and takes Harry through his entries, "This is where we caught 'em, and what day it is, and if it's like warm and sunny."

"Oh, excellent!" Harry is enthusiastic, speaking quickly, "Time of day and conditions, locations. That's good, that's important, that's key. 'Cause if you just have a bug on a pin, well, that's nice, it's pretty but it doesn't have, there's no information. You don't know where you collected it, what time of year. That stuff makes your collection so much more valuable."

"We left some blank spaces in, for looking up information later," Jay continues. He is clearly very proud to have earned Harry's praise.

"That's a good idea," Harry nods his approval, "because then you can write down all the information you can about them. What kind of bug it is, how old it was. The thing about bug collecting is, unless you get mites in your collection and other bugs eat them, they'll last forever. We have some bugs in our collection that are 100 years old. A scientist went on a trip and collected bugs, wrote down all of his notes, and put 'em in our collection. And it was 100 years ago, 1898. So it's really important to have information like the year and the location and all of that stuff because 100 years from now, somebody could look at your collection and say, 'Oh that species of bug existed in that place at that time,' and that could be really valuable information."

Jay leans forward from his seat at Harry's desk, "Do you know, sometimes after they was dead they came back alive?"

"Oh no!" Harry chuckles, "And they were wiggling on the pin? That's horrible. I hate that. That means they need to stay in your kill jar longer." Harry and Jay trade collecting stories for the next several minutes, then Harry asks, "Do you know how to quickly tell damsel from dragonflies?"

"I think I know," Jay answers. "The tail is different."

"Yes, that's true but there's an even easier way. What's the most obvious difference between this one and this one?" Harry points to a damselfly and a dragonfly in Jay's collection.

"Size," Jay says quickly.

"What else?"

"Their wings stick to their back."

"Yes. Dragonflies always hold their wings out flat and damselflies fold their wings up over their back."

"They both have big old eyes," Jay adds.

"Well, do you know what they eat?"

"Mosquitoes. Kathleen said not to kill too many 'cause they eat mosquitoes."

"So if you eat something that flies fast and is small, having big old eyes to see them with," Harry pauses expectantly.

Jay finishes his statement, "Is a good thing."

I've packed a picnic lunch and we spend the next 4 hours happily hiking through a park near the university, collecting specimens at five different sites, which Harry advises Jay to identify with letters. After each insect is caught and killed, Harry places it in a small envelope made of wax paper. Before we leave each site, he shows Jay and Tasheka how to record site information on a larger envelope and then place all of the small envelopes within it. This is a much easier method than taking Jay's wooden collection boxes with us everywhere, which is what we have been doing.

When we return from hunting, Harry sets Jay up at his desk with a microscope. Jay has his insect journal and pencil out, ready. Harry slides the first specimen, a damselfly, from its cellophane envelope, and places it on the microscope tray. "OK, which things are the things that you wanna take notes on?"

Jay, seated at the desk, looks up at Harry standing next to him, "What do you mean?"

"What are some of the things you're gonna wanna remember for later?"

Harry helps Jay focus the microscope, which has two eyepieces, and continues, "You can't focus on everything at once so pick one, pick one structure. Like say just the eyes, and focus on the eyes. Let's make a list of which things you want to take note of. Which body parts do you want to remember?"

"His eyes and his body?" Jay asks.

"OK. Which part of his body, his head, his thorax, or his abdomen?"

"Is that the thorax or the abdomen?" Jay points to the thorax of the damselfly.

Harry points to each part of the insect's body, "First his head, then his thorax, then his abdomen. The thorax is where the legs are attached."

Jay ponders this decision, "His head won't change too much so I don't need to observe that."

Harry agrees, "His head won't change too much but his eyes *will* change color."

"Yeah," Jay nods thoughtfully.

"So make sure that you," Harry pauses again, waiting.

"Observe the eyes. And the thorax," Jay responds.

"Let's make a little list," Harry bends over Jay at the desk, sliding Jay's journal over to him, "Write down the places on the bug that you're gonna take notes on. So, for all of these damselflies, you're gonna write down the color of the eyes, the color of the wings, the color of the thorax, whatever you want."

Jay makes a vertical list in his journal, writing "eyes, thorax, abdomen, wings" down one side of the paper.

"OK," Harry nods, "now you have to write down each insect. This is because you've got a bunch of damselflies. So should we number the insects too?" Harry looks at the numbers in Jay's collection box, "This was place A, so maybe this is bug A34?" Jay agrees to this system and begins writing while Harry sets Tasheka up in a similar manner at a second microscope.

Jay works alone for 7 minutes, then asks Harry to point out the abdomen again. Harry takes a grasshopper from his own collection and uses it to point out the head, thorax, and abdomen. Jay returns to writing and observing for several more minutes, then turns to Harry again, "Don't we have to write the date?"

"Nope. We recorded all that stuff. Remember this is place A, right? So we have all that stuff under place A." He peeks over Jay's shoulder to his notebook and notices that Jay is writing in full sentences, "You don't have to write that for each one. See, suppose you're gonna wanna come back and identify these in the future. What are you gonna wanna know? You gonna know what color were the eyes, what color were the wings, so you don't have to write it out in sentence form. You can just take notes for yourself and say thorax, green; eyes, green."

"All right." Jay nods, "But I'm gonna finish this one 'cause I already started it."

"It's your notebook. You can make as many scratch marks as you want," Harry advises.

There was a distinct difference in the character of the interactions that Harry was able to have with Jay and those that I had. Whereas Jay and I were learners entering the entomology inquiry together ("Oh, what is this grasshopper leg doing all by itself?" "That's not a grasshopper leg. Whose leg is it?"), Harry had the expertise and experience to be able to guide Jay's activity and discourse. In being so explicit about the habits of mind and practices of entomology, Harry scaffolded Jay's participation in a way that I, as a novice, was unable to do.

What does this mean for teachers engaged in guided inquiry instruction? Although a teacher might never gain the facility with the tools of a community of practice that a full-fledged member like Harry has, to guide students' inquiry the teacher must have an understanding of what those tools are, as

Sample pages from Jay's entomology notebook.

well as an understanding of what the collected knowledge (substantive understanding) of that inquiry area is. As Dewey wrote, the teacher must be able to see ahead to where the child's inquiry path may take him or her, and thus be able to guide that child along the way. Guidance or scaffolding is not an external structure or order of thought imposed on a child but a sort of map that helps the child connect where she is on her inquiry path with where she might be if she continues:

> *Guidance is not external imposition. It is freeing the life-process for its own most adequate fulfillment … Really to interpret the child's present crude impulses in counting, measuring, and arranging things in rhythmic series involves mathematical scholarship—a knowledge of the mathematical formulae and relations which have, in the history of the human race, grown out of just such crude beginnings. To see the whole history of development which intervenes between these two terms is simply to see what step the child needs to take here and now; to what use he needs to put his blind impulse in order that it may get clarity and force. (Dewey, 1902/1990, p. 195)*

Dewey argued that this form of assisted observation required that teachers "psychologize" subject matter so that material was developed to reflect the child's interests and experiences.

This was consistent with Vygotsky's (1987) emphasis on the importance of ontological history in influencing learning and development, particularly as expressed through his constructs of spontaneous and scientific concepts. For Vygotsky (1987), spontaneous, or everyday concepts developed from humans' concrete activity "outside any definite system; it tends to move upwards towards abstraction and generalization" (p. 168). Spontaneous concepts were those derived from children's being-in-the-world and therefore influenced actions and understandings but might not have been raised to consciousness. In contrast, scientific concepts began with the abstract, verbal definition and "as part of an organized system, this verbal definition descends to the concrete" (p. 168). Scientific concepts were thus distinguished by their expression within a "system of relationships of generality" (p. 236). Vygotsky recognized scientific concepts as part of a symbol–symbol relation, whereas spontaneous concepts develop directly from experience with material reality.

From the perspectives of these theorists, then, Jay and I were both engaged in a dialectic between our own concrete experiences and understandings, experienced both prior to and while engaged in our entomology inquiry, and the agreed-on conventions and practices of entomologists. Although we tried to scaffold ourselves (and each other) through reading texts, Harry was able to facilitate the dialectic much more effectively because he could, as one further along the path, see where we needed to turn.

15

"Church Is Not a Game!"

When I pull into Jay's gravel driveway, I see him standing near the shed, his insect collecting equipment gathered near his feet and his field guide in his hand. Jay steps toward the car eagerly and has the passenger door open almost before I'm parked. Equipment in the trunk and Jay buckled into the passenger seat, we are quickly on our way to Axleton Park. Jay pulls a blue flyer out of his field guide and waves it toward me as I drive, "I have something that I want you to go to."

"Oh, yeah? What is it?"

"It's Church Fest! See, this even has the directions on it." Jay points to the text printed at the bottom of the blue flyer.

I knew that Jay's church played a very important role in his life, and I was touched that he invited me into this context that was so personally important to him. I also wondered how Jay's skills in oralcy supported his participation in this context. Early in my collaborative work with Jay, I had shared my observations about Jay's ways of interacting with text with his uncle, Bruce. Bruce later reported that he noticed Jay used the same approach, mediating his understanding of written text through oral interactions, during Bible study at the church. Although I wouldn't be attending Bible study with Jay, perhaps I could gain some further understanding of who he was by observing him in this context. Jay's invitation to his church picnic was an opportunity, I hoped, to learn more about his participation in another discourse community outside of Laura's classroom, one that held personal meaning and interest for him.

I was unsure whether the picnic was a public event and called Jay's grandmother, Jennifer, to confirm that it was appropriate for me to attend.

Unaware of Jay's invitation, Jennifer chuckled a bit when I told her and as-
sured me that I was welcome. She also gave me directions to Safe Haven
Church of God in Christ, Jay's church. His great-grandfather founded Safe
Haven in the 1950s, and its first location was a rented building in Andover
City. After several years, Jay's family was able to purchase a vacant church
in a small town approximately 20 miles southeast of Axleton, and this is
where I drove for the picnic.

Safe Haven is located in a neighborhood of a single-family homes with
small yards. Next to the church is a vacant lot that Jay's uncles have turned into
a grassy playground, and when I arrive at 1:00 in the afternoon the yard is full
of children playing a game that looks like tag. The street in front of the church is
blocked off with white saw horses so I park down the block. As I walk up to
Safe Haven I am aware that, although both Black and White residents of the
neighborhood are out in their yards, I am the only person at the picnic who is
not Black. A group of young adults, dressed in matching purple t-shirts and
denim shorts, are rehearsing a step routine in the open area of the street. Their
shirts pledge their allegiance to a church in a neighboring town. I pause briefly
to watch them, mesmerized by the rhythm and joy of their dancing.

As I approach the church, Jay's Aunt Cecilia and Uncle Bruce welcome
me and introduce me to the other adults, Jay's other aunts and uncles, who are
gathered in lawn chairs and standing in groups outside the front entrance of
the church. I learn that Jay's great grandmother has 12 children, and they are
nearly all present with their families. Jay comes running up to greet me then,
breathless and excited. He stops just short of hugging me and seems really
happy that I am there in time to see the step competition and have brought my
camera to take pictures of the drill team. "Come on see us practice!" he urges,
drawing me toward the group of children entering the church.

Jay's Aunt Georgia stands at the front of the church in a white shirt and
shorts, a whistle around her neck. The Safe Haven drill team, Jay's cousins,
line up in the wide center aisle, rows of wooden pews on either side of them.
"Act like soldiers!" Georgia tells the children, who square their shoulders
and stand up straight. Jay helps his younger cousins line up, straightening
the lines. The children are all dressed in white t-shirts. When Georgia blows
the whistle, the routine begins. The children burst into song, accompanied
by their rhythmic clapping and stepping:

> Blessed.
> Blessed.
> We're blessed in the city,

We're blessed in the fields.
We're blessed when we come and when we go.
We have passed every struggle,
The devil is defeated,
We are blessed.

Jay grins through the entire routine, his body a blur of energy and movement. He appears totally in his element: moving, clapping, stepping, and singing in perfect rhythm in a manner so joyful I am suddenly reminded of our first day chasing insects in the park, Jay grinning and running with his net raised in the air.

The Safe Haven drill team runs through two different routines several times each. When the younger children step out of line or become off rhythm, Jay steps over and quietly corrects them. He is one of the oldest and tallest children in the group. Finally they are ready for their public performance, and the children spill out of the church to get a lemonade before finding a seat on the curb to watch the visiting team dance first.

The visiting team is significantly older than Jay's team and it is evident that the churches have combined for other events in the past as people call and greet each other again. During their performance, members of Jay's church call out their support ("You go!" "Break it down, girl!") and clap in rhythm to the steppers. When it's time for his team to perform, Jay again grins the whole time he dances, clearly having a great time. The visiting team lines the curb and calls out their support while the children dance. When they are finished, all of the children are served ice cream cones.

The rest of the afternoon is consumed by relay races, a three-legged race and numerous games of tag spontaneously organized by the children. Jay's aunts organize the races and award candy to the winners. Jay's athleticism serves him well and he wins several races. Jay's uncles are in charge of the grill and cluster around it, cooking hot dogs and hamburgers. Paper plates, cups, napkins, lemonade, potato salad, and macaroni salad are set out on a folding table near the grill. After the children eat, Jay's Aunt Georgia blows her whistle and commands their attention again. The final game, she announces, will be a scavenger hunt—the winner will be the child who finds and picks up the most trash from around the grounds of the church. Children immediately scatter around the yard, snatching up napkins, cups, candy wrappers, and any other trash they can find.

Jay races off with them, then returns in a moment. "You said the winner finds the most trash?" he checks with his aunt. She nods assent, and Jay breaks into a grin. I can all but see the wheels turning in his head—something is up but I don't know what. Jay turns quickly and marches around the corner of the building. He returns with his arms wrapped around a giant clear plastic trash bag, full of the day's waste, which he has pulled from the metal trash can behind the building. He grins and marches down the center of the street, where the drill team marched earlier, hugging the bag of trash close to him. "You said the winner's got the most trash! Guess I'm the winner!" he announces to the adults lining the street. His aunts and uncles chuckle and grin, "That boy!" Although they clearly appreciate Jay's sense of humor, they also insist on his following the implicit rules of the contest, and Georgia sends him marching back to return the plastic bag to its container. Jay grumbles a bit over losing the contest but grins all the while, cutting his eyes over to the adults as he passes them, making sure his performance is appreciated. He seems more concerned with having his wit acknowledged than with getting the candy prize.

Jay's great-grandmother, Lillian, observes the festivities from a chair in the shade in the entrance of the church. When the stepping performances and races are over and Jay goes off to play tag with his cousins, I sit down with Lillian. She is nearing 80 years old, having moved north from Mississippi with her husband when she was 17, because her brother, whose move preceded hers, told her of work opportunities in the steel mills. Her husband subsequently got a job working for Henderson Steel in Maple Cove. Lillian and her husband lived briefly in both Maple Cove and Anderson City but she really didn't like "the city" and so they decided to move "out to the country." They built a house "about 10 miles from Axleton." She describes raising 12 children in that house, and emphasizes that four of her daughters have now built houses on the land as well. One of her sons is the current pastor of the church, having taken on that role when her husband passed away 2 years earlier.

"How do you like living in Axleton?" I ask.

She appears startled, "I don't live *in* Axleton. I *never* lived in Axleton. We live out in the country." She smiles and adds how much she loves it there, because "it's real quiet." When I tell her about my work with Jay, she describes teaching Jay and his cousin Tasheka to read. Lillian recalls cutting out words from magazines and advertisements and pasting them to large sheets of poster paper, and she describes working with the children until they recognized all of the words and sounds.

About 6:00, as evening approaches, several of Jay's older cousins arrive in a van. They are young adults and teenagers and, after a quick meal from the grill, they move into the church. Soon the sounds of a keyboard and a set of drums fill the air. Jay comes running up to where I sit with Lillian, "Are you stayin' for the concert?" I assure him I'll stay. Several minutes later Jay's cousin Reggie, Tasheka's older brother, steps out of the church door and announces that the band is ready.

I hang back a bit as everyone enters the church, unsure of where to sit. Jay gathers up his younger cousins—the drill team—and leads them into the church, where they file into a front pew on the left side of the church. Jay sits on the aisle. I slide into the pew behind them. The other adults fill in the back and right side of the church so that the seats are approximately two-thirds full.

The plain white walls and polished wooden pews and floors reflect the late afternoon sun pouring through the windows of the church. Across the front is a low, raised platform. Reggie sits at a keyboard on the right and another of Jay's cousins sits at a drum set in the center of the platform. I sit facing the front of the church, and a green chalkboard with a list of several Bible references hangs high on the wall to my left. The wall behind the platform bears a plain stained-wood cross with a deep purple felt banner, which proclaims, "Rejoice!" in bold, gold lettering. There are no prayer books or hymnals in the pews.

Jay's uncle Joseph, the pastor, wearing his long black robe, takes his place in the center of the front of the room, in front of the platform. A microphone on a stand rests near him, and he picks it up now. Pastor Joseph welcomes everyone and then invites the band to begin to lead us in song and celebration. The music is energetic and joyful. Reggie calls out each line into a microphone mounted at the keyboard and then the congregation sings it back to him. I recognize the chorus from the drill team's performance:

> I been there,
> I done that,
> I ain't gonna do it again.
> Oh - oh
> I been there,
> I done that,
> I ain't gonna do it again.
> I ain't going back to the world.

Physical movement is an important part of participating in this song and those that follow. Jay leads his younger cousins through the concert, signaling them when to stand up, sit down, when to clap, and how to respond to the music. I, too, follow his cues, not wanting to make a mistake as Reggie urges the importance of "showing your spirit." At one point, though, Jay apparently misses a cue to stand and sits down passively during a response period. Georgia quickly moves up from the back of the church and whispers in his ear. Jay responds by quickly standing up and joining in the clapping and singing, and he signals the rest of his cousins to do so as well.

As we near the end of an hour of singing, group performances punctuated by solos from two of Jay's older female cousins, Joseph comes back up to the front and takes the microphone again. He offers a prayer of thanks, and we close our eyes and bow our heads to pray with him. He then asks if anyone would like to "testify" about God's role in his or her life. Perhaps our newcomer would like to share the story of how God brought her here today?

My heart skips a beat, just as it did when I was concerned about the response of Jay's class to his eagle oral report, except today I am worried about myself. I am the only newcomer there today—is Joseph expecting to me to step up and say something? What will I say? I begin hastily composing words of thanks for allowing me to spend the day with their family while reviewing my childhood experiences in the Catholic Church. Although I have attended many different churches since then, I am decidedly uncomfortable with the idea of public proclamations of faith. As a guest here, how do I respond? What is the appropriate way for an ethnographer to respond? In the moments of silence that follow Joseph's invitation, I open my eyes and peek out at him. However, he is looking past me, toward the back of the church. I turn and see an older, heavyset White woman with long gray hair standing at the end of the last row. Where did she come from? I notice everyone's eyes are open and they are all turned toward this newcomer.

Unlike me, the visitor has no doubt about whether Joseph means her. She steps forward and takes the microphone from his hand. In a lilting, rhythmic voice, somewhere between singing and chanting, she tells the story of a recent rainstorm. The congregation supports her with frequent "Amens" and "uh-huhs" and, once, "tell it, sister." She was driving in the storm with her two grandchildren in the back seat. The rain was pouring down, and thunder and lightning filled the sky. She was driving that brown 1979 Oldsmobile Cutlass out there (here she points out the window to a car parked at the curb) when suddenly the car died. She prayed over the car and for the safety of her grandchildren when a loud crack filled the air and a huge oak tree fell to the ground across the road—right over the very spot where she would have been had the car's engine not died. She knew, when she drove by today and heard the singing, she had to come in and give thanks.

The response to her story is tremendous. Jay's family rises up and embraces her, and amid hugs urges her to return to worship with them. As I file past her out of the church with Jay and the children, I wish for a moment that I had been the one to elicit such a response.

Many studies have documented students' out-of-school literacies and the ways in which they can intersect with school-based discourse practices in supportive or contrastive ways (see comprehensive reviews in Cazden, 1986, and Hicks, 1995). Perhaps the most often cited study was Heath's (1983) Ways With Words: Language, Life, and Work in Communities and Classrooms, *a ground-breaking ethnographic analysis of the intersections between home and school literacy practices. Over a period of 10 years, Heath worked with three groups of people, residents of Roadville, residents of Trackton, and townspeople (who did not live solely in one geographically identified community) in the Piedmont Carolinas to document the communicative practices within each group. Heath was particularly concerned with how children in each community were socialized into particular language practices, or "ways with words," and described the intimate relation between communities and literacy practices. Heath's study illustrated the complexity of interactions, particularly among participants of different communities and cultures, and the embeddedness of language practices in sociocultural contexts. Additionally it demonstrated, through her own ethnographic work and that of the students and townspeople with whom she worked, one approach to "encourag[ing] the flow of cultural patterns" between classroom and communities, and thus improving the opportunities for students of various linguistic and cultural backgrounds to participate, and succeed, in school.*

In another important project that linked home and school literacy practices, Au and her colleagues at the Kamehameha Elementary Education Program drew on the community-based discourse patterns of children who spoke Hawaiian English as their first language. They identified a discourse pattern known as "talk-story" and then developed classroom participation structures that reflected students' home discursive practices. This led them to create the experience–text–relationship model for reading instruction, and to structure classroom discussion in ways that more closely mirrored children's turn-taking practices at home (Au, 1979, 1980, 1990; Au & Jordan, 1981; Tharpe & Gallimore, 1988).

In a similar manner, Moll and his colleagues developed schooling practices that reflected Latino students' community-based "funds of knowl-

*edge" and drew on their strengths in biliteracy (Moll, 1992; Moll &
Dworin, 1996; Moll & Greenberg, 1990; Moll & Whitmore, 1993). Rather
than participation structures, however, Moll's work focused more directly
on the substantive knowledge and expertise of Latino community members,
and the way in which teachers can draw on this knowledge to enrich classroom learning (Moll, 1992). Additionally, his work related to Latino students' biliteracy emphasizes analysis of classroom activity settings that
support students in using their biliteracy "deliberately, consciously, to access and manipulate resources for intellectual and academic purposes"
(Moll & Dworin, 1996, p. 238).*

*Dorsey-Gaines and Garnett (1996) advocated consideration of the liter-
acy practices Black children bring with them to school, especially those
practices that resulted from participation in the practices of the Black
church. Dorsey-Gaines and Garnett discussed the sociohistorical development of the Black church and its literacy practices, tracing its beginnings as
"the invisible church of slavery" (p. 253). The oral discourses of the Black
church, they argued, developed out of necessity for survival, and because
written discourses were more easily thwarted. In addition to the emphasis
within the Black church on oral literacies, through practices such as
call-and-response and hymn lining, one of the most central aspects of participation in the Black church was through music, especially song, which
was always accompanied by active movement (Dorsey-Gaines & Garnett,
1996; Lincoln & Mamiya, 1990). Dorsey-Gaines & Garnett (1996) argued
for more literacy research that explicated the role of the Black church as "a
nexus of literacies in the Black community" and explored ways that schools
might draw on these literacies (p. 263).*

*Awareness of this body of literature on home and school discourses and
literacy practices perhaps heightened my focus on Jay's discursive participation in Church Fest. Certainly the discursive features identified by
Dorsey-Gaines and Garnett (1996) and Lincoln and Mamiya (1990) were
important parts of Church Fest. In church, Jay was able to draw on a range
of ways of participating, including oral and physical expression, that were
unavailable to him in Laura's classroom.*

*However, another important feature of Jay's participation in this context
was his role in the church community as compared to his role in the classroom
community. In the church, Jay was a responsible, contributing member
whose participation was valued and supported by others in the community.
He took charge of his younger cousins and was a leader. He was appreciated
for his wit and humor. In contrast, he was silenced, excluded, and ignored by*

his classroom community. Jay's case suggests that social positioning within the classroom community is at least as important as "culturally appropriate teaching" (Au & Jordan, 1981). Ladson-Billings (1995) discussed this issue in some depth, arguing that teachers who were successful in teaching and supporting Black students "believed that all students were capable of academic success," "demonstrated a connectedness with all of the students," "developed a community of learners," and "encouraged students to learn collaboratively and be responsible for one another" (pp. 478–480); all aspects that were lacking from Laura's teaching.

Shortly after Church Fest, I ask Jay, "How does participating in church compare to participating in school?" We are seated on a picnic bench at the park, his insect collection spread out around us.

"You know, it's just like a game," Jay says casually.

"Church is like a game? Or both are?"

"No!" Jay looks at me and states firmly, "Church is not a game! Period."

"School is like a game?"

"School is not a game either," Jay laughs.

"Well, what did you mean?"

"Well, they are both kinda like a game because once you get the catch of it, you know how to do it." Jay speaks slowly, trying to explain his thoughts to me.

"Oh, like the rules?"

"Yeah, the catch. You know?"

"I see. So do you think church has a similar catch or rules as school or is it different?"

"Well, it's not really, really different. We go to classes in both places."

"When like, Mrs. Bozek or another teacher is talking, and you participate in the learning, is that the same or different as participating in church?"

"Sunday morning we don't do that. Tuesday and Sunday night in Bible study we answer questions and we ask questions like school. Sometimes what they do is, they, they, um, read something out of the book and then they read a scripture out of the Bible. And then we talk on it. We read, but we don't write."

"Do you, do you like that part? When you have to say what you think it means after you read it?"

"We don't, we don't *have to,* but I usually do. I like to explain my feelings and things."

"About the reading?"

"Yeah. About the *scriptures.*"

16

"I Think That's Why We Became Very Good Friends."

The late afternoon light has already taken on a dusky hue when I pull into Jay's driveway at 4:00 in the afternoon. Since school started several weeks earlier we are back on our every-other-week after-school meeting schedule. Today our plan is not to collect insects but to work on our reading about Charles Henry Turner.

Jay's grandmother, Jennifer, greets me at the door and signals for me to follow her into the kitchen of her brand new home. It is my seventh visit since the family moved into this home, but the first time I have been invited into the kitchen. Usually Jennifer meets me in the foyer and Jay, anxious to leave, stands beside her and waits impatiently for us to exchange pleasantries.

The kitchen is decorated in soft shades of blue, which complement wedgewood carpeting in the living room, dining room, and hallway and re-mind me of the colors within my parents' home. The kitchen is immaculate, and the polished surfaces of appliances gleam in the late afternoon sun. Jennifer turns to face me, leans back against the counter, and crosses her arms, "Have you had problems with him disrepectin' you?"

I am surprised by the question. "Disrespect? No."

"Does he be back talkin', tryin' to argue with you? Asking questions, challenging you?"

"Oh, no. I've really enjoyed our time together."

"His teachers say he's been tryin' to argue with them, askin' questions, callin' out."

Jay enters the kitchen behind me, carrying his planner. He crosses the kitchen, glances over at me, and, clearly uncomfortable, hands the planner to his grandmother. She turns to face the counter and opens Jay's planner. "Hmm," she begins reading, "Fair. Made effort to stay in seat and raise hand." She turns to Jay, "Did you finish your homework?"

"Yes, Ma'am," Jay speaks clearly, and shifts his weight from foot to foot. His grandmother hands the planner back to him, and Jay leaves the kitchen without looking at me again.

Minutes later Jay and I are driving down the dirt road that leads away from his house and toward town, a road that is deeply rutted from the tires of tractors and trucks and along which I navigate my 8-year-old Nissan Sentra with caution. Too much caution, according to Jay, who regularly remarks on how slowly I travel this road. Today, though, he is unusually quiet, and I glance over at him anxiously.

"Are you OK today?"

"Yeah."

"Did something happen at school?"

"No. I had a good day today. Didn't get in trouble. Finished all my homework." He turns from the window, where he has been gazing out at the cornfields lining the road, sentinel stalks marking the boundary between the core and periphery of the community of Axleton. Jay looks over at me, "You said we could go see Mrs. Cleminson? Can we go today?"

"Well, I said sometime. I don't know if she'll have time to see us today. We really should call first." I look over at Jay, and he is slumped deeper into his seat, looking out the window again. "She may not even be there, because sometimes teachers have meetings and things right after school."

Jay does not respond for a long moment, and then mumbles, "She probably don't remember me anyway."

We are approaching the intersection where, if we are going to visit Faith at her elementary school, we need to turn off. I glance over at Jay again. He is holding his pocket tape recorder and an unwrapped tape in his hands, which are resting in his lap. I consider his grandmother's questions, Jay's desire to visit his former first-grade teacher, and his subdued mood. Clearly something unusual has happened and it is important to him that he see Faith. I put my left blinker on and pull into the turn lane. "Well, if Mrs. Cleminson isn't there, or she has to go to a meeting or go home, don't be disappointed. 'Cause we're surprising her, and she might have plans, OK?"

Jay sits up straighter, "OK."

Faith is not in her classroom when we get there, but music emanates softly from a CD player on her desk and her light brown leather satchel rests on the seat of the chair behind it. "Mozart. We used to listen to that," Jay whispers softly as he looks around the room. "Let's surprise her! I'll hide." He unwraps the new tape as he speaks and fits it into his tape recorder, stuffing the cellophane wrapper into his coat pocket and sliding himself in the space between the open door and the wall, seemingly all at once.

"OK. But remember, she might be busy. She might be in a meeting." I am standing in the middle of the room, hoping that Faith will be back soon and that Jay won't be too disappointed if she isn't. This is the second year of my work with Faith as part of a school–university research project, and as I look around, her classroom feels warm and familiar to me. Student work fills the two bulletin boards at the back of the room. Desks are arranged into three tables of eight desks each. The classroom is carpeted, and a large open area ("the big space") in front of the chalkboards provides room for large-group instruction and class meetings. Faith's desk is off to the right of this area. Low shelves and cabinets around the perimeter of the room hold an array of books and materials. A door in the far corner of the room leads to a private bathroom. The wall opposite the entrance to the classroom is lined with windows that provide a view of a plant-filled courtyard. When filled with children, Faith's classroom has the look and feel of organized productivity, with students moving about and using various facilities and tools purposefully.

"Oh, hello, Kathleen!" Faith walks into her classroom, carrying an armload of brightly colored paper that she has cut into the appropriate size for assembly into student journal covers. I remember that Faith usually begins daily journal writing with her first graders in November, and wonder if she started earlier this year because she is teaching second grade. I smile, and before I can say anything, Jay steps out from behind the door, grinning. "Well, hello there, Jay!"

"You remember me?"

"Of course I remember you! You are working with Kathleen now?"

Jay nods. "For re-search," he explains, drawing out the "e" sound. He holds his tape recorder, its little red light glowing, with his right hand and keeps it close to his body.

Faith appears unfazed by the tape recorder. She glances down at it, "Are you ready with the sound?" Jay nods, and Faith continues. "I remember the first book you read, *Teeny Tiny.*" She puts her armload of paper down and crosses over to the student bookshelf in front of her desk. It is a low, display-type shelf that holds books with their covers facing out, toward the room. Faith regularly changes the books on the shelf, which are available to the students during reading or any time when they have completed their other assignments. She pulls out *Teeny Tiny,* a picture book, and reminds Jay of how his voice would get louder as he read the end of the story to her. Jay sits down at a desk and examines the book carefully, turning the pages slowly and looking at each one. While he is engrossed in the book, Faith and I confirm our plans to meet on the upcoming Saturday to work on a conference paper.

Jay looks up, cocking his head to the side, "Is this the same?"

"Yes. Do you remember this? I'm glad you did."

"That's the first thing he said when we came in the room. 'Oh, Mozart. We used to listen to that.'"

"That was the first thing," Faith says softly. "So, what else do you remember? This is now a second-grade room."

"You're teaching second grade?" Jay's eyes widen.

"I'll teach first grade again next year."

Jay looks around again, "You gonna keep teaching after next year?"

Faith laughs, "Well, I think so. I hope so. I'm still gonna be teaching for 5, 10 years. I like kids. I miss them when I'm not teaching. And I like to remember people like you." Jay grins and I laugh, relieved to see his spirits lifting. Faith continues, "Especially when they remember me, too. You know, that's very exciting for a teacher."

"Hmm," Jay sounds doubtful.

"Hm-mm." Faith goes on, "And when you remember the book that they first read, oh, that is very, very exciting."

"Yeah. I read a lot of books now."

"Oh, good!"

"I remember, I didn't, I used to get in trouble in first grade."

"Oh, a little bit. And I think that's why we became very good friends." Faith laughs, and I join her, but Jay just grins. Faith turns to me, "So what are you up to today?"

"Well, we're on our way to McDonald's, where we're getting a snack," I explain.

"Oh, good."

"And we're gonna do some talking. We're reading, we haven't read it in a while so we need to get back to it, we're reading a book about an entomologist."

"Oh, wow. Wow."

"Um, named Charles Henry Turner."

Faith turns back to Jay, "What is an entomologist?"

"It's like, a scientist that collects bugs, and studies them, and does research. And he was the first Black man who became an entomologist," Jay explains.

"Wow." Faith sounds impressed, and Jay grins again.

"Well," I am wary of taking too much of Faith's time. "We just wanted to come in and say hi."

"Oh, I'm really glad you did. If you ever have another chance, stop by."

"I'm glad we caught you. We didn't know your schedule."

"Bye-bye, Mrs. Cleminson."

We get back in the car, and Jay rewinds the tape he has just made. Holding the player up to his ear, he plays the recording of his visit with Faith, rewinds the tape, and plays it again. He listens to the tape three times before we get to McDonald's.

Dusk is approaching as I pull into Jay's driveway. He pulls an unwrapped cassette tape from his coat pocket and places it on the dashboard. He then ejects the tape from his player and, picking up the tape from the dashboard, hands both of the tapes to me, "For your research. See you next week?"

"I think we agreed to make it every other week when school's in session, right?"

He grins. It's become something of a game between us—he pushes for more meetings and I remind him of our agreement. "Right. Week after next." He closes the car door and I watch him climb the wooden stairs to the second-floor deck and enter his house through the back.

I don't push the tape Jay gave me into dashboard player until I am on the highway, traveling smoothly and swiftly back to my own apartment in a university town nearly an hour from Jay's house. I expect to hear Jay's voice describing the insects he's collected lately. Instead, a woman's voice fills my car.

"You all sit over there. Right there." There is a screech made by metal furniture scraping across a linoleum floor. "We called you because we thought it'd be best if we all got together to try to help Jay have a successful school year. He's starting off sixth grade having some problems. Self-control. He's quite disruptive. He'll call out, or not raise his hand. Constantly just talkin' and whatnot, and comments and whatever. So we're trying to, you know, get some help in curbing that. So we can get some instruction done in the classroom without any disruptions."

As a second woman begins speaking, I realize I am listening to a tape of a conference with Jay's sixth-grade teachers. "And it's also happening with, she has him half the day and I have him the other half, and it's definitely in my classroom also. Jay has a lot of good ideas. Sometimes, you know, like I

I would think so —

said, he likes to share his ideas, and I don't mind him sharing those with us, but there's an appropriate way to do that, you know ... "

The teacher in my heart urges me to call Jay, to call his teachers and his grandparents, to become even more involved than I already am; the researcher in my head reminds me that I am supposed to maintain "objectivity," that it isn't my job to interfere, that maybe I am already too close to this little boy to conduct "good research."

I try to honor both voices. I sit down and transcribe the tape. Then I write a journal entry about my interactions with Jay that day, and record my reactions to the tape. Then I turn off my computer, and I call Jay's grandmother.

Five days later, on a bright fall morning with a touch of apple-pie crispness in the air, I am standing on Jay's back porch. The leaves on the oak and maple trees bordering the expansive backyard are just beginning to change, providing only a hint of the riotous reds and golds to come. It won't be long before our insect hunting is curtailed by frost, I think, as I knock on Jennifer's door.

I have with me a videotape containing excerpts of Jay's participation in guided inquiry (the same tape I showed his classmates, Ned and Maria), a transcript of the tape (the same transcript I shared with Laura), and several artifacts of my work with Jay, including the eagle report, our poems, Jay's insect journal, and photos of us collecting insects. I am hoping to discuss my work with Jay and the sixth-grade parent–teacher conference with Jennifer. I want to share my observations of Jay and to learn from her understanding of him. I am also hoping that Jay's work with me will provide counter-evidence to the way he was portrayed by his sixth-grade teachers.

We sit down together on the couch in the living room of Jennifer's new home. As usual, everything is spotless. A wicker basket of *Jet* and *Ebony* magazines sits next to the fireplace, directly across from us. Jennifer, unsurprised by the existence of the audiotape, is not interested in watching the videotape, or in reading the transcript. She is, however, very excited about the eagle report and the grade on it, an A+, and asks how Jay wrote it. I explain our writing process, and the use of the computer. Then I try to steer the conversation back to Jay's ways of interacting and his sixth-grade teachers' perceptions of him as disruptive.

Jennifer emphasizes that she is very concerned that Jay learn discipline because he will need this for college. When I point out how disciplined he is in church, Jennifer explains that when Jay knows what's coming next he can participate appropriately. Jennifer repeats the idea she voiced in the parent–teacher conference, that Jay should practice his handwriting. I reply that in my view it is important that Jay not be made ashamed of his handwriting. When I suggested that perhaps his teachers could consider some of his strengths, Jennifer insists that it is Jay who needs to change to accommodate the expectations of his teachers.

Jennifer returns to the theme of respect: "His thinking is good. He can think. He just needs to learn respect. He speaks out too much in class, and that's disrespect." She emphasizes that she does not want him tested or identified. "There ain't nothin' wrong with his thinking, his learning. He just needs to learn respect."

When her sister, Tasheka's mother, arrives, Jennifer becomes more light-hearted and begins to describe Jay's growing-up years. She describes an award he received in first grade for speaking out in class. Tasheka's mother points out that her son got a similar award in first grade. She grins proudly, "It runs in the family."

Jennifer chuckles, "Yeah, the boys in this family can talk."

On my way to pick up Jay from school, I pass the entrance to Axleton's police station, and remember my recent conversation there with Officer Butler. I first met Officer Butler, a large, friendly man in his early 30s, in Jay's classroom, when he came in with five "role models" from the high school. The high school students sat across the front of room in front of the chalkboard, and the fifth-grade students asked them questions about what high school was like. What captured my attention was Officer Butler's response to a question Jay asked: "Are there any bullies in the school?" One of the high school students, a boy, replied that there are some gang members at high school. Officer Butler extended this answer with, "There are a few hard-core gang members who moved from Andover City or something like that but in Axleton there are mostly wannabe's."

I wondered about this assertion, and about what it might mean for Jay and his experiences in Axleton as a child "from Andover City." I scheduled an interview to ask Officer Butler more about his perspective on Axleton. When I arrived at the police station for the interview, Officer Butler welcomed me into the officers' break room and reached into a bowl of individually wrapped caramels, the soft kind that stick to your teeth and make your jaw ache. Removing a handful, he offered them to me and seemed disappointed when I turned them down. He commented that the children love for him to bring them candy, and he always has some tucked into his uniform pockets when he visits the school. He loves working with children in the Axleton schools, he added, although he always wears his gun belt into the classrooms because "it's best to be armed when I go in there, with all the stuff that's been happening in schools these days." He unwrapped a caramel and popped it in his mouth, fingering the cellophane wrapper between his fingers as he continued talking.

The DARE program was Officer Butler's special project, and he was eager to talk about it. He asserted that it had been quite successful in Axleton, that "gang activity and marijuana use would be much higher without DARE." He stressed that the crime in Axleton stems primarily from "spillover" from Andover City, gang members "who come down here to try to recruit members." Officer Butler asserted that there are no real problems in Axleton related to economic or racial diversity, "Everybody sees each other just as people. We don't see color."

The rest of Main Street holds reminders of similar conversations I've had in the last month: the office of the *Axleton News*, where I spoke with the associate editor; the coffee shop, where I met with the town historian and former police chief; the turn that will take me down the street to the school board offices, where I met with the superintendent; the park constructed with tax money collected from the largest industry in town, Axleton Plastics, in whose plant I met with an engineer and a community relations manager (Jay's grandmother, Jennifer, recently retired from this plastics plant); and, right on Main Street, the restored historical home that is now the site of Axleton Community Aid, where I met with the director, Ruby Lee.

Although I hoped to find general themes in these interviews, which were designed to elicit each person's perspective on Axleton, I was surprised by the lack of diversity in the ways people described Axleton (see sample questions in the Appendix). With the exception of Ruby Lee, every person I interviewed asserted that Axleton is a small, quiet town with few problems, that people in Axleton "don't see color," and observed that the problems faced by children and teens in Axleton, as well as the crimes that do occur, are instigated by "gangs from Andover City."

Perhaps because her job for the last 22 years has been to work with those who would otherwise "fall through the cracks," Ruby Lee expressed a different view of Axleton. As director of a nonprofit agency, Axleton Community Aid, Ruby oversees 120 volunteers who help her provide services to those in need in the community. These services range from emergency food programs and various forms of counseling to "self-help" programs such as the distribution of seeds in the spring. From this perspective, Ruby described Axleton as a "community of the working poor" who are "just getting by each month." Rather than the influence of gangs, Ruby observed that it is the higher cost of living that is fanning out from nearby Andover City and exacerbating the economic problems of many families and children in Axleton. Ruby also observed that Axleton is "racially divided," and when I asked what she meant she explained that residents of the central areas of Axleton, near downtown, are nearly all White, whereas many residents of outlying areas, particularly Sanguine Hill, are Black. A volunteer at the center, an older Black woman, leaned over to us at Ruby's desk, and chuckled ruefully, "Don't no services go out to us in darky town."

That afternoon Jay and I walk down Main Street in Axleton. We've skipped McDonald's today, opting instead to go to a small ice cream shop near the park. As we enter the shop, I point to the red brick building next door, a funeral parlor. "Did you know," I ask him, sharing knowledge I had recently gained from the town historian, "that building was Axleton's first doctor's office?"

"Yeah, my great-grandpa told me. He told me lots of stuff. Did *you* know not too many Blacks lived here then? We were almost the first, I think." Jay slides into a booth as he finishes.

After we get our cones, I ask Jay about the tape of the meeting with his sixth-grade teachers. He looks both angry and sad, and says softly, "Teacher said I was wrong for yelling out." He pauses, then looks away from me, down at the table, and adds softly, "Maybe she thinks I'm dumb."

"Did you think it was wrong to yell out?"

"No."

"Why?"

"'*Cause!*" Jay looks as upset as I've ever seen him. "She doesn't *call on me!*"

"Is it wrong to talk when you're not called on?"

"Yeah, but, still." Jay relaxes and looks at me a bit sheepishly. He continues, some measure of confidence returned to his voice, "Sometime things need to be said. You should always say what you're thinking it if it's something good."

17

Ability Profiling
and School Failure:
Learning From Jay's Story

Society establishes the means of categorizing persons and the complement
of attributes felt to be ordinary and natural for members of each of these categories. Social settings establish the categories of persons likely to be encountered there. The routines of social intercourse in established settings
allow us to deal with anticipated others without special attention or thought.
When a stranger comes into our presence, then, first appearances are likely
to enable us to anticipate his category and attributes, his "social identity" ...
While the stranger is present before us, evidence can arise of his possessing
an attribute that makes him different from others in the category of persons
available for him to be, and of a less desirable kind—in the extreme, a person
who is quite thoroughly bad, dangerous, or weak. He is thus reduced in our
minds from a whole and usual person to a tainted, discounted one. Such an
attribute is a stigma, especially when its discrediting effect is very extensive;
sometimes it is also called a failing, a shortcoming, a handicap.

—Goffman (1963, pp. 2–3)

There are those who will read this work, and then ask, "Yes, but is Jay learning disabled or emotionally impaired?" There are others who will exclaim
fervently, "Oh, but Laura is just racist!" Both responses to Jay's story are responses I made at different times while conducting this research, and both
responses miss the opportunity to uncover and understand the complexity
of the issues raised by Jay's story. To reduce this complexity to a deficit
within Jay or within Laura is to obscure the real lessons it offers.

While working with Jay, I found myself repeatedly reflecting on my own time as a public school teacher. The year that I completed my work with Jay was the same year that the last class of freshmen I taught graduated from high school. While pouring through the artifacts of my work with Jay, I was also receiving and responding to letters from my former students. Over and over again as I analyzed and wrote about my work with Jay, my mind returned to my memories of working with them. Jay's struggle to be seen as competent mirrored the struggle of so many of my students to be seen as whole people, and in his resilience I saw reflections of their resistance to internalizing the categorical labels through which the school system, and society, defined them.

Memories of one particular conversation shaped my thinking about how Jay was perceived in school. It was lunchtime, and like many other teachers I spent this free time in my classroom, preparing for my afternoon classes. Students who wanted a quiet place to work, to help out with yearbook production, or simply a moment to talk or get some extra help frequently joined me for lunch. On this particular day Larnell, (pseudonym), a tall, athletic, articulate, and intelligent 17-year-old Black man, burst into my room, visibly upset. I had known Larnell for 4 years, initially through my work with the freshman football team and later as a student in my English and photojournalism classes. I knew him to be thoughtful, patient, determined, and extremely bright. Larnell cared deeply about the impression he made on others, and he always wore impeccably pressed dress shirts and slacks to school. Having given up football to devote more time to his studies, he also cared deeply about getting into a 4-year university. Larnell's attire, completed with a pair of elegant wire-rimmed glasses, his usually reserved demeanor, and his focus on grades, gave him the air of a scholar, and his classmates respected him as such and gave him the nickname "Doc."

"Ms. Collins!" he burst out as he tossed his usual load of books and notebooks across a nearby desk.

"What is it?" I looked up, startled by the emotion in his voice. Larnell was clearly angry, but he also looked deeply hurt and was obviously struggling to retain his composure. He took a deep breath, and began, "I got pulled over last night."

"What happened?"

Larnell sat down, and began a long story about being stopped by the police while driving a classmate to her home in a nearby affluent neighborhood. Larnell, like most of the students who attended our high school, lived in one of two very low-income neighborhoods. His friend and classmate, a 17-year-old

White woman from an affluent family, lived a new housing development. Fighting to keep his voice level, he explained that he had been "profiled."

Later that day, Larnell shared his experiences with our English class during a discussion of Lorraine Hansberry's *A Raisin in the Sun*. Waves of anger, fear, and frustration broke through the classroom as other students recounted similar stories of the ways in which they had been profiled by police, school administrators, teachers, and counselors for being either Black, Latino, male, female, an adolescent, poor, or some combination of these traits, which, in our community, stigmatized them. At 16 and 17 years old, these students expressed deeply personal understandings of the ways social positioning is enacted through daily discursive practices.

As Goffman (1963) asserted almost 40 years ago, we assign social identities to people based on how we "read" the combination of traits we observe in them—traits ranging from styles of dress to ethnicity and including, of course, their facility with various social discourses and literacies. This is a process of cognitively comparing an individual with a schema or image we have of that "type" of person, and expecting them to enact that schema. Goffman reminded us that this human impulse to categorize becomes problematic—and harmful—when the schematic lens through which we view a person is colored by deficit thinking.[1] In these cases, individuals are profiled against a schema or cultural narrative, a "stigma-picture" (Delgado, 1995) that portrays them as lacking in some way, and they are treated as such.

The assumption that informs this kind of typological thinking is that "individuals are merely errors (deviations) from an underlying, ideal type" (Gelb, 1998, p. 496). Typological thinking is an artifact of intelligence testing that underlies many approaches to schooling in the United States, including the current standards and assessment movements, which position individuals in terms of the "score" against an "ideal" norm (see discussion in Collins, Dutro, & Collins, in preparation). This typological system of social practices works to establish order by identifying and drawing boundaries between differences.

Laura can thus be viewed as acting as the agent of an institution that encourages her to "profile" her students according to their perceived abilities, a system that will rank and sort her and her school in a similar manner. The push for homogeneity in Laura's classroom might have been further exacerbated by the cultural practices of the local community. She lives, works, and

---

[1]This matter, always a contentious one in the United States, has received renewed attention since the September 11, 2001 attacks on the World Trade Center in New York City. See, for example, "Americans Give in to Race Profiling," by Verhovek (2001).

teaches in a community where student scores on state-mandated standardized tests are published in the paper and online, as well as reported on local TV. Axleton is a town where, in the words of Faith Cleminson, "If you stick out, you get squashed." When I asked her to elaborate, Faith added, "If you think outside what is normal for that community you stick out, you're weird, and it's threatening. They think that what is different should not exist."

From this perspective, it is less surprising that Laura's exclusion of Jay from full membership in the classroom community was mirrored in her exclusion of the other students who deviated in some way from her expected norms for behavior.[2] Each of the students who Laura, by the end of the year, positioned outside the core community of the classroom was described by her as "different" in some way from those who made up the core community. Here race also intersected with other ways of being different, such as class and poverty, learning differences, and physical differences (e.g., a hearing impairment). In the process of marking these students as different and subsequently assigning them to a position of failure or low achievement, Laura engaged in an institutionally and socially sanctioned form of discrimination and segregation, ability profiling. That is, she identified a deficit within each if these students that, in her view, marked them as "low ability," and assigned them to a position of marginality as a result.[3]

Jay's story also illustrates the ways in which ability profiling draws on cultural narratives and deficit discourses regarding children of color in general, and Black males in particular. From his first day in the class, Jay was excluded and positioned as different, as an outsider to Axleton who was from Andover City. One of the shared cultural narratives in Axleton is that crime, violence, and things to be feared come from gangs from Andover City. Because Andover City has a significantly higher proportion of Black residents (during the 1997–98 school year, 49% of Andover's schoolchildren were Black, as contrasted with Axleton's 8%) than Axleton, this narrative intersects with a narrative shared by the larger culture of the United States, in which young Black males are associated with gangs and perceived as dangerous.[4]

---

[2]Assuming the best interpretation of this push for homogeneity, the physical exclusion of these students could perhaps be understood as a kind of "benign exclusion" where, for their own benefit, Laura positioned these students on the margins so that she was able to get to their desks more easily. However, as portrayed in the narrative, there was no evidence that Laura did go to their desks more frequently, and ample evidence that this physical exclusion contributed to the social isolation of these students.

[3]See the discussion in Kliewer and Fitzgerald (2001) regarding disability oppression.

[4]This larger cultural narrative and the ways in which it negatively impacts the educational experiences and opportunities of Black males has been the focus of much recent attention in both the popular and academic press. See, for example "Learning While Black" by Morse (2002) and *Bad Boys: Public Schools in the Making of Black Masculinity* by Ferguson (2001).

As with all cultural narratives, there are discourses present in the community of Axleton that could be used to uphold the positioning of Andover as dangerous. Shortly after I conducted my interviews with community members in Axleton, a newspaper serving both communities ran a 4-day series focusing on "the crackdown against gang activity in the Andover City area" (Nash, 1998a, 1998b, 1998c, 1998d). Throughout the series, the title "Gangs: A Second Look" was printed below the title of each article, with the word *gangs* in red, capital letters, a knife-like slash hanging from the bottom of the *N*. The first article in this series was published on a Sunday, when the paper was assured of its largest circulation, and ran on the front page with the headline, "Police Zero in on Another Andover City Gang." Another was titled "The Night Police Became Victims." Photos of White police officers and Black community members ("a mother whose son got caught up in the allure of gangs," Nash, 1998d, p. 1) accompanied the articles. This series held the potential to validate Axleton's identification of Andover City as a place where gangs, and potential violence, crime, and danger, stem from.

Thus when Laura, not realizing Jay's deep family roots in Axleton, positioned him as an outsider from Andover City and a potential problem within her classroom community (and, "an increasing problem almost everywhere he is"), it was possible that her subsequent expectations for his behavior were influenced by her situatedness in the community of Axleton. There was evidence of this in her description of Jay as a "bad-ass" when he entered her classroom community, and in her concern that "he could so easily get caught up in a gang, or in being a bad-ass again, or, you know, going down that other path." This was also reflected in her willingness to see Jay as impaired or disabled in some way, and in her positioning of his family as deviant.

The assertion of colorblindness on the part of Axleton community members raises similar issues regarding the interrelated nature of cultural narratives and daily practices. Color blindness is also often viewed as benign, a way of demonstrating that one is not racist. However, color blindness is *blindness*—it results in not seeing the gifts offered by the uniqueness of different participants. Thompson (1998) argued that perpetuating colorblindness in teacher education programs contributes to racism and the erasure of the potential contributions of Black culture and experience:

> Politely pretending not to notice students' color makes no sense unless being of different colors is somehow shameful. Colorblindness, in other words, is parasitic upon racism: it is only in a racist society that pretending not to notice color could be construed as a particularly virtuous act. In a society that is both culturally diverse and racist, colorblindness is a willed ignorance of

color that, although well intended, insists on assimilating the experiences of people of color to that of whites. (p. 524)

Thompson brought this perspective on colorblindness to bear on an examination of theories of care. As one of three themes she identified in her critique of theories of care, Thompson (1998) asserted that a Black (womanist) standpoint recognizes that "the reference point of knowledge is not the solitary individual but the committed member of the community" (p. 536) As part of this commitment, there is along tradition of "othermothering" in the Black community. From this standpoint, Jay is lovingly cared for by an extended network of caregivers. This is very different from Laura's colorblind standpoint, from which she perceived Jay's family as deviant. Operating from a colorblind standpoint, Laura pathologized Jay's family structure, his cultural way of being.

The deficit view that undergirds this form of pathologizing is thus itself a form of oppression that contributes to the positioning of students of color in marginalized categories. Loury (2002) described this process as "discrimination in contact." The symbolic violence inflicted by the categorizing, labeling, and sorting of children is sanctioned by a system of schooling operating from a capitalistic, profit motive. The ethic of competition that informs this system is not consistent with an ethic of care. In contrast, the teaching and learning contexts in which Jay excelled were all informed by an ethic of care for him, his gifts with orality, his interests, his needs, and his social positioning as a Black child. In each of the contexts in which Jay participated successfully: (a) his use of discursive (written and oral) reasoning tools was explicitly introduced and scaffolded, (b) his attempts to participate were responded to favorably by others in the context, (c) the activities reflected community values, and (d) Jay was interested, although to a greater or lesser extent, in the focus of the activity. None of these contexts was extraordinary except that, operating from an ethic of care, they made visible the ways in which Jay was "at promise" rather than "at risk."

hooks (1994, 2001) wrote that without justice there can be no love, that oppressive relationships of any kind—within families, classrooms, schools, communities, or countries—destroy the possibilities for love. Jay's story illustrates that this relationship is synergistic and dialectical, not linear. If we—on individual and societal levels—don't act from an ethic of love, an ethic of care, we cannot achieve justice.

Epilogue

Jay is no longer the boy he was when I began this project. At 12, he is poised on the brink of adolescence, and stands at almost exactly my height (he would claim he's actually taller than me because I usually wear shoes with a heel). In our conversations, his former exuberance is tempered with a quiet maturity, and our talk is more liberally peppered with reflective pauses. Jay continues to collect insects, and is a member of the Young Entomologists Society. He also continues to love the blues, and recently started saxophone lessons. He is absolutely thrilled with the sound of his own music.

After reconnecting with his first-grade teacher, Faith Cleminson, Jay wrote to her and they have continued to correspond. Unaware of Jay's own description of school and church ("Well, they are both kinda like a game because once you get the catch of it, you know how to do it"), Faith reported to me that she responded to Jay and told him that school "was like a game" and that he would succeed by "figuring out the rules of your teacher."

I am thrilled that two of them are corresponding, especially because I can no longer be present in Axleton for Jay. Jay is working on compiling a portfolio, a project suggested by Dr. Jean McPhail, of the ways in which he learns best. I have sent him documentation of our work together to include in this portfolio. Ultimately our goal is for him to share this with his teachers.

The day before I left for California, over lunch at McDonald's with his cousins, Jay and I celebrated his birthday and reflected on our work together. I asked him what lessons he wanted teachers to learn from our work. He paused thoughtfully, then said, "Tell 'em kids might not learn anything if you just give 'em a paper and tell 'em what to do. They need to express their feelings. And they should have fun. There's no reason to be stuck in the classroom all the time. Like when we did the bugs, that was tight." Jay paused again, then looked at me and smiled, "That's a way to go. You're tryin' to make a difference in school."

Before leaving, we composed another blues poem, which Jay then stood up and performed (flamboyantly) for his cousins. He composed the last verse spontaneously during his performance:

> I was walkin' in the rain.
> I was walkin' in the rain.
> Just felt so lonely,
> I thought I'd go insane.
>
> I got the blues. ((simulated saxophone solo))
> I got the blues. ((simulated saxophone solo))
> The saddest, bummiest, wet-head,
> Ain't got no umbrella blues.
> ((simulated saxophone solo))
>
> Ain't got no place to go.
> Ain't got no place to go.
> Ain't got no friends to see.
> And now I'm soaked.
>
> I'm at McDonald's with Kathy,
> She's making me really happy.
> We're gonna be friends forever,
> Don't ever say never.

Appendix: Approaches to Inquiry, Analysis, and Representation

Clearly, when I observed, experienced, recorded, interpreted, and wrote Jay's story, it was not only through the lenses of social constructivist theory, but also through a personal lens ground from my own experiences. In this sense, all research is the construction of an author or authors, an *interpretation* of some set of data, even seemingly transparent statistical analyses. The questions we ask, those that awake us in the night and move us to conduct research, are borne in our hearts and motivated by our own interests and experiences. As asserted by Coles (1997), "We notice what we notice in accordance with who we are" (p. 2). More so than any other work I've conducted, this research—both in its foci and its methods—represents who I am in the world, what I care about, and the changes I want to facilitate in education and in society.

Inherent in my research with Jay was a tension between my position and role as "researcher" and my concern regarding the effects of educational exclusion on Jay and his opportunities to participate successfully in school. I was faced with a series of decisions regarding whether to behave as a distanced researcher or as an advocate with the responsibility to work for social justice, a responsibility Smith (1999) identified as endemic to all research conducted with historically oppressed peoples. My teacher sensibility clashed with my researcher sensibility on more than one occasion during this work, and these tensions are made visible throughout the narrative. In this appendix, I discuss these tensions explicitly and explain my decision-making processes.

METHODS OF DATA COLLECTION

My work with Jay spanned 18 months, during which I spent an average of 1 day a week with Jay and additional time learning about his community. In total, I spent approximately 700 hours collecting data in Jay's school, home, and community. My approaches to data collection were informed by qualitative inquiry, particularly case study designs that draw on a broad range of data collection methods to understand a single case (Stake, 1994). Although this was not an ethnographic study in the sense that I was engaged in intervention as well as in conducting research, my data collection procedures as I sought to understand the cultures and practices of Jay's classroom, school, church, and town communities were informed by ethnographic and anthropological approaches to inquiry. My specific methods of data collection included observation and field notes; video and audiotaping; structured, unstructured, and stimulated recall interviews; collection of textual and graphic artifacts (e.g., the community newspaper and Jay's school work); still photography; and participant observation in classroom, community, and church events.[1]

After the guided inquiry program of study, which lasted 11 school days, I asked Jay if he would participate in an interview about his participation. This was a stimulated recall interview in which I selected videotaped excerpts that depicted the range of his participation in the floating and sinking inquiry. While viewing the tape with him, I asked Jay to comment on three questions after each clip:

1. What were you thinking during this activity?
2. Do you think the responses of the other people to what you had to say in this clip were helpful to your thinking? Why or why not?
3. How did you experience the activity represented in this clip? What did you like? What did you not like? Why?

---

[1]In addition to the 700 hours of data collection described here, I also spent time with Laura as part of our work together as members of the Guided Inquiry Community of Practice. These meetings provided unstructured occasions for me to speak with Laura about my work with Jay, and structured occasions to examine and reflect on the participation of children with special needs in guided inquiry instruction. All of these meetings were videotaped.

After Jay viewed all of the clips, I asked him to respond to several additional questions:

4. How is learning by investigation similar to or different from other learning experiences you've had?
5. How does this type of learning suit you? What type of learning do you like best?
6. What do you enjoy about learning by investigation? What is difficult about this type of learning?

I videotaped this conversation with Jay. Two weeks later, I met with Jay again and we reviewed the transcript of the interview together. At that time, Jay suggested that we meet with two other students in class, his partner, Ned, and a girl named Maria, because he thought their questions had been really helpful to him. Jay and I subsequently repeated the stimulated recall interview (using the same questions) with these two students, and I videotaped this interview as well.

When I began documenting Jay's perspective on his participation, I hoped that sharing his perspective with Laura would support our collaborative reflection on her teaching, particularly her interactions with Jay. Increased understanding of Jay's perspective on his participation in GIsML contexts would, I hoped, motivate Laura to consider the ways in which different instructional and interactional contexts shaped her interpretation of Jay's ability, achievement, and identity. I thought that this research project could interrupt the institutional biography of Jay as a child with a problem. At the very least, I was sure that Laura would see him differently.

It became clear, however, that Laura's assessment of Jay was unlikely to permanently change based only on my work with Jay relative to GIsML instruction. Rather, it seemed to fluctuate and change in response to the contexts in which they both participated. I wanted to further understand the contextual influences on Laura's assessment and interpretation of Jay's participation. I also wanted to learn more about those contextual features that influenced Jay's own understanding of his participation. Therefore, after Laura's guided inquiry investigation concluded, I continued to videotape, 1 day a week, Jay's participation in other instructional contexts.

The days I videotaped the instruction in Laura's classroom varied each week according to Laura's schedule, but were most often Wednesdays. I began in February and filmed once a week until school ended in June. Each time I taped the entire school day, beginning before the first bell and stopping only after all the children had gone home for the day (Erickson, 1992). During these days of taping I tried to engage Laura in reflection regarding Jay's participation, and we had several informal conversations at times when the students were out of the classroom. In addition, at the end of each day of taping I asked Laura to reflect on the typicality of the day's events and interactions. I videotaped all of these informal conversations with Laura.

During the same time period, at Jay's suggestion, I continued to meet with him once a week after school. I videotaped these meetings as well. We began our work together by working on a research report that he was assigned by Laura. At this time, I loaned Jay a pocket tape recorder as part of a writing strategy. After that, we moved on to composing blues poetry and songs, which were particular interests of his. During this time, Jay brought me a tape, which he had recorded at home. His spontaneous observations of insects, recorded on the tape, launched our entomology inquiry, which we continued over the summer and the following fall. Our entomology work was documented through audiotapes, still photographs, and journal entries, which I completed when I returned home after each insect hunting adventure.

As my relationship with Jay deepened, I learned about his personal and family histories. I had the opportunity to conduct informal interviews with his aunt and uncle, his cousin, his great-grandmother, and his grandmother. These were open-ended interviews without formal prompts, focused on learning about Jay's personal and family history, and I documented them with field notes. I also had the opportunity to attend a day-long picnic and service at Jay's church, which I documented with a journal entry written afterward.

During my observations of Jay at school, an Axleton police officer, Officer Butler, regularly visited the class as part of a drug prevention program. In his conversations with the students, he characterized the crime in Axleton as committed by "outsiders" and "gang members" from Andover City. Early in my work with Laura, she had emphasized that Jay was an outsider to Axleton, and that he was from Andover City. What was it like for Jay to live in a community where the negative influences were labeled as coming from the city he came from himself? Based on these conversations with Laura and Officer Butler, I wanted to learn more about the community of Axleton and what it was like for Jay to live there. I also wondered about the relationship between the community of Axleton and the schools. I set out to learn about Axleton's history and culture through semistructured interviews with community leaders (Officer Butler, the newspaper editor, the school superintendent, two community-relations managers at the largest industry in town, the town historian, and the leader of a community aid program). Each interview was guided by the same set of questions, which I adjusted slightly to make them specific to each person. I documented these interviews with field notes and later analyzed them for themes. An example of the questions appears here:

Ruby Lee
Axleton Community Aid
June 8, 1998

1. How long has Axleton Community Aid existed?
2. What is its role in the community?
3. What is your role? How long have you worked for Axleton Community Aid?
4. Based on your experiences working for Axleton Community Aid, what are your perceptions of Axleton as a community?
5. What effects do you think Axleton Community Aid has had?
6. What relationship, if any, does this organization have with the school system?
7. What is your sense of the ways in which people of different racial and/or economic backgrounds relate to each other in Axleton?
8. Do you live in Axleton? What do you think life is like for children who grow up in Axleton?

To search for confirming and disconfirming evidence relative to what I learned through the interviews, I also conducted textual analyses of the town's historical documents and newspapers. The town of Axleton was first settled in the late 1700s, and first became a town in 1831. The town library has maintained a reading room with historical documents dating back to that time, including personal items, such as journals and letters of community members, as well as "official" documents, such as the charter for Axleton's first school, a one-room log structure built in 1837.

In addition to the data sources already described, my unimagined portrait of Jay was also informed by data collected independently by him. Early in our work together, Jay kept a written journal, which evolved into audio recordings of his thoughts about school that he recorded at home at the end of each day. Jay also recorded his independent entomology work. Working with his cousin, he spontaneously composed and recorded prayers for church and blues songs and poetry. As our relationship evolved, Jay took increasing responsibility for what would be documented in his story.

NARRATIVE ANALYSIS

"Romantics in science," wrote Luria (1979), "want neither to split living reality into its elementary components nor to represent the wealth of life's concrete events in abstract models that lose the properties of the phenomena themselves" (p. 174).[2] In his own work in the romantic tradition, *The Mind of a Mnemonist* and *The Man With a Shattered World,* Luria drew on the tools of observation, description, and narrative to paint "unimagined portraits" of "an individual and the laws of his mental life" (1968/1987, p. 178). His view was that science is about exploring relationships, and not about observing objects, events, or psychological phenomena in isolation:

> The more we single out important relations during our description, the closer we come to the essence of the object, to an understanding of its qualities and the rules of its existence. And the more we preserve the wealth of its qualities, the closer we come to the inner laws that determine its existence.... When done properly, observation accomplishes the classical aim of explaining facts, while not losing sight of the romantic aim of preserving the manifold richness of the subject. (pp. 177–178)

Luria's writing was particularly inspiring for me as I pondered how to tell the story of my experiences with Jay, my 11-year-old coresearcher, subject, informant, and friend. The more common models of research and academic writing I tried out seemed to peel away the richness of Jay's life and experiences, and to privilege the "abstract models" Luria wrote of over the complexity of the "living reality" of my time with Jay. Reading Luria's work made it clear that the story of my explorations with Jay was best told in the tradition of romantic science, drawing on the tools of narrative analysis. Only narrative analysis truly expresses the layers of complexity inherent in Luria's (and my own) views of science; that is, the observation and exploration of relationships and not of decontextualized phenomena or of isolated "subjects."

As I searched for additional models of romantic science, I was further inspired by the work of neurologist Sacks, who also acknowledged an intellectual debt to Luria. Sacks strove to construct cases that include the personal histories of his patients, and of his time with them. He asserted that we need narrative cases to understand the lived experiences of people. "To restore the human subject at the center—the suffering, afflicted, fighting human subject—we must deepen a case history to a narrative or tale: only

---

[2]Luria credited German scholar Max Verhorn with developing the terminology "romantic" and "classical" science. Verhorn, Luria (1979) noted, asserted that these two orientations not only described "the scholar's general attitude toward science but his personal characteristics as well" (p. 174).

then do we have a 'who' as well as a 'what,' a real person, a patient, in relation to a disease—in relation to the physical" (Sacks, 1970, p. viii). Sacks's argument for employing the tools of narrative to inform medical research applies to education as well: we need more work that restores the human subject to the center of our inquiries.

Romantic science as practiced by Luria and Sacks illustrates the appropriateness of narrative analysis for research that seeks understanding of human agents in relationship with their worlds. Narrative or "storied" analysis is a form of textual representation that both positions the human subject at the center of inquiry and provides a way for investigators to locate themselves as the interpreters and coconstructors of the research story. In this spirit, I tell the story of my time with Jay, presenting an "unimagined portrait" that provides a view of the relationships between Jay and the teaching and learning contexts of his life. Through Jay's story, we witness the contextualized, jointly created, and contested nature of three aspects of subjectivity or personhood: ability, identity, and achievement. As the writer of the story, my interpretations and observations of Jay are grounded in my roles as coresearcher, teacher and friend. In my role as narrator, I am able to make visible the challenges and opportunities I faced in this work, and the decisions I made in response to them. In addition, narrative analysis is the only form of academic writing that comes close to depicting the kind of dynamic interdependence of relationships posited by sociocultural theory. As noted by Polkinghorne (1995), "narrative is the linguistic form uniquely suited for displaying human existence as situated action" (p. 5).

Polkinghorne (1995) identified two broad categories of narrative research, *analysis of narratives* and *narrative analysis*.[3] Elsewhere, Polkinghorne (1988) made a similar distinction between *descriptive* and *explanatory* narrative inquiry. Polkinghorne (1988; 1991; 1995) argued that both analysis of narratives and narrative analysis rest on the assertion that constructing a narrative is a meaning-making, analytical process (see also Bruner, 1986; 1996 on narrative cognition and self). When a researcher conducts life story interviews, for example, the researcher relies on his or

---

[3]"Narrative research" encompasses a broad range of approaches to inquiry about participants' lived experiences, including life stories, biographies, and "hybrid" approaches such as auto/biography and interpretive biography (Denzin, 1989), among others. Here I discuss those strands of this diverse body of work that are most relevant to my own work with Jay. For a discussion of narrative studies in education, especially relating to feminist epistemologies, see Casey's (1995) review of recent narrative research. Also, see Denzin's (1989) *Interpretive Biography* for an overview of the terminology associated with different approaches.

her "informant's" ability to use narrative as a tool for constructing, order-ing, and expressing the meaning of his or her life. Similarly, researchers who employ narrative analysis assume that their own construction of a plot from a variety of data is a valid way of constructing and expressing their in-terpretation of the data. Polkinghorne (1988) contended that "the basic fig-uration process that produces the human experience of one's own life and action and the lives and actions of others is the narrative" (p. 159).

According to Polkinghorne (1995), the purpose of descriptive narrative in-quiry (analysis of narratives) is to identify and describe the features of narra-tives expressed by an individual or group. This form of inquiry begins with narratives as data and "produces paradigmatic typologies or categories" (p. 5) of those narratives through analysis. However, even among scholars whose work falls into the same general category of analysis of narratives, the type, degree, and focus of such analysis varies widely. For example, within educational research, a strand of descriptive narrative inquiry has recently emerged that places less emphasis on identifying the features of narratives and more emphasis on exploring the functions of narrative discourse within specific classroom communities (cf. Hicks, 1994; Kyratzis & Green, 1997).[4] What unites these studies is that their data consist of narratives.

In contrast, studies that employ narrative analysis draw on a variety of data, including "actions, events, and happenings, but *whose analysis pro-duces stories* (e.g., biographies, histories, case studies)" (Polkinghorne, 1995, p. 6; italics added). Its purpose is to "explain through narrative why something happened" (Polkinghorne, 1988, p. 161). The "why" is of course the researcher's interpretation of the data, as represented through the story. Therefore, the process of emplotment is the primary tool of narrative analy-sis. In narrative analysis, diachronic data are integrated through the devel-opment of a plot, which depends on hermeneutic movement between the data and the developing plot. Polkinghorne (1995) noted that, "the final story must fit the data while at the same time bringing an order and meaningfulness that is not apparent in the data themselves" (p. 16).

Although the data I collected in my work with Jay (described earlier) in-cluded dialogues in which participants created narratives, and I could therefore have conducted a descriptive analysis of these narratives, the form of analysis I employed is narrative analysis. This form of analysis is consistent with my in-quiry regarding the interaction of context and the coconstruction of Jay's abil-

---

[4]For a recent and informative collections that include a wide range of approaches to and perspec-tives on narrative inquiry, see *Narrative in Teaching, Learning, and Research* (McEwan & Egan, 1995) and *Representation and the Text: Reframing the Narrative Voice* (Tierney & Lincoln, 1997).

ity, achievement, and identity. As noted earlier, through emplotment and narrative configuration, narrative analysis seeks to understand and represent human action in context (Polkinghorne, 1995). Therefore, this method of analysis is also consistent with the goal of sociocultural theory.

Further, in an effort to represent postpositivistic epistemologies regarding knowledge generation, such as social constructivist and sociocultural perspectives, Polkinghorne (1997) asserted that qualitative researchers should employ narrative analysis to represent the diachronic (as opposed to synchronic) unfolding of events in time. Drawing on Bourdieu (1977; 1990), Ricoeur (1984; 1992), and Bruner (1990), Polkinghorne argued that qualitative research follows the logic of practice and that narrative is the form most suited to capturing and expressing this logic. Given the congruence between the goals of sociocultural theory, those of narrative analysis, and my own goals for this inquiry, narrative analysis is a clear choice for this work. In addition, as noted in my discussion of sociocultural theory earlier, the unit of analysis for a study informed by this perspective is the agent acting with a cultural tool. Narrative analysis is also well-suited for my research because it supports such a unit, without "split[ting] living reality into its elementary components" (Luria, 1979, p. 174).

In an argument similar to Polkinghorne's (1997), Zeller (1995) contended that although many educational researchers have rejected positivistic epistemologies, their writing is still structured by the discourse conventions of this approach to research. Drawing on Brazerman (1987), she identified these conventions and asserted that they were designed to give the appearance of objectivity (see also Marshall & Barritt, 1990). Narrative analysis, she argued, provides a way of presenting nonpositivistic, naturalistic research that is more reflective of the underlying assumptions regarding objectivity and causality of this form of research:

> Naturalistic researchers, who see objectivity as an impossible goal, reap a second advantage in constructing case narratives: they can depict clearly their own interaction with the site and the resulting biases. Another advantage pertains to the issue of causality: since naturalists do not accept the idea of linear causality, they can use the case report to describe or demonstrate the range of mutually shaping influences on the case. (Zeller, 1995, p. 212)

The analytic task of narrative analysis is constructing a plot that provides coherence among the data. The purpose of a plot is to illustrate a relationship among elements or events, not to simply list them. The first step in developing a plot is to arrange all of the data in chronological order, although it will not all be present in the final plot (Polkinghorne, 1995). For my study, I developed two chronologies by printing summaries of events in the narrative on index cards and then posting the index cards on two different walls of my apartment as I worked. One depicted the chronological order of my work with Jay; that is, the order in which I came to learn about the events in his life. The other depicted the "real-time" chronological order of the events in his life as he experienced them. The reason for first constructing a chronology is to make visible relationships among events that might not otherwise be apparent.

In moving from these chronologies of the data to the development of a plot, I was guided by Polkinghorne's (1995) suggestion to begin with a question such as *"Why* did *this* come about?" (p. 15, italics added). Before responding to this question, I transcribed all of the recordings I had made (video recordings were first transferred to audiotape to simplify transcription). I then reviewed all of the transcripts, as well as my own field notes and my research journal, to identify the outcomes of Jay's story.

The process of identifying the outcomes of my work with Jay was painful for me in that it forced me to recognize and acknowledge that this research had not been successful in all of the ways that I had initially hoped it would. As I described earlier, I developed this project in the context of a larger professional development effort. I had hoped that one of its outcomes would be Laura's recognition of the ways in which she contributed to Jay's demonstration of [dis]ability by designing learning contexts that did not allow him to use his intellectual and interactional strengths. This change, I had planned, would then result in her positive representation of Jay to his sixth-grade teachers and the withdrawal of her referral of him for special education assessment. Instead, one outcome of this story was Jay's continued referral for special education assessment by his sixth-grade teachers, and his continued identity within the school as "difficult." Another related outcome was my own realization of the complexity and pace of teacher change and professional development.

Careful examination of the data and the chronologies helped me to recognize another outcome of this work: Jay's own expression of his capabilities as a reader, writer, composer of blues music, and budding entomologist increased. As we worked together, Jay was more explicit about challenging the negative identities constructed about him at school, and became more active in seeking out ways to reconstruct these identities by providing evidence of his abilities.

I chose to begin the plot with a scene that suggests both of these outcomes and raises the major themes and tensions in the story. By beginning the plot in this manner, I invited the reader to ask Polkinghorne's question,

"How did this come about?" How did it come about that Jay's teachers see him as disabled, and his behavior as deviant? How did it come about that I see him so differently? How did it come about that Jay makes an audio recording of the description of himself provided by his first-grade teacher and uses it as counter-evidence to challenge the description produced by his sixth-grade teachers? The suspense these questions create was intended to propel the reader through the story.

After deciding on this scene as representative of the outcome of Jay's story, I needed to configure the rest of the plot in response to it. The next step in narrative analysis is to determine which elements of data contributed to the outcome. In selecting data to include in the plot, the writer moves recursively between the data and the plot-in-progress (Polkinghorne, 1988). In this process, I drew on both chronology charts to determine relationships between events and the outcomes of the story. In this step of the analysis I was guided by a list of emerging tensions between participants, which evolved into the identification of five interrelated themes:

- Laura and Jay ascribe to different epistemological philosophies that reflect different values regarding community and individual achievement, as evident in their different preferences in classroom activities.
- Laura positions Jay as an outsider (to the classroom community and the community of Axleton) very soon after his arrival; this colors her expectations of him and her assessments of his work and behavior as "different" (identification as EI or LD).
- As a result of this positioning Jay is increasingly excluded from the classroom community.
- Jay exhibits increasing awareness of the ways he is positioned across contexts and the connection to language differences; he attempts to reposition himself within the classroom community.
- In out-of-school-contexts where Jay is not positioned as an outsider (and that reflect his values and interests) he participates successfully.

I then began to construct a plot outline, moving between the plot, themes, and the data, seeking representative events and interactions that illustrated the emerging themes in Jay's story. I initially identified all of the evidence (and counter-evidence) for each theme, using colored highlighters to mark my transcripts and ethnographic video notes. I envisioned each theme as a colored strand of yarn as I did this, and pictured my task as first gathering the strands and then weaving them together to create the narrative.

I included in the plot all of the interactions I had with Laura about Jay, as well as all of the discursive interactions within out-of-GIsML contexts in which Jay was a central participant. This was possible because neither of these was a very frequent event as Laura grew increasingly reluctant to engage in conversation about Jay, and her out-of-GIsML teaching was predominantly "monologic" as opposed to dialogic. Including all of these interactions ensured that I was not just excerpting from the data those interactions that painted particular pictures of Laura and Jay. Further, I included all of the classroom interactions that might have provided support for Laura's perspective of Jay as emotionally impaired or learning disabled, such as a moment when he fell out of his chair, which Laura herself cited as evidence of her "diagnoses." Other classroom interactions represented in the narrative were selected to represent typical interactions within a range of different activity settings across Jay's school day.

In the process of constructing the plot, I was looking not only for representative elements of data, but also for elements of data that challenged the emerging relationships I was constructing. These elements of data provided "counter-evidence," which then influenced my construction of the plot as I adapted my interpretations to account for them. For example, one of the emerging themes I was documenting was a dialectical pattern of response through which Jay, Laura, and the other students positioned Jay as an outsider. This interpretation was complicated by counterevidence in the form of instances where Laura responded to Jay in an inclusive manner, such as an interaction when she laughed with him rather than disciplining or ignoring his discursive contribution.

In this example, Laura had just announced that the class would begin sharing their vocabulary homework. Each student was to go to the front and share the word they looked up, the definition they found, and a sentence that demonstrated the correct use of the word. Jay, who was supposed to go first because of the placement of his seat in the upper left corner of the classroom, appeared to ignore Laura's instructions as he got out of his seat and stood at the wastebasket with his back to Laura and the class, blowing his nose repeatedly. When her general instructions to the class elicited no response from Jay, Laura called on him directly:

Laura:	Go up to the front please.
Jay:	Me? ((*standing at the trash basket, turns to face Laura and speaks from behind a wad of tissues*))
Laura:	Yes.

Jay: While I'm blowing my nose? *((still speaking from behind a wad of tissues))*

Laura: Shall I come back to you or are you finished?

Jay: I'm finished. *((throws out his tissues, picks up his paper and walks to the front of the room))* Furious. "He gave a furious shout." Furious means a violent rage. *((pauses and looks up from his paper at the class, and gives himself a drum roll))* Dat-da-da! I got furious when I took the test.

Laura: When you took the test? The test gave you violent rage? *((laughs))*

In this interaction, Laura did not get angry or frustrated with what might have been interpreted as Jay's bids for attention or flamboyant behavior. Rather, she joined in his performance, publicly recognizing and communicating her appreciation of his sense of humor. In contrast to the theme of exclusion I documented in the developing plot, this example provided an illustration of Laura including Jay in the classroom community. When Laura laughed, the other students joined in her laughter and Jay smiled good-naturedly. The plot thus had to be reconfigured to include examples like this that complicated developing thematic interpretations of the data.

Polkinghorne (1988) likened the process of plot construction to the part–whole movement of the hermeneutic circle, and I found this to be an accurate description as my movement between the elements of data and the plot in progress was continuous as well as recursive. In addition, I needed to analyze all of the data available to me; as Polkinghorne (1999) noted, "Things we didn't understand at the time can bubble with meaning later." I found this especially true as I reviewed videotapes after constructing a working plot: Interactions that had not seemed especially meaningful at the time I initially observed them did indeed "bubble with meaning" when viewed later.

In narrative analysis, the location of events and data within the plot is what gives them meaning relative to the whole story and its outcome. As asserted by Polkinghorne (1988), "emplotment composes meaning out of events by a process similar to the process that grammar employs to develop meaning from words" (p. 159). It is the location of events within the plot that encourages the reader of the story to build interpretive links between the events. Consistent with anthropologist Van Maanen's (1988) description of narrative approaches to ethnography, my intention in creating the plot was to support the reader in making these interpretive links:

The intention is not to tell readers what to think of an experience but to show them the experience from beginning to end and thus draw them immediately into the story to work out its problems and puzzles as they unfold. (p. 103)

As suggested by the works of Polkinghorne (1988), Ricoeur (1984; 1992), and Bruner (1990), the reader's active engagement in "work[ing] out the problems and puzzles as they unfold" is made possible because of the primacy of narrative cognition. Narrative cognition, as a primary mode of human meaning making, drives us to order and make sense of events through constructing relationships between them. Narrative text supports the reader's interpretive activity because, unlike other forms of academic writing that take great pains to structure and defend one interpretation of a set of data, narrative more fully represents the complexity of lived experience.

Strengths and Limitations of Narrative Analysis

Scientific practice and scientific theories may be considered a kind of story-telling practice—a rule-governed, constrained, historically changing craft of narrating the history of nature. Scientific practice and scientific theories are embedded in particular kinds of stories.... Scientific practice is above all a story-telling practice in the sense of historically specific practices of interpretation and testimony. (Haraway, 1989, p. 4)

Haraway, like other anthropologists of science (cf. Cohn, 1987; Latour, 1987; Latour & Woolgar, 1979/1986; Martin, 1991, 1994), argued for analysis of the discursive practices of scientists to make visible the ways in which these practices shaped both the research that was conducted and the knowledge claims that were made. Haraway used the metaphor of storytelling to illuminate the situated, contested, and socially constructed nature of truth—even in the "hard" sciences. As Latour and Woolgar (1979/1986) noted, "Argument between scientists transforms some statements into figments of one's subjective imagination, and others into facts of nature ... reality is the *consequence* of the settlement of a dispute, rather then its *cause*" (p. 236).

Phillips's (1995) critique of current applications of narrative analysis raised similar points, although from a very different perspective, when he asked "Will any old story suffice?"(p. 15). Like Haraway and Latour, Phillips recognized the need for agreed-on conventions and criteria for the truth claims of scientists; unlike these scholars, Phillips maintained that, properly developed, the conventions could represent "truth." The criteria of adequacy determined by the narrative community of practice, Phillips claimed, are inadequate in that they don't distinguish between truth and fiction:

The point is that if action is taken on the basis of an incorrect narrative, even if disaster does not always ensue, at least it will be likely that we will end up with consequences that we neither anticipated nor desired; we are more likely to act successfully if we act on the basis of correct information (p. 17).

Phillips (1995) similarly critiqued the emphasis of narrative on documenting emic accounts of events: "There are many cases in the social sciences (including educational research) in which the beliefs—and resulting narratives—of the individuals concerned are not particularly insightful or causally enlightening" (p. 19).

These criticisms of narrative research (both narrative analysis and analysis of narratives) illustrate the difficulty researchers from this perspective have had in making their truth claims and the purposes of their work clear to those who are informed by different paradigms. What has happened is that scholars who conduct narrative research have tried to employ the constructs of nonnarrative and most especially quantitative approaches, such as "validity," to argue for the rationality of narrative research. This has been unsatisfying to scholars like Phillips because there are essentially no analogs between the paradigms. For example, scholars of narrative such as Bruner have argued for determining the value of a narrative by the value of the vicarious experience it provides:

> With science, we ask finally for some verification (or some proof against falsification). In the domain of narrative and explication of human action, we ask instead that, upon reflection, the account correspond to some perspective we can imagine or "feel" as right. (Bruner, 1986, p. 52; see also Connelly & Clandinin, 1990)

Returning to the argument of the anthropologists of science, it is clear that scholars like Phillips and Bruner are operating within totally different discursive worlds, and their "storytelling" practices are fundamentally different. I can imagine Bruner cringing at Phillips's remarks about emic perspectives failing to be "causally enlightening," and I can also imagine Phillips's consternation at Bruner's assertions that we judge a narrative based on whether the "feel" is right. Each scholar has to be considered within his own paradigm to understand his argument for verification or truth.

What does this mean for the validity of work such as my own? What does one story contribute to our general understanding of teaching and learning? I believe that the presentation of my work with Jay as a narrative case study is one of its strengths: Jay's story illustrates the complexity of understanding teaching and learning interactions in their social and institutional contexts. By closely portraying one student and the factors that contributed to his successful (and unsuccessful) participation in diverse teaching and learning contexts, this study challenges the notion that deficit and competence are static properties of individuals. Instead, Jay's story focuses attention on the interactions between individuals and the constraints and affordances of their environments.

In addition, I provide connections between the themes of Jay's story and related research literature in two ways. First, I weave discussions of specific studies and their findings into the body of Jay's story through the use of both references within the text and footnotes. The reader is thus invited to incorporate findings from other works within his or her interpretation of Jay's story and to determine the significance of the contributions of Jay's story to other forms of inquiry. Second, I conclude this work with a final chapter in which I reflect on the story and its implications for educational research and practice. Thus I avoid what Van Maanen (1988) identified as a shortcoming of narrative analysis; that is, that it too often includes "little or no mention of previous work in the same area or a similar one" and is presented as though in a "scholarly vacuum" (p. 135).

Regarding the issue of truth, as Van Maanen (1988) noted, the audience cannot be sure that the plot I constructed reflects actual events. There must be a certain amount of trust, as in any form of research, that I have engaged in data collection and analysis in rigorous ways. I have made every effort to make my research methods (data gathering, triangulation, analysis, and writing process) visible to the reader, and it is up to the reader to determine whether it "feels" true. Further, the plot itself is an analytical construction, not "raw data":

> To ask of a narrative "What really happened?" is to assume that plots are simply representations of extralinguistic realities and that they can be investigated empirically by recapturing those extralinguistic realities. (Polkinghorne, 1988, p. 159)

Representation of Data Within the Story Frame

We need to conduct research informed by the theoretical and empirical literature relative to our inquiries, to participate in and contribute to the discourse community of educational research. However, it is not enough to talk only with other researchers: The subject of our inquiries is too important. We need to find a way to communicate with practitioners, parents, and students, to construct a discourse that is inclusive and relevant to all stakeholders.

My central goal in designing this study was to document the particulars of one student's learning across multiple contexts. By illustrating the immediate contextual features that influenced Jay's opportunity to learn and to display his learning, I hoped to contribute to our understanding of how ability, achievement, and identity are coconstructed in particular activity settings. Further, by placing these analyses within a consideration of the larger sociohistorical contexts in which they occurred, I sought to deepen our understanding of the factors beyond the immediate setting that contributed to the construction of Jay's identity and ability in the classroom.

In addition, I wanted to tell this story in a way that invited teachers to reflect on their own practices. Through reading Jay's story, my hope is that teachers will recognize and reflect on the role they have in shaping what forms of ability, achievement, and identity are constructed in the teaching and learning contexts of their classrooms. I believe that the narrative format of this work is a step toward the construction of a discourse that is inclusive and relevant to all stakeholders (Barone, 1992; Carter, 1993; Connelly & Clandinin, 1990). As asserted by McEwan and Egan (1995), "the philosophy of teaching and the empirical study of teaching have kept themselves at a distance from the practice of teaching and a narrative approach can provide a step forward in seeking a long-needed reconciliation" (p. 166).

For these reasons, the voice of this research is different from the academic voice most often associated with social science research. This variance from more conventional forms created its own set of challenges, however. One such challenge was how to represent the spoken data I had recorded. The transcription conventions used within academic texts to represent various features of spoken discourse would make the data in my research at best cumbersome to read, and at worst inaccessible to many readers. With this in mind, I had to (by referring to my evolving plot and list of themes) decide what features of spoken language were most important to represent in writing, and how to represent them.

As explained earlier, the construct of positioning was central to my sociocultural analyses of these data. As in the examples within Davies and Harré (1990), positioning has often been used to analyze the content of discursive interactions. Although this was an important aspect of positioning for my analysis as well, I also found I needed to represent the interactive style of different participants. Pauses, false starts, interruptions, talking over another speaker in a louder voice, or working with another speaker to jointly produce oral text were important features of interactions that also contributed to understanding how participants were attempting to position each other or to reposition themselves.

Drawing on the conventions of narrative storytelling, I decided to embed my interpretation as a participant/observer/scholar within the text, without the use of transcription symbols. There is some precedence for this in Heath's (1983) *Ways With Words* (see transcription notes, pp. 15–16). Table A.1 represents the range of narrative representations I employed.

TABLE A.1
Narrative Representations Employed

Transcription Convention	Representation in Narrative
: turn start	" " says, exclaims, speaks, and so on
@@@	laughs, chuckles, and so on
[] overlap	Embedded in narrative description and use of—
	Example 1 where first speaker stops speaking and reacts as though interrupted "They might. Just some—" Mrs. Armstrong begins "Yes. For handwriting." Jay's grandmother answers Mrs. Simpson." Just some," Mrs. Armstrong repeats, her voice growing louder.
	Example 2 where first speaker continues after start of second speaker "Pressure from your thumb pushes the air," Jay continues. "Lack of air." Molly announces, overlapping the last part of Jay's explanation.
(()) action	Embedded in narrative description "I'm finished." Jay throws out his tissues, picks up his paper, and walks to the front of the room.
stressed words	italics (e.g., "Don't you *think* so?")
\ falling intonation	. when final; otherwise embedded in narrative (e.g., "says softly")
/ rising intonation	? when final; otherwise embedded in narrative (e.g., "his voice rising as he spoke")
= latching	...Example "And she took him to the university. She would take him to the places ... " " ... and she would buy him, and treat him," her husband goes on
...(6 sec.) pause	, when less than 1 second; otherwise embedded in narrative (e.g., "The room is silent for six seconds.")

Deciding on the conventions with which to represent oral discourse as conversation also involved careful consideration of how to represent phonological features of spoken language. There were differences in the spoken dialects employed by the participants in this research that were important to the plot. For example, in the first chapter Jay and his grandparents meet with two of his sixth-grade teachers. Here, representation of differences in spoken language helps make visible to the reader the ways that his teachers positioned Jay's family as outsiders to the world of education. In the context of this meeting, power, authority, and knowledge of Jay as a learner were intimately tied to language use through such features as volume, speed and rhythm, time on the floor, and dialect. Further, such representations were important to understanding the contextual features that, as described in my earlier discussion of sociocultural theory, were critical to fully appreciating the relationships between context, positioning, and personhood.

In addition, making visible the positioning that took place in the meeting in chapter 1 helps the reader appreciate Jay's awareness of the intimate relationship between dialectical variance and membership in a historically and culturally situated speech community. The building of connections across time and place in this manner is one of the unique affordances of the narrative form, and it is critical to understanding Jay's ontological history and his approach to learning in the diverse teaching and learning contexts studied.

To represent the phonological variation that resulted from differences in the speed and rhythm and dialect of participants' spoken language, I drew on respelling of standard orthography. For example, within this text the reader will find the following forms of representation:

> "Constantly just talkin' and whatnot … " (chap. 1, allegro speech)
> "Everybody, you know, be wonderin' what's goin' on." (chap. 2, dialect and allegro speech)
> "I'm just gonna plunk you right here." (chap. 2, allegro speech)
> "Or do you just think you got too much energy you just hafta bust out everywhere?" (chap. 2, eye-dialect)

Having made the decision to represent phonological variation, I sought to represent such differences for all of the speakers. In doing so I realized that I am, like the participants of my research, a situated listener, and might be more likely to index certain forms as different, and was wary of any tendency to do so.

I did not make the decision to use such respelling lightly. There is evidence that readers stigmatize speakers whose oral speech is represented in nonstandard written forms (Preston, 1985). Further, there is also evidence that the speech of Blacks and Appalachians is most often "respelled" in scholarly work, especially among folklorists, contributing to the representation of these groups as "different" or even "exotic" (Preston, 1982). Preston argued further that any form of respelling negatively indexes the speaker.

I certainly did not want representational choices I made to contribute to the denigration of any of the participants in my research. However, as described earlier, one of the central tensions in this work, the tension between Jay's home and school contexts, was evidenced through language use. For example, to change his grandparents' speech to standard phonological representation would change who they were in the eyes of Jay's teachers, and thus misrepresent the interactions among the participants in that meeting. To make this tension between Jay's home and school contexts visible, as well as to provide the rich contextual details that support the reader's building of thematic connections across contexts, I felt compelled to represent spoken language differences. Further, this decision was consistent with Jay's awareness of and attention to such differences, demonstrated through his question about being "proper" and comments regarding certain forms of language stemming from "slavery times" (as in chap. 13) and through his use of an array of discourses when recording his own oral speech, such as his TV news announcer voice.

Simply put, changing the spoken language of the participants in this work would have eliminated my ability to represent the power dynamics operating within the interactions. The hegemonic practices of the teachers, and their roots in a culturally sanctioned deficit view, would have been rendered invisible. This would have served to protect those who held power, and thus contributed to the replication of the very power relationships that positioned Jay as "disabled" and relegated him to the margins of the classroom. This was, and remains, an unacceptable choice for me as a scholar, as a teacher, and as Jay's friend.

REFERENCES

Anderson, C., Holland, D., & Palincsar, A. (1997, March). Canonical and sociocultural approaches to research and reform in science education. *Elementary School Journal*, 359–383.

Artiles, A. (1998). The dilemma of difference: Enriching the disproportionality discourse with theory and context. *The Journal of Special Education, 32*, 32–36.

Artiles, A., Aguirre-Munoz, Z., & Abedi, J. (1998). Predicting placement in learning disabilities programs: Do predictors vary by ethnic group? *Exceptional Children, 64*, 543–559.

Artiles, A., & Trent, S. (1994). Overrepresentation of minority students in special education: A continuing debate. *Journal of Special Education, 4*, 410–438.

Artiles, A., Trent, S., & Kuan, L. (1997). Learning disabilities empirical research on ethnic minority students: An analysis of 22 years of studies published in selected refereed journals. *Learning Disabilities Research and Practice, 12*, 82–91.

Au, K. (1979). Using the experience–text–relationship method with minority children. *Reading Teacher, 32*, 677–679.

Au, K. (1980). Participation structures in a reading lesson with Hawaiian children: Analysis of a culturally appropriate instructional event. *Anthropology and Education Quarterly, 11*, 91–115.

Au, K. (1990). Changes in a teacher's views of interactive comprehension instruction. In L. Moll (Ed.), *Vygotsky and education: Instructional implications and applications of sociohistorical psychology* (pp. 271–286). New York: Cambridge University Press.

Au, K. (1998). Social constructivism and the school literacy learning of students of diverse backgrounds. *Journal of Literacy Research, 30*, 297–319.

Au, K., & Jordan, C. (1981). Teaching reading to Hawaiian children: Finding a culturally appropriate solution. In H. Trueba, G. P. Guthrie, & K. Au (Eds.), *Culture in the bilingual classroom: Studies in classroom ethnography* (pp. 139–152). Rowley, MA: Newbury House.

Bakhtin, M. M. (1981). *The dialogic imagination: Four essays by M. M. Bakhtin* (C. Emerson & M. Holquist, Trans.). Austin: University of Texas Press.

Bakhtin, M. M. (1986). *Speech genres and other late essays.* Austin: University of Texas Press.

Barone, T. (1992). A narrative of enhanced professionalism: Educational researchers and popular storybooks about school people. *Educational Researcher, 21*(8), 15–24.

Behar, R. (1993). *Translated woman: Crossing the border with Esperanza's story.* Boston: Beacon.

Behar, R. (1996). *The vulnerable observer: Anthropology that breaks your heart.* Boston: Beacon.

Bourdieu, P. (1977). *Outline of a theory of practice* (R. Nice, Trans.). Cambridge, England: Cambridge University Press.

Bourdieu, P. (1990). *The logic of practice* (R. Nice, Trans.). Cambridge, England: Polity.

Brazerman, C. (1987). Coding the social scientific style: The APA Publication Manual as behaviorist rhetoric. In J. Nelson, A. Megill, & D. McCloskey (Eds.), *The rhetoric of the human sciences: Language of argument in scholarship and public affairs* (pp. 125–144*)*. Madison: University of Wisconsin Press.

Brown, N., Palincsar, A., & Magnusson, S. (1999). The quiet quadrant: Inter and intra reflection in a community of practice. Unpublished manuscript.

Bruner, J. (1986). *Actual minds, possible worlds.* Cambridge, MA: Harvard University Press.

Bruner, J. (1990). *Acts of meaning.* Cambridge, MA: Harvard University Press.

Bruner, J. (1996). *The culture of education.* Cambridge, MA: Harvard University Press.

Carter, K. (1993). The place of story in the study of teaching and teacher education. *Educational Researcher, 22*(1), 5–12, 18.

Casey, K. (1995). The new narrative research in education. In M. Apple (Ed.), *Review of research in education* (pp. 211–253). Washington, DC: American Educational Research Association.

Cazden, C. B. (1986). Classroom discourse. In M. Wittrock, (Ed.) *Handbook of research on teaching* (pp. 432–463). New York: Macmillan.

Cazden, C. B. (1988). *Classroom discourse: The language of teaching and learning.* Portsmouth, NH: Heinemann.

Cobb, P. (1994). Constructivism in Mathematics and Science Education. *Educational Researcher, 23*(7).

Cohn, C. (1987). Sex and death in the rational world of defense intellectuals. *Signs, 12*(4), 687–718.

Cole, M. (1996). *Cultural psychology: A once and future discipline.* Cambridge, MA: Belknap Press of Harvard University Press.

Cole, M., Engestrom, Y., & Vasquez, O. (1997). *Mind, culture, and activity: Seminal papers from the Laboratory of Comparative Human Cognition.* New York: Cambridge University Press.

Coles, R. (1997) *Doing documentary work.* Oxford, UK: Oxford University Press.

Collins, J. L. (1998). *Strategies for struggling writers.* New York: Guilford.

Collins, J. L., & Collins, K. M. (Eds.). (1997), *Handbook of strategic writing lessons.* Buffalo: Graduate School of Education Publications, State University of New York at Buffalo.

Collins, K. M. (1997, December). *Talking about light: The construction of a shared discourse by first grade students in guided inquiry science.* Paper presented at the annual meeting of the National Reading Conference (NRC), Scottsdale, AZ.

Collins, K. M. (1998, November). *The case of Robert: Influences of one students' ability to negotiate verbal, print, and scientific discourses on the construction of shared knowledge in guided inquiry science.* Paper presented at the annual meeting of the National Council of Teachers of English, Nashville, TN.

Collins, K. M., & Collins, J. L. (1996). Strategic instruction for struggling writers. *English Journal, 85,* 54–61.

Collins, K. M., Dutro, E., & Collins, J. L. (in review). *Discourse and educational equity: Positioning literacy instructions for the standards movement and beyond.* Guilford Publications.

Collins, K. M., MacLean, F., Palincsar, A. S., & Magnusson, S. (2000). The role of discourse in guided inquiry science. *ENC Focus: A Journal for Classroom Innovators, 7*(1), p. 42–44.

Collins, K. M., Palincsar, A. S., & Magnusson, S. (1998). *Metaphor, mediation, and meaning: Dialectical knowledge construction in guided inquiry science.* Paper presented at the annual meeting of the American Educational Research Association, San Diego, CA.

Connelly, F., & Clandinin, J. (1990). Stories of experience and narrative inquiry. *Educational Researcher, 19*(5), 2–14.

Davies, B., & Harré, R. (1990). Positioning: The discursive production of selves. *Journal for the Theory of Social Behavior, 20,* 43–63.

Delgado, R. (1995). *The Rodrigo chronicles.* New York: New York University Press.

Denzin, N. (1989). *Interpretive biography.* Thousand Oaks, CA: Sage.

Dewey, J. (1913). *Interest and effort in education.* Boston: Houghton-Mifflin.

Dewey, J. (1990). *The child and the curriculum.* Chicago: University of Chicago Press. (Original work published 1902.)

Dorsey-Gaines, C., & Garnett, C. (1996). The role of the black church in growing up literate. In D. Hicks (Ed.), *Discourse, learning and schooling* (pp. 247–268). New York: Cambridge University Press.

Driver, R., Asoko, H., Leach, J., Mortimer, E., & Scott, P. (1994). Constructing scientific knowledge in the classroom. *Educational Researcher 23*(7), 5–12.

Englert, C. S. (1992). Writing instruction from a sociocultural perspective: The holistic, dialogic, and social enterprise of writing. *Journal of Learning Disabilities, 25,* 153–172.

Englert, C. S., & Raphael, T. (1989). Developing successful writers through cognitive strategy instruction. *Advances in Research on Teaching, 1,* 105–151.

Englert, C. S., Raphael, T., & Anderson, L. (1992). Socially mediated instruction: Improving students' knowledge and talk about writing. *The Elementary School Journal, 92,* pp. 411–449.

Englert, C. S., Raphael, T., Anderson, L., Anthony, H., & Stevens, D. (1991). *American Educational Research Journal, 28,* 338–371.

Erickson, F. (1987). Transformation and school success: The politics and culture of educational achievement. *Anthropology and Education Quarterly, 18,* 335–356.

Erickson, F. (1992). Ethnographic microanalysis of interaction. In *Handbook of qualitative research in education* (pp. 202–225). New York: Academic.

Erickson, F. (1996). Going for the zone: The social and cognitive ecology of teacher–student interaction in classroom conversations. In D. Hicks (Ed.), *Discourse, learning and schooling* (pp. 29–62). New York: Cambridge University Press.

Ferguson, A. A. (2001). Bad boys: Public schools in the making of Black masculinity. Ann Arbor: University of Michigan Press.

Fleming, R. (no date). Lady beetles (Entomology Note No. 6). Michigan Entomological Society. http://insects.unmz.lsa.umich.edu/MES/notes/endnotes6.html.

Ford, D. (1998). The underrepresentation of minority students in gifted education: Problems and promises in recruitment and retention. *Journal of Special Education, 32*(1), 4–14.

Forman, E., Minick, N., & Stone, A. (Eds.). (1993). *Contexts for learning: Sociocultural dynamics in children's development.* New York: Oxford University Press.

Gavelek, J., & Palincsar, A. S. (1988). Contextualism as an alternative worldview of learning disabilities: A response to Swanson's "Toward a metatheory of learning disabilities." *Journal of Learning Disabilities, 21,* 278–281.

Gee, J. P. (1996). *Social linguistics and literacies: Ideology in discourses* (2nd ed.). Bristol, England: Taylor and Francis.

Gee, J. P. (1991). What is literacy? In C. Mitchell & K. Weiler (Eds.), *Rewriting literacy: Culture and the discourse of the other* (pp. 3–12). Westport, CT: Bergen & Garvey.

Gee, J. P., & Green, J. L. (1998). Discourse analysis, learning, and social practice: A methodological study. In P. D. Pearson & A. Iran-Nejad (Eds.), *Review of research in education,* (Vol. 23, pp. 119–165). Washington, DC: American Educational Research Association.

Gelb, S. (1998). One number fits all? Why typology is poor science. *Mental Retardation, 36,* 496–498.

Goffman, E. (1959). *The presentation of self in everyday life.* New York: Anchor.

Goffman, E. (1963). *Stigma: Notes on the management of spoiled identity.* New York: Simon & Schuster.

Goffman, E. (1981). *Forms of talk.* Philadelphia: University of Pennsylvania Press.

Green, P. (1999). Separate and still unequal: Legal challenges to school tracking and ability grouping in America's schools. In L. Parker, D. Deyhle, & S. Villenas (Eds.), *Race ... race isn't: Critical race theory and qualitative studies in education* (pp. 231–250). Boulder, CO: Westview.

Greenfield, E. (1988). *Nathaniel talking.* New York: Black Butterfly.

Guitierrez, K., & Stone, L. (1997). A cultural-historical view of learning and learning disabilities. *Learning Disabilities Research and Practice, 12,* 123–131.

Gumperz, J. (1982). *Discourse Strategies.* Cambridge, UK: Cambridge University Press.

Gumperz, J. (1992). Interviewing in inter-cultural situations. In P. Drew and J. Heritage (Eds.), *Talk at work* (pp. 302–330). Cambridge, UK: Cambridge University Press.

Haraway, D. (1989). *Primate visions: Gender, race, and nature in the world of modern science.* New York: Routledge.

Harry, B., & Anderson, M. (1994). The disproportionate placement of African American males in special education programs: A critique of the process. *Journal of Negro Education, 63,* 602–619.

Harry, B., & Anderson, M. (1999). The social construction of high-incidence disabilities: The effect on African American males. In V. C. Polite & J. E. Davis (Eds.), *African American males in school and society: Policies and practices for effective education* (pp. 32–50). New York: Teacher College Press.

Heath, S. B. (1983). *Ways with words: Language, life, and work in communities and classrooms.* New York: Cambridge University Press.

Hicks, D. (1994). Individual and social meanings in the classroom: Narrative discourse as a boundary phenomenon. *Journal of Narrative and Life History, 4,* p. 215–240.

Hicks, D. (1995). Discourse, learning, and teaching. In M. Apple (Ed.), *Review of research in education* (Vol. 21, pp. 49–95). Washington, DC: American Educational Research Association.

Hicks, D. (Ed.). (1996). *Discourse, learning and schooling.* New York: Cambridge University Press.

Hicks, D. (1997). Working *through* discourse genres in school. *Research in the Teaching of English, 31,* 459–485.

hooks, b. (1994). *Outlaw Culture.* New York: Routledge.

hooks, b. (2001). *All about love: New visions.* New York: Morrow.

Hymes, D. (1974). *Foundations in sociolinguistics: An ethnographic approach.* Philadelphia: University of Pennsylvania Press.

Hughes, L. (1994). *The dream keeper and other poems.* New York: Knopf.

John-Steiner, V., & Mahn, H. (1996). Sociocultural approaches to learning and development: A Vygotskian framework. *Educational Psychologist, 31,* 191–206.

Keller-Cohen, D. (1994). The web of literacy: Speaking, reading, and writing in 17th and 18th century America. In D. Keller-Cohen (Ed.), *Literacy: Interdisciplinary conversations* (pp. 155–176). Cresskill, NJ: Hampton.

Kliewer, C., & Fitzgerald, L. (2001). Disability, schooling, and the artifacts of colonialism. *Teachers College Record, 103*(3), pp. 450–470.

Kyratzis, A., & Green J. (1997). Jointly constructed narratives in classrooms: *Co-construction of friendship and community through language. Teaching and Teacher Education 13*(1), pp. 17–37.

Ladson Billings, G. (1995). Toward a theory of culturally relevant pedagogy. *American Educational Research Journal, 32,* 465–491.

Lave, J., & Wenger, E. (1991). *Situated learning: Legitimate peripheral participation.* Cambridge, England: Cambridge University Press.

Latour, B. (1987). *Science in action.* Cambridge, MA: Harvard University Press.

Latour, B., & Woolgar, S. (1986). *Laboratory life: The construction of scientific facts.* Princeton, NJ: Princeton University Press. (Original work published 1979.)

Leahy, C. (1987). *Peterson first guide to insects.* New York: Houghton-Mifflin.

Lemke, J. (1990). *Talking science: Language, learning, and values.* Norwood, NJ: Ablex.

Lincoln, C. E., & Mamiya, L. (1990). *The Black Church in the African American experience.* Durham, NC: Duke University Press.

Loury, G. (2002). *The anatomy of racial inequality.* Cambridge, MA: Harvard University Press.

Luria, A. R. (1972). *The man with a shattered world: The history of a brain wound.* New York: Basic Books.

Luria, A. R. (1979). *The making of mind: A personal account of Soviet psychology* (M. Cole & S. Cole, Eds.). Cambridge, MA: Harvard University Press.

Luria, A. R. (1968/1987). *The mind of a mnemonist: A little book about a vast memory.* Cambridge, MA: Harvard University Press. (Original work published 1968.)

MacMillan, D., & Reschly, D. (1998). Overrepresentation of minority students: The case for greater specificity or reconsideration of the variables examined. *Journal of Special Education, 32*(1), pp. 15–25.

Magnusson, S., & Palincsar, A. S. (1995). The learning environment as a sight of science education reform. *Theory Into Practice,* 34(1), 43–50.

Marano, N., Palincsar, A., & Magnusson, S. (2000). *The emergence of a community of practice: The dynamics of shared understanding.* Unpublished manuscript.

Marshall, M. J., & Barritt, L. S. (1990). Choices made, worlds created: The rhetoric of AERJ. *American Educational Research Journal, 27,* 589–609.

Martin, E. (1991). The egg and the sperm: How science has constructed a romance based on stereotypical male–female roles. *Signs, 16,* 485–501.

Martin, E. (1994). *Flexible bodies: The role of immunity in American culture from the days of polio to the age of AIDS.* Boston: Beacon.

McDermott, R. P. (1993). The acquisition of a child by a learning disability. In S. Chaiklin & J. Lave (Eds.), *Understanding practice* (pp. 269–305). New York: Cambridge University Press.

McDermott, R. P., & Varenne, H. (1995). Culture *as* disability. *Anthropology and Education Quarterly, 26,* 324–348.

McDermott, R. P., & Varenne, H. (1996). Culture, development, disability. In R. Jessor, A. Colby, & R. Shweder (Eds.), *Ethnography and human development: Context and meaning in social inquiry* (pp. 101–126). Chicago: University of Chicago Press.

McEwan, H., & Egan, K. (Eds.). (1995). *Narrative in teaching, learning, and research.* New York: Columbia University Press.

McPhail, J., Pierson, J., Freeman, J., Goodman, J., & Ayappa, A. (2000). The role of interest in fostering sixth grade students' identities as competent learners. *Curriculum Inquiry, 30*(1), 43–70.

Mehan, H. (1979). *Learning lessons: Social organization in the classroom.* Cambridge, MA: Harvard University Press.

Mehan, H. (1993). Beneath the skin and between the ears: A case study in the politics of representation. In S. Chaiklin & J. Lave (Eds.), *Understanding practice* (pp. 241–267). New York: Cambridge University Press.

Michaels, S., & Collins, J. (1984). Oral discourse styles: Classroom interaction and the acquisition of literacy. In D. Tannen (Ed.), *Coherence in spoken and written discourse* (pp. 219–244). Norwood, NJ: Ablex.

Michaels, S., & O'Connor, M. C. (1990). *Literacy as reasoning within multiple discourses: Implications for policy and educational reform.* Paper presented at the summer institute of the Council of Chief State School Officers. July; Washington, DC.

Miller, J. (1999, May 30). Schools address race differently. *Ann Arbor News,* p. A1.

Moll, L. (Ed.). (1990). *Vygotsky and education.* New York: Cambridge University Press.

Moll, L. (1992). Literacy research in community and classrooms: A sociocultural approach. In R. Beach, J. Green, M. Kamil, & T Shannahan (Eds.), *Multidisciplinary perspectives in literacy research* (pp. 211–244). Urbana, IL: National Conference on Research in the Teaching of English.

Moll, L., & Dworin, J. (1996). Biliteracy development in classrooms: Social dynamics and cultural possibilities. In D. Hicks (Ed.), *Discourse, learning and schooling* (pp. 221–246). New York: Cambridge University Press.

Moll, L., & Greenberg, J. (1990). *Creating zones of possibilities: Combining social contexts for instruction.* New York: Cambridge University Press.

Moll, L., & Whitmore, K. (1993). Vygotsky in classroom practice: Moving from individual transmission to social transaction. In E. Forman, N. Minick, & A. Stone (Eds.), *Contexts for learning: Sociocultural dynamics in children's development* (pp. 19–42). New York: Oxford University Press.

Morse, J. (2002, May 27). Learning while Black. *Time*, pp. 50–52.

Nash, A. (1998a, June 15). Neighbors fight gang presence in West Willow area. *Ann Arbor News*, pp. A1, A6.

Nash, A. (1998b, June 17). The night police became victims. *Ann Arbor News*, pp. A1, A6.

Nash, A. (1998c, June 14). Police zero in on another Ypsilanti gang. *Ann Arbor News*, pp. A1, A13.

Nash, A. (1998d, June 19). Son's fall into gang life is wrenching experience for family. *Ann Arbor News*, pp. A1, A16

Nieto, S. (1999). *The light in their eyes: Creating multicultural learning communities.* New York: Teachers College Press.

Oakes, J. (1985). *Keeping track: How schools structure inequality.* New Haven, CT: Yale University Press.

Oakes, J. (1995). Two cities' tracking and within-school segregation. *Teachers College Record, 96,* 681–690.

Oakes, J., Wells, A. S., Jones, M., & Datnow, A. (1997). Detracking: The social construction of ability, cultural politics, and resistance to reform. *Teachers College Record, 98,* 483–510.

O'Connor, M. C., & Michaels, S. (1993). Aligning academic task and participation status through revoicing: Analysis of a classroom discourse strategy. *Anthropology and Education Quarterly, 24,* 318–335.

O'Connor, M. C., & Michaels, S. (1996). Shifting participant frameworks: Orchestrating thinking practices in group discussion. In D. Hicks (Ed.), *Discourse, learning and schooling* (pp. 63–103). New York: Cambridge University Press.

Orenstein, P. (1994). *Schoolgirls: Young women, self-esteem, and the confidence gap.* New York: Anchor Doubleday.

Palincsar, A. (1986). The role of dialogue in scaffolded instruction. *Educational Psychologist, 21,* 71–98.

Palincsar, A. S. (1998). Social constructivist perspectives on teaching and learning. *Annual Review of Psychology, 49,* 345–375.

Palincsar, A., & Brown, A. (1984). Reciprocal teaching of comprehension fostering and comprehension monitoring. *Cognition and Instruction, 1,* 117–175.

Palincsar, A., Brown, A., & Campione, J. (1993). First grade dialogues for knowledge acquisition and use. In E. Forman, N. Minick, & A. Stone (Eds.), *Contexts for learning: Sociocultural dynamics in children's development* (pp. 43–57). New York: Oxford University Press.

Palincsar, A., Collins, K., Marano, N., & Magnusson, S. (1998). *Methodological choices in the design and conduct of case-based research.* Paper presented at the National Reading Conference, December. Austin, TX.

Palincsar, A. S., Collins, K. M., Marano, N. L., & Magnusson, S. (2000). Investigating the engagement and learning of students with learning disabilities in guided inquiry science teaching. *Language, Speech, and Hearing Services in Schools, 31,* 240–251.

Palincsar, A. S., Magnusson, S. J., Collins, K. M., & Cutter, J. (2001). Making science accessible to all: Results of a design experiment in inclusive classrooms. . *Learning Disabilities Quarterly, 24*(1), 15–32.

Palincsar, A. S., Magnusson, S., Collins, K. M., Marano, N. L., & Hapgood, S. (1999). *Making rigorous curricula accessible to all students.* Paper presented at the annual meeting of the American Educational Research Association, April. Montreal, Canada.

Palincsar, A. S., Magnusson, S., Marano, N., Ford, D., & Brown, N. (1998). Designing a community of practice: Principles and practices of the GIsML community. *Teaching and Teacher Education, 14*(1), 5–19.

Patai, D. (1993). *Brazilian women speak: Contemporary life stories.* New Brunswick, NJ: Rutgers University Press.

Philips, S. U. (1972). Participation structures and communicative competence: Warm Springs children in community and classroom. In C. Cazden, V. John, & D. Hymes (Eds.), *Functions of language in the classroom* (pp. 370–394). New York: Teachers College Press.

Phillips, D. C. (1995). The good, the bad, and the ugly: The many faces of constructivism. *Educational Researcher, 24*(7), 5–12.

Polkinghorne, D. (1988). *Narrative knowing and the human sciences.* Albany: State University of New York Press.

Polkinghorne, D. (1991). Narrative and self-concept. *Journal of Narrative and Life History, 1*, 135–153.

Polkinghorne, D. (1995). Narrative configuration in qualitative analysis. *Qualitative Studies in Education, 8*(1), 5–23.

Polkinghorne, D. (1997). Reporting qualitative research as practice. In W. Tierney and Y. Lincoln (Eds.), *Representation and the text: Re-framing the narrative voice* (pp. 3–22). Albany, NY: SUNY Press.

Polkinghorne, D. (1999). *Narrative analysis and semiotics.* Invited address given to the American Educational Research Association, Montreal, Canada.

Poplin, M. (1988a). Holistic/constructivist principles of the teaching/learning process: implications for the field of learning disabilities. *Journal of Learning Disabilities, 21*, 401–416.

Poplin, M. (1988b). The reductionist fallacy in learning disabilities: Replicating the past by reducing the present. *Journal of Learning Disabilities, 21*, 389–400.

Poplin, M. (1995). Looking through other lenses and listening to other voices: Stretching the boundaries of learning disabilities. *Journal of Learning Disabilities, 28*, 392–398.

Preston, D. (1982). 'Ritin' fowklower daun 'rong: Folkorists' failures in phonology. *Journal of American Folklore, 95*, 304–326.

Preston, D. (1985). The Li'l Abner syndrome. *American Speech, 60*, 326–336.

Pugach, M. C. (2001). The stories we choose to tell: Fulfilling the promise of qualitative research for special education. *Exceptional Children, 67*, 439–453.

Pugach, M. C., & Seidl, B. L. (1996). Deconstructing the diversity–disability relationship. *Contemporary Education, 68*(1), 5–9.

Pugach, M. C., & Seidl, B. L. (1998). Responsible linkages between diversity and disability: A challenge for special education. *Teacher Education and Special Education, 21*, 319–333.

Purcell-Gates, V. (1995). *Other people's words: The cycle of low literacy.* Cambridge, MA: Harvard University Press.

Rich, A. (1984). *The fact of a door frame: Poems selected and new, 1950–1984.* New York: W. W. Norton and Company.

Ricoeur, P. (1984). *Time and narrative* (Vol. 1, K. McLaughlin & D. Pellauer, Trans.). Chicago: University of Chicago Press.

Ricoeur, P. (1992). *Oneself as another* (K. Blamey, Trans.). Chicago: University of Chicago Press.

Rogoff, B. (1990). *Apprenticeship in thinking: Cognitive development in social context.* New York: Oxford University Press.

Rogoff, B. (1994). Developing understanding of the idea of communities of learners. *Mind, Culture, and Activity, 1*, 209–229.

Rommetveit, R. (1974). *On message structure: A framework for the study of language and communication.* New York: Wiley.

Rommetveit, R. (1979). On codes and dynamic residuals in human communication. In R. Rommetveit & R. M. Blakar (Eds.), *Studies of language, thought, and verbal communication* (pp.163–175). Orlando, FL: Academic.

Ross, M. E. (1997). *Bug watching with Charles Henry Turner.* Minneapolis, MN: Carolrhoda.

Sacks, O. (1970). *The man who mistook his wife for a hat and other clinical tales.* New York: HarperCollins.

Sacks, O. (1995). *An anthropologist on Mars.* New York: Vintage.

Santa Barbara Classroom Discourse Group. (1994). Constructing literacy in classrooms. In R. Rudell, M. Ruddell, & H. Singer (Eds.), *Theoretical models and processes of reading* (pp. 124–154). Newark, DE: International Reading Association.

Schiffrin, D. (1996). Narrative as self-portrait: Sociolinguistic constructions of identity. *Language in Society, 25,* 167–203.

Schwab, J. (1964). Structure of the disciplines: Meanings and significances. In G. W. Ford & L. Pugno (Eds.), *The structure of knowledge and the curriculum* (pp. 6–30). Chicago: Rand McNally.

Sleeter, C. (1986). Learning disabilities: The social construction of a special education category. *Exceptional Children, 53,* 46–54.

Smith, L. T. (1999). *Decolonizing methodologies: Research and indigenous peoples.* New York: Zed Books.

Stake, R. (1994). Case studies. In N. Denzin & Y. Lincoln (Eds.), *Handbook of qualitative research* (pp. 236–247). Thousand Oaks, CA: Sage.

Stone, A., & Reid, D. K. (1994). Social and individual forces in learning. *Learning Disability Quarterly, 17*(1), pp. 72–86.

Stone, C. A. (1993). What is missing from the metaphor of scaffolding? In E. Forman, N. Minick, & A. Stone (Eds.), *Contexts for earning: Sociocultural dynamics in children's development* (pp. 169–183). New York: Oxford University Press.

Taylor, D. (1991). *Learning denied.* Portsmouth, NH: Heinemann.

Tharpe, R., & Gallimore, R. (1988). *Rousing minds to life.* New York: Cambridge University Press.

Thompson, A. (1998). Not the color purple: Black feminist lessons for educational caring. *Harvard Educational Review, 68,* 522–554.

Tierney, W., & Lincoln, Y. (Eds.). (1997). *Representation and the text: Reframing the narrative voice.* Albany: State University of New York Press.

Trent, S., Artiles, A., & Englert, C. S. (1998). From deficit thinking to social constructivism: A review of theory, research, and practice in special education. In P. D. Pearson & A. Iran-Nejad (Eds.), *Review of research in Education,* (Vol. 23, pp. 277–307). Washington, DC: American Educational Research Association.

Van Maanen, J. (1988). *Tales of the field: On writing ethnography.* Chicago: University of Chicago Press.

Vaughn, S., Gersten, R., & Chard, D. (2000). The underlying message in LD intervention research: Findings from research syntheses. *Exceptional Children, 67*(1), 99–114.

Verhovek, S. H. (2001, September 23). Americans give in to race profiling. *New York Times,* p. 1.

Vygotsky, L. S. (1978). *Mind in society: The development of higher psychological processes.* Cambridge, MA: Harvard University Press.

Vygotsky, L. S. (1981a). The genesis of higher mental functions. In J. Wertsch (Ed.), *The concept of activity in Soviet psychology* (pp. 144–188). New York: M. E. Sharpe.

Vygotsky, L. S. (1981b). The instrumental method in psychology. In J. Wertsch (Ed.), *The concept of activity in Soviet psychology* (pp. 134–143). New York: M. E. Sharpe.

Vygotsky, L. S. (1987). *The collected works of L. S. Vygotsky,* (Vol. 1). New York: Plenum.

Wells, G. (1999). *Dialogic Inquiry: Towards a sociocultural practice and theory of education.* New York: Cambridge University Press.

Wertsch, J. (1991). *Voices of the mind: A sociocultural approach to mediated action.* Cambridge, MA: Harvard University Press.

Wertsch, J. (1998). *Mind as action.* New York: Oxford University Press.

Wertsch, J., Tulviste, P., & Hagstrom, F. (1993). A sociocultural approach to agency. In E. Forman, N. Minick, & A. Stone (Eds.), *Contexts for learning: Sociocultural dynamics in children's development* (pp. 336–356). New York: Oxford University Press.

Wood, D., Bruner, J., & Ross, G. (1976). The role of tutoring in problem solving. *Journal of Child Psychology and Psychiatry, 17,* 89–100.

Zeller, N. (1995). Narrative rationality in educational research. In H. McEwan & K. Egan (Eds.), *Narrative in teaching, learning, and research* (pp. 211–224). New York: Teachers College Press.

Author Index

Subject Index